Eperon's Guide to the Greek Islands

Arthur Eperon is one of the most experienced and best-known travel writers in Europe. Since leaving the RAF in 1945 he has worked as a journalist in various capacities, often involving travel. He has concentrated on travel writing for the past twenty-five years and contributed to many publications including *The Times*, *Daily Telegraph*, *New York Times*, *Woman's Own*, *Popular Motoring* and the *TV Times*. He has also appeared on radio and television and for five years was closely involved in Thames Television's programme *Wish You Were Here*. He has been wine writer to the RAC publications and a number of magazines.

He has an intimate and extensive knowledge of France and its food and wine, as a result of innumerable visits there over the last forty years. In 1974 he won the Prix des Provinces de France, the annual French award for travel writing.

Also by Arthur Eperon in Pan Books

Travellers' France
Le Weekend
The French Selection
The British Selection
Eperon's French Wine Tour

First published in Great Britain 1988 by
Pan Books Ltd, Cavaye Place, London SW10 9PG

9 8 7 6 5 4 3 2

© Arthur Eperon 1988
Photographs © Fanny Dubes 1988
Illustrations © Mary Fraser 1988
ISBN 0330 29993 X
Phototypeset by Rowland Phototypesetting Ltd
Bury St Edmunds, Suffolk
Printed and bound in Spain by
Mateu Cromo SA, Madrid

ARTHUR EPERON

EPERON'S GUIDE TO THE GREEK ISLANDS

Photographs by Fanny Dubes

Illustrations by Mary Fraser

PAN BOOKS
London, Sydney and Auckland

Acknowledgements ⸺

My thanks to Harry Goodman, chairman, and Peter Smith, managing director, of ILG (International Leisure Group) for great practical help over the two years in which I have revisited the Greek Islands. Also Eileen Hills of Intasun and Lancaster, for help in organizing journeys, and to George Dabnos of Hellas Agency in Athens and my old friend Norman Duckworth of Intasun in Athens and their staffs for unstinting help in Greece, to John Boyle of Falcon Holidays for real practical help, and Peter Analytis of the Greek Tourist Office in London for great help and encouragement.

And my thanks and congratulations to photographer Fanny Dubes, whose beautiful photographs appear in this book.

Contents

INTRODUCTION

Magic for Dreamers

Greek islands are magic to dreamers, purgatory to planners and organizers. If you want your world to be tidy and efficient, if you fuss if a bus does not run on time or admire people who can serve you a three-course meal in twenty-five minutes dead, don't go past Athens.

Beauty, friendship, conversation matter more than efficiency in Greek islands. After a few days, things which seem important at home don't matter any more. No Greek islander would whine about 'pressures'. Those are for Americans or Athens ship owners. Relaxation takes over. You learn the art of just standing and staring. You don't want to go home. You can sit and watch the intense light making patterns on the blue sea, the sun on the white houses, fishermen languidly checking their nets. You can follow one fishing caique from leaving the quay and watch it until it disappears over the horizon. You can take pleasure in patterns of light on bare rocks and in wind rippling water. But if you travel with set itineraries and follow timetables rigidly, you will be frustrated to desperation. Wind, weather, the sea and the gods control life on these islands as in ancient times.

A friend on Seriphos who has spent much time in the US told me that when young Greeks go to America, they catch the American fever of working all hours and all days to build up a business and make money. They are often good at it. But those who come home again with their savings soon drift back into the Greek way of life. 'They are usually much happier,' he said.

I started touring the Greek islands at the end of the 1940s when there were few inter-island ferries. You found out when a supply-caique was going vaguely in your direction and travelled sitting on wine casks or jumbo bottles of olive oil, probably next to a goat or sheep. Usually someone played a guitar and everyone drank from a bottle of wine which was passed round.

I remember landing on Sikinos and, as the only foreigner on the island, was received like a long-lost cousin. As Ben Jonson said of Shakespeare, I have 'small Latin and less Greek'. But there is always someone who fought with the British Army in the '39–'45 war or who has worked in London, New York, Vancouver or Sydney, very willing to interpret freely, so I was soon a member of the taverna set, meeting mid-morning for ouzo and dominoes and leaving only for a mid-afternoon siesta.

Soon they knew my history, my family, my job, the size of my house, and my approximate income. It is polite to ask such questions on Greek islands.

Then one morning I said that I was leaving next day. To where? they asked. Ios, the next island, I said.

They looked astounded and worried. They all started talking at once and gesticulating. Then they explained.

I would be in danger. The men of Ios were pirates. They would rob me.

Ios was a very quiet place then, before the 1960s invasions of flower-children and hippies. I found the Ios pirates sitting in a little taverna by the quay, sleepy with sun, ouzo and wine. They gave me the same cousinly welcome. Where had I come from? Sikinos, I said, and I got the same astounded reaction. 'Weren't you robbed? They're all thieves and robbers on Sikinos.'

The place to find out where to stay, where to eat and when boats were going was the barber's shop. Many Greek men went to the barber's for a morning shave, a cup of coffee and a chat, and it was like a local broadcasting station. I have had many hair cuts that I did not need.

Better inter-island transport and tourism have changed attitudes somewhat. I actually found a Cretan working as a waiter on Kos recently, and to Cretans, Kos barely rates as a Greek island. It was occupied so often until 1947. But the differences between isles have not vanished. Remember that almost every Greek island has a different history and often different culture, influenced by occupations over centuries. Corfu was long under French and British rule, and like the other Ionian isles was under Venetian rule for so long that it was until recently regarded as partly Italian. Rhodes and the other Dodecanese islands were under Turkish rule right up to 1912, then under the Italians, and did not join the modern Greek state until 1948. The islanders have at least one thing in common – a strong suspicion of Athens and everything Athenian.

The Turks, of course, ruled most of Greece from the fifteenth century until 1829 with their accustomed harshness. They forbade schooling in the Greek language, so education was kept alive secretly by monks in monasteries. They levied crippling taxes to pay for the Turkish army and navy and took away quotas of pretty girls each year for their harems, so that Greek mothers prayed that their daughters would be ugly. And they took the eldest son from every family as young boys to be janissaries – brought up as Muslims and trained to be soldiers or sailors fighting for Turkey.

There is no such confectionery as Turkish Delight in a Greek's vocabulary. It is Greek Delight. The truth is that most 'Greek' cooking came from the Turks, but *never* hint of that.

The islands vary vastly in scenery. Corfu is lush and green. Much of Santorini is a lunar landscape of volcanic dust and rock. Some isles are arid rock, with a sprinkling of scrub and stunted trees. Others look like that as you approach from the sea, but hide lush valleys between their rocky hills. The sea is extremely important to Greece. It changes between groups of isles and its mood can change dramatically in a few hours. I arrived in 1987 in Athens in late March intending to make for the Cyclades – for Siphnos, Seriphos, Kythnos, Milos, Kea. Not a ferry was running. Gales had made sailing them suicidal. I got no further than Aegina and Hydra. Yet another year we were island hopping in a yacht in late March. I like to go to most islands in late April or May, when they have awoken after the winter but not many visitors have arrived. You risk a few wild winds, but you see some beautiful wild flowers.

Selective weedkillers are used little on the Greek isles, edges of fields often run wild, so do fields and terraces on rocky hillsides which are no longer economic to work. Each island has its own flowers but on most you can see wild poppies flourishing prolifically in cornfields, hayfields or just by the roadside as they did in England when I was a boy. With them are often the beautiful, delicate-looking purple flowers of Venus's looking glass. On Siphnos in early May I have seen a profusion of the two-coloured crown daisy with yellow centre encircled by white petals and alongside the rosy purple sunrose and white rockrose.

Buttercups come in several colours from March to May – yellow, of course, but also a deep red, looking like an anemone, with sepals, white, pink and cream slightly streaked with pink. There are red wild anemones, too, and on some more cultivated islands chamomile grows as thickly as daisies in Britain.

Look too for Neapolitan garlic, like a cluster of tiny snowdrops, in April and May, and the delicate mauve corn flag, called sometimes the sword lily. It grew from the blood of Hyacinth, who was accidentally killed by his friend the god Apollo while throwing the discus. In autumn you can find wild crocus and even in winter beautiful, delicate little sweet-scented narcissi.

I am saddened when I hear people who do not know them very well dismiss the Greek islands as 'spoiled'. Spoiled for whom? Tourism, time and the motor car have changed them, of course, and in some places not for the better. Parts of Corfu, Rhodes, Crete, even Paros and a small part of Kos have become saturated with tourists and tourist development and have lost their Greek charm. But these carpers cannot have explored very far on any island nor thought at all about the needs of the Greek people. They certainly cannot have gone into the hinterlands of the islands. That is where you get away from tourists even in high season. Often, I admit, on awful roads.

With or without tourists, the Greek islanders could not have stayed in the primitive poverty which was picturesque to the few with enough time and money to travel to them, but impossibly frustrating to the Greek people. The islands were already becoming denuded of young people. They had lived for centuries from the sea and the land. The sea was becoming overfished by big boats. The terraced hillside farms with poor soil had no chance of competing for food markets with big, highly mechanized farms of wealthier areas, and modern transport had made it possible to import food fairly cheaply. The young made for the US, Canada and Australia. Since the tourist boom, many have come back, especially from Australia. You will find them on most islands but particularly on Crete, Kos and Kalymnos, where they are called 'Australians' and often live in the best and most modern houses.

Tourism has provided money for farm machinery and cars, jobs not only in cafés and restaurants and hotels, but in the building industry, building hotels, self-catering flats and villas, and roads to reach them. Motor cars and aircraft have revolutionized the Greek islands as they have revolutionized the world. The islands with poor roads remain poor and primitive – what some writers still call 'genuinely Greek'. Genuine Greeks would prefer more roads, more machinery to help them look after those terraced patches on hillsides, water from taps, heating and less backache. Laden donkeys may make pretty pictures to take home but the Greek farmer would prefer a truck.

I arrived in Benitses, in Corfu, when it was a real fishing village, known mostly because the German Kaiser had had a house nearby where he sat on a saddle instead of a chair at his desk and crossed to a private jetty for his yacht by a private bridge over the road. I stayed at one of two tavernas run by a young ex-army officer almost inevitably called Spiros after the local saint. He received me as porter, took off his peaked cap and became receptionist, then sat at a desk marked 'Spiros Boss' and welcomed me as manager. Next he reappeared as waiter, offering us a 'small snack' in mid-afternoon, then as chef in a toque with a massive, beautifully decorated fish to keep away starvation until dinner. After he had cooked and served dinner for twenty, he became disc jockey and cabaret act, dancing with a wooden table between his teeth.

Now he has turned his taverna into a successful bar-disco, he owns blocks of holiday apartments, and is unofficial boss of a Benitses taken over by international youth. I preferred Benitses the old way.

The change in Corfu started long before with the building of the first post-war luxury beach hotels like the Korkyre Beach, and the gradual invasion of Athenians, British and French buying up villas and cottages in the wake of Lawrence Durrell. It was the rich who first started to play at peasants on the Greek islands, not back-packing tourists.

When Paleokastritsa was a fishing village little known to visitors, the owner of one of the two tavernas high above the beach was showing me in his kitchen fresh-caught fish for lunch when a tall, greyhaired Englishman in faded, torn denims dropped in for his post. To my astonishment I found myself faced with a man I had last seen wearing a Savile Row suit sitting behind a vast desk in the heavily carpeted top-director's office of a big magazine group. He got a platinum handshake a few months later and retired early to Corfu.

Despite its package-tour popularity, Corfu still has hideouts which you can reach only by boat or along old mule tracks of shingle into which your car will surely dig itself deep if your driving technique falters. You'll be pulled out by a mule as likely as a tractor. That is the trick in Greece – if you hate sharing a place with other tourists, keep ahead, however bad the roads or primitive your bedroom.

If I appear to be subjective, please forgive me. Greek islands *are* subjective. They are a personal experience. Even if you go on a package tour, your experiences will be quite different from other people on the same trip. That is one of the joys of Greek travel. However much a harassed rep may count you to make certain no one is left at the airport, you are never a number.

Even in a modern Athens transit hotel where airline pilots stay overnight, and where I had stayed three nights when there was freak snow in March and gales had stopped the ferries, the barman greeted me when I returned after three months with: 'Did you ever get to Seriphos?'.

The Way to Go

There are three basic ways of seeing Greek islands. You can take a package to a big island such as Crete, Rhodes or Corfu and explore that one thoroughly in fair comfort, taking a few excursions to other isles. Or you can pick bed and breakfast or just a bed on a central isle which has ferries to three or four others, staying overnight in rooms at any of these if you want or if you cannot get a ferry back. You will find more ferries run from about mid-May to early September and that in June, July and August there may be many extra excursions to other islands which will return the same day but will give you a chance for a quick look round. You can sometimes take an excursion, jump ship, then return on a ferry a day or two later. But do tell the excursion ship's purser that you are not returning, or they may wait for you. It's a good idea to book a bed-and-breakfast or self-catering package even if you don't use your bedroom all the time. You can leave most of your luggage in it and travel light to other islands. It may not cost you any more on a package than if you booked the room yourself for fewer days.

Island hopping is quite different. It needs as much time as you can spare and an easy-going nature. Stay in a room in a private house or a small hotel, just bed or bed and breakfast if they insist. I would try to avoid booking half-board on a Greek island. It curtails your freedom. Eating out at different tavernas or beachside or village café-bars is the best way to get talking to people. Do not expect to see many isles in a fortnight. Ferries to and between smaller isles are not as frequent as that, and they can be cancelled because of ill winds at some times of year. But if you can't get a ferry ask around and find if a caique or some small delivery boat is going. Because of ferry times you can often see twice as many isles in three weeks as in a fortnight, and a lot more still in four weeks. I would sooner see fewer islands and spend three or four days exploring each one. You have to find out how to get off the tourist tracks and to see the hidden treasures, and with some small islands you can get to know people if you stay a few days.

Cheap flights by tour companies have made island hopping a much better proposition than it used to be, when you had either to book a full package holiday with hotel or villa or pay high scheduled air fares.

There are very few charter flights from the US to the Greek isles except Rhodes and Crete. Nearly all go to Athens. It may pay you to fly to London, Amsterdam or Frankfurt on a cheap flight, then pick up a 'flight only' or package with simple room, to Greece. By far the most extensive package and flight programmes – and the cheapest trips – are from London.

To comply with air regulations, you are given a voucher for 'accommodation' – a pitch on a campsite – when you book a charter flight.

People often ask me the best time to go to Greek islands. It must be a personal matter, but I would certainly try to avoid July and August, when weather can be too hot for walking or sightseeing much of the day, there are often too many people in places which are uncrowded at other times, and local people just do not have so much time to talk or help. In high summer rooms can be difficult to get, especially on small islands. People make a rush along the quay as ferries land to grab those available. Get something for the first night right away in mid-summer. Don't be too choosy. Some islands, such as the Cyclades, can be windy in April. The weather is unpredictable. May is more settled, June starts to get hot, September is excellent in many isles and October balmy and pleasant in more southerly isles, with few other tourists about.

If you are going to smaller islands or hopping around a lot, you must be something of a back-packer. I do not usually believe in travelling too light. When you have run out of trousers in Prague or had to attend a big mayoral dinner in a pair of yellow Moroccan slippers in Lisbon because over-zealous hotel staff have taken away your shoes to be cleaned and mislaid them below stairs, you tend to play safe. Few professionals travel very light. But if you are going to climb around ferries and wander little towns looking for rooms, you must not take more than you can carry comfortably. Do include spare shoes, a sweater, and a complete change of clothes. With the eccentricities of water supplies in private rooms, small hotels, apartments or villas in Greece, anyone who counts on washing their shirts or socks each night and putting them on next morning is gambling. Anyway, you will be lucky to get hot water when you want it for washing and there is no guarantee that nights will be warm enough to dry your clothes. It's different for people who sleep in the sun on the beach all the morning. They hardly need dry clothes. I know people who boast that they can get around Greece in the clothes they stand up in. I try to avoid sitting next to them in buses or bars. Wine and food tasting have given me a keen sense of smell.

Do take paperbacks, unless you can live on a diet of James Hadley Chase, murder and spy stories. Those are the only books shops seem to stock in English.

Even if you have a timetable, do check ferries. They can be cancelled, changed or held up for a variety of reasons. I waited half a day for one which had been switched to another island because there was a fête there. Barbara took a very small ferry to a remote isle, to return that night, and found the whole island en fête. The captain started to drink with friends, announced around midnight that the weather wasn't fit for the return journey, kept sending over bottles of wine to Barbara's table, then suggested that she and he should go down to the beach to finish the celebrations.

For bigger ferries, you must buy your ticket from the local agent – often the grocer's shop. But don't rely on the agent for information about ferries. Agents look after rival companies and will not tell you that another boat exists. Ask in a taverna, or, better, ask the port police. They are friendly and helpful but often speak very little English, so you need paper and pencil.

Big ferries from Piraeus (Athens port) often have several classes – perhaps 1st, 2nd, Tourist and Deck. Prices are reasonable. Tourist class is quite adequate and excellent value except perhaps on a long run in mid-summer heat when boats are crowded. Then it is worth taking the more expensive luxury ferries when available or going first class even with a cabin. Tourist areas can be massed with luggage and people. Boats do range from terrible tubs (happily disappearing now) to comfortable modern boats with air-conditioning, clean lavatories and hot water. First class fares bring better loos.

Buses vary enormously from island to island and routes obviously depend on the standard of roads. Timetables are usually posted up in a taverna or café window by the main stops, but don't take them too literally. Buses can be early or late. In mid-summer they are always very crowded. You may have to stand on one foot and will almost certainly have quite a fight getting off at intermediate stops. Getting on is not that easy in high summer, too. As the bus pulls up, you may be one of five people waiting. By the time it has emptied, an army of people will have appeared from nowhere. In early May, however, you might have the bus to yourself.

In high summer, share taxis. They cost more, of course, but have a dozen advantages – not least that the driver will probably tell you about passing interests. If you want to make a tour of an island's sights in a day, try to find three or four

people to share a taxi with you. Negotiate the cost before you set out. And try to pick an English-speaking driver who can tell you about places.

The amount of Greek money you can import is very small. Many islands have no banks, so change money as soon as possible. Some mini-markets and ferry agents change foreign money and a few change travellers' cheques, but don't rely on Euro-cheques. Only certain banks will change them, usually on busy islands in the port or bigger towns. Only posher tourist hotels or restaurants will accept credit cards.

On smaller islands, there are few hotels and pensions. You will see notices such as 'room rent' on private houses. In mid-summer, especially when the ferry arrives late in the day, take almost any room for the first night. At other times make sure that you see the room first. Some people, often young teenagers, meet the ferry and offer rooms, saying 'follow me'. Chances are that you will walk a long way, probably up a hill and out of the village, or in a dark backstreet. And the room will almost certainly have no loo or shower. If you cannot find a room at all, ask at a taverna – after you have bought a drink. I arrived after dark at Poros, the smaller port of Cephalonia, and was assured that there was not a vacant room in the place. I ordered a bottle of wine in a taverna and asked the owner. He sent his young daughter out and she came back to take me to a backstreet house where a smiling old lady led me up a rickety outside wooden stair to a little room opened with an enormous 'mediaeval dungeon' key. Bare floor but tidy and clean, with a shower-loo next door where the water was luke-warm – not freezing. The loo door didn't lock, but you can't have everything, can you? The price was so low I gave the old lady double. And I had the bonus of meeting a statuesque blonde German girl running for the loo in the night wearing her birthday suit. That is another possibility of village rooms.

I have stayed in rooms akin to the solitary cell in Oflag XXI B in Poland with which I became quite familiar. But I have also had delightful surprises. Whatever the room, the owners have always been friendly and helpful. And even when floors are bare boards and beds basic, the rooms have always been clean. One hazard in village rooms is the seatless loo. The Greeks have a way with showers. Most have immovable heads and some joker has often pointed these so that your towels and any clothing you have been foolish enough to take in the room will be washed (and the loo paper) and the floor flooded to a depth of 3 inches.

So I do recommend paying a little extra and whenever possible booking into a pension or small hotel. In July and August, try to book ahead. *Someone* will phone for you! On islands such as Corfu, Kos, Rhodes and mostly on Paros these are likely to be reasonably modern and comfortable and very good value. On smaller isles they can be basic, but you may well have your own loo and shower and they cost a fraction of prices in other countries. Hotels down to 'B' grade have rooms with shower and loo. 'C' grade usually have some such rooms.

Water is precious on some smaller islands and in mid-summer may well go off completely for part of the day. That is why washbasins often don't have plugs. Visitors have a habit of putting in the plug, turning on the tap and, if no water comes, leaving them both. When water comes on, it floods the room and the one below. In some hotels you get hot water morning and evening only.

Self-drive transport can be a problem on islands with rough roads. Motorbikes are difficult unless you are already an accomplished rider – and steady. Mopeds can be death. Deaths and injuries from among visitors who hire mopeds happen every year, even on good roads. It is terrifying to see young people maimed for life because of a moped accident. Do not hire one unless you have ridden them many times before, and preferably owned one. This is not old man's talk. Some tour operators specifically discourage moped hire. And look at those little shrines on the roadside to accident victims and ponder. If you do hire one, make absolutely certain that the brakes are good. Greeks are not devoted to servicing vehicles. The same goes, of course, with a motorbike 'or car. Italian mopeds are giving way to Japanese automatic models – easier until you start tackling steep hills or trying to go up quite reasonable hills with two adults aboard. They may stop or, worse, jump out of gear. Some of the local hired crash helmets are more for playing spacemen than for safety. You will surely have been intelligent enough to take out medical insurance before going to Greece. Before you hire any vehicle, make certain that you are covered on this insurance for accidents. Some policies are void for motorbike and particularly moped riding. Some even exclude car accidents. It is best to have a policy which includes a medical care flight home. It is very difficult to get anything but third party insurance on a moped.

Car hire is expensive compared with some countries. But it is quite the best way of seeing islands and almost imperative if you want to get into the villages of the hinterlands to see the old Greece. But you must have care and courage on those old dirt mule tracks which now pass for roads. The rewards are way beyond the cost. If alone, try to find English-speaking companions to share the cost and enjoyment. Quoted hire prices can be misleading. Mileage is rarely included and that can mount up. Then there is the 'collision waiver' which you *must* have, otherwise you can be charged outrageously even for a little scratch and, in some contracts, up to £500 (or about 800 US$) of repair bills whether the damage was your fault or not. On top of this, there is an 18% tax (it used to be nearly 30%). You may be able to cut costs by finding a small local car hirer. But he may refuse the accident waiver clause, his cars may be badly serviced, and if you break down it will be heaven's own job to get him interested. Do try brakes and inspect tyres. I always when possible pay a bit more for an Avis, Eurocar or Hertz car. They will replace the car quickly if it breaks down. And you can pay by credit card.

Some local island maps are a joke. Uncompleted roads or even roads merely planned for the future may be marked; hard-earth mule tracks are marked as roads, too, because that is what local people use them for. Don't shy away from them or you'll miss a lot. They can be driven with care, but watch for projecting boulders waiting to tear off sumps and transmission! Watch especially those which are marked with dotted lines. Michelin's map 980 of Greece is very useful but it does not show these minor local roads which you will need to explore properly. Don't worry if you get lost on an island. There are not enough roads for you to be lost for long – except perhaps on Rhodes or Crete. Fill up with petrol whenever possible. Filling stations are rare.

Eating and Drinking ————————————

No one goes to Greece for the food or the wine. Eating is a family or social occasion – cheerful and informal, often rather noisy, not the serious matter it is in France. The food seems almost incidental to the conversation.

With mostly Turkish origin, you would expect Greek food to be very spicy. They do use herbs quite a lot, especially oregano, but not as much as the Italians, and they use much less salt and pepper than we do. This may be the reason for so many tourists thinking that the food has little taste. You notice the scarcity of salt and pepper particularly in meatballs (*keftedhes* – made with veal or veal and pork mixed), and the pleasant cheese pie, *tiropita*, which many Greek families buy hot from the baker and which makes a good snack lunch. Greeks make many pies – with pastry – spinach (*spanakopita*), chicken (*kotopita*), courgette (*kolokithopita*), and a pie of their favourite meat, lamb (*arnaki*).

There are few complicated dishes. Meat is casseroled with vegetables or grilled, fish fried or grilled, and apart from tomato, sauces are rare. A squeeze of lemon replaces them. Big or very tasty fishes are often baked. So is lamb, regarded as rather a luxury.

For Sunday lunch, families who can afford it usually eat roast lamb, often baked for them by the local baker. Traditionally, the family went to church, then mother and daughter went home to get the vegetables ready, Dad went to the taverna to sink a few glasses of ouzo or wine and collected the joint from the baker on his way home.

Friends of mine who run a taverna on Siphnos cook their Sunday lamb with onions, lemon juice, lots of garlic and other herbs (especially rosemary) in olive oil in a very low oven for twenty-four hours! The lamb is very tender, but frankly the meat has little flavour; the juice is gorgeous, though.

Shishkebab (*souvlakia*) of meat, tomatoes and onions grilled on a skewer, is usually pork these days, though sometimes you can get lamb or veal. Pork is now the cheapest meat in Greece, as it is over most of Western Europe.

Fish is usually fresh and superb on the isles. Alas, it is also now expensive. I am against the fashion for half-raw fish, taken by the French from the Japanese, but I don't want it grilled dry, either, and some Greek tavernas are careless when grilling. The son of the taverna owner on Siphnos has grilled me baby red mullet to perfection – when he has been paying attention! But sometimes he tries to do too many things at once and overcooks the fish and cutlets. And in the evenings he is sometimes diverted by his vendetta against a big fish in the harbour. When this old veteran is attracted to the quayside by the taverna lights, he leaves his grill, grabs his gun and tries to shoot it! Meanwhile the smaller fry in the taverna may burn.

My own favourite Greek dish is still moussaka – when well made. I still prefer the minced meat to be lamb, though you get beef very often. And there should be a lot of aubergine, very little potato.

Intricately patterned loaves of bread for sale on Crete

I love Greek starter salads, which are mostly quite simple to make. *Taramosalata*, the paste of smoked fish roe, is delicious with bread and wine before the main course. *Tzatsiki* (dip of yoghurt, garlic, grated cucumber and olive oil) is at its best when made with local farm yoghurt (preferably from sheep's milk) and I am sorry to notice that even on small isles many tavernas use large tins of it sent from Athens. Tomato and cucumber salad (*angour domata*) is best when it includes a little green and red pepper. But the great salad is the Greeks' and tourists' standby. Called Greek salad by British tourists, village salad by most tavernas and *horiatiki* by Greeks, it is usually made of wedges of tomato and cucumber, sliced onion, red and green peppers, black olives, mixed with oregano, salt and pepper in olive oil, topped with thin slices of feta cheese sprinkled with oregano. You can put in other vegetables of the season, such as slices of deseeded courgette. Greek olive oil is important. With any other it tastes different. Don't bother with Greek butter. It is almost tasteless.

On smaller Greek islands, there are very few posh restaurants with white tablecloths and 'international' menus. Tavernas are the best place to eat Greek food, and the best ones invite you into the kitchen to see the fish and meat on a slab waiting to be cooked, and other dishes bubbling in copper pans on the stove.

Don't order all your meal at once or it will arrive all together and get cold – especially as Greeks rarely heat plates. Try a salad or two with some wine, then go and choose your fish or meat to be cooked or your dish off the stove. Fruit is so good that many tavernas don't serve desserts except ice cream. But you might get honeycakes (*baklavas*), honey puffs (*loukoumades*), a semolina cake with almonds, cinnamon and lemon (*halvas*), cream caramel, or yoghurt with honey and walnuts.

Menus are more a rough guide than a bill of fare. Restaurants and tavernas rely very much on what is good and fairly priced in the market and several items marked on the menu may be 'off'. A taverna owner will come forward with a special fish just bought from a boat or lamb chops bought from a farmer. Dish of the Day! Deep-frozen dishes are marked KAT. I wish that we had a symbol like that. Prices are controlled according to the grade of restaurant. There are two prices. You pay the second, bigger one which includes tax and service. A bill is *logaristhimo* and will be a long time coming.

By the way, Greece is the last country in which to snap your fingers to call a waiter, waitress or anyone else, whereas smiles work wonders. It is no good being impatient in a restaurant or taverna. It will get you nowhere. Forget slick city service. Lie back and settle for Greek indolent enjoyment.

There is no Turkish coffee in Greece, of course. It is called Greek coffee – and don't drink the bitter dregs. Nescafé (usually genuine) is sometimes called 'Nes', sometimes American coffee. Ice cold instant coffee is the local version of French café frappé. The Greeks think they invented it.

Ouzo, the local pastis, in its cruder forms more like Arab arak, is served iced with water added and, like Pernod, you either like it or don't.

I cannot love retsina, the resinated wine. I once brought down the wrath of every Greek from New York to San Francisco by writing in the *New York Times* that retsina tasted as if a tom cat had taken exception to a camphor ball. But at least retsina is one of the few remaining links between ancient and modern Greek. It originated 3000 years ago when Greece was making its fortune by exporting oil and wine in jars with no corks, sealed with a mixture of plaster and pine resin. The resin was wrongly believed to preserve the wine.

Many other Greek wines have improved recently, with better methods of growing and wine making. The longer you are there, away from French and Italian wines, the better they taste!

The Peloponnese on the mainland makes the most wine. There are reliable brand wines which you can buy on all except the smallest isles, such as Demestica (red and white), Santa Helena (one of the better dry whites), and Achaia Clauss wines. Dry white Hymettus from near Athens is often available. Otherwise most islands drink their own wine and import a little from an island nearby. White and red wines are produced on Kos, Thasos, Andros, Naxos, Ios and Milos. Reds in particular come from Corfu (try Ropa), Lefkas (very dark wine called Santa Mavra), Lemnos (Mavro Kalpaki), Euboea (Halkidas), Paros (good deep red, made from Mandilari grape), Ikaria, Santorini (very strong wines around seventeen per cent – Santorin and Vinsanto, much sought by Greeks themselves, and especially sweet Thira, grown on that little isle), and a big producer of powerful red wines, Crete (Malvazia, Mavro Romeika, Peza, Daphnes, Creta).

Mavro means black, but red when applied to wine. Some *are* nearly black. Mavrodaphne, the strong sweet red wine, is made mostly in the Peloponnese but drunk almost everywhere in Greece. Some is made on the Ionian isle of Cephalonia, which also makes the best white wine of Greece, Robola, and a Muscat sweet white very similar to the renowned Muscat of Samos. Rhodes, too, makes a sweet Muscat and two pleasant dry whites, Lindos and Rhodos. Zakynthos (Zante) has a refreshing dry white 'green' (young) wine called Verdea.

The Fix brewery no longer makes Fix beer, so the bad jokes have stopped. Beers of Greece are made now by French, Danish, Dutch and Scandinavian brewers. It's cheaper to stick to wine.

Greek brandies are useful for making mixed drinks, like brandy sour and Alexander (brandy with crème de menthe and cream). Metaxa makes 3, 5 and 7 star brandies. Raki is schnapps. So is the very potent Cretan *tsikoudhia*, especially when made by local farmers for their own drinking.

Some very palatable fruit-flavoured spirits are made, some sweet as liqueurs, others drier as aperitifs. Apricot versions are especially good.

Information and Explanations

Place names – I cannot pretend that there is much logic in spellings of places that I have used – they are the ones best known in the travel trade, although these vary from brochure to brochure, guide to guide. The problem stems, of course, from translating the Greek alphabet into Roman script. Twice the Greek government has issued official spellings based on scholarly research but almost no one outside Greece has paid much attention. There are also alternative names for some islands.

Hotels and restaurants – I have not recommended very many hotels or restaurants because, apart from the international package-tour hotels, which are not truly Greek and could be in any country, these vary so much in standards and availability from island to island and place to place. Furthermore, so many travellers prefer rooms in private houses or tiny pensions for their atmosphere and low cost. Just go and see what you can find. In the bigger islands like Rhodes and Crete you will find some restaurants with 'international' cuisine but that is not what Greek islands are about. The best advice is to pick the taverna with the nicest smells, walk into the kitchen and literally see what's cooking. This is normal.

Ferry times, bus routes – It is impossible from year to year, even month to month, to give these accurately and only a brave man would try. There is a series of guides by such brave men – called *GROC's Candid Guides to the Greek Islands* (Willowbridge). They cover only certain isles and inevitably much of the information is dated within a year – especially comments on tavernas and the timetables. But they are quite the best *practical* guides. They are strictly for back-packers on a budget and regard £10 a night for a double room with shower as being very expensive.

Maps – The Greek Tourist Offices in London and New York publish free a good map of all Greece but on each island you will need to buy a map on arrival. Don't be surprised if roads marked 'paved' are *not*.

IONIAN ISLES 1

Corfu

Gentle and smiling, green and lush, Corfu is the garden isle of Greece, coveted by men and nations through ages. Other isles are harsh and strong. Corfu is soft and seductive.

Before package tour jets arrived, it was the dream island for the great escape from noise, rush and crowds. Now it is the isle of laughter, enjoyment and escape from dull routine. Gradually the young and lively have taken over from the retired and retiring.

Lawrence Durrell, whose book *Prospero's Cell* about his life on Corfu did much to create the escape dream, suggested that it was Prospero's Isle of *The Tempest* – 'full of noises, sounds and sweet airs that give delight and hurt not.' The airs that come now from the discos and the holiday villas and apartments are sweet to the young but not, I confess, to me. But I am passing old. I sigh for the old Corfu I knew. But the young folk have a right to enjoy their holiday in their own way, so long as the Corfiot people don't mind. And obviously they don't, or they would not have tolerated so many changes.

For me there is still the hinterland, the rolling hills, luxuriant gardens, the mountains of the north-east, the dark huge old olive trees contrasting with the brighter greens of fruit trees and the oranges and lemons. The varying coastline washed by a sea which changes from vivid blue to a dark violet as the clouds gather, means more to me than staking out a patch of sand.

Despite cars and mopeds in profusion in season, the scent of Corfu is still of pines, herbs, and orange and lemon groves. Roses, clematis and marguerites still grow wild on hillsides and in hedgerows of the rich plains of Corfu's centre. There's still plenty of room to grow apples, pears, tomatoes and figs. A lot of vines, too, to make good dry white wine and sweet, strong red, blessedly not resinated. But huge olive trees dominate the island scenery – four million of them, unpruned and grown like forest trees. It was the wise if autocratic Venetians, who ruled Corfu from 1205 to 1797, who persuaded the Corfiots to plant the olives by subsidizing every tree.

The Venetians left behind tall narrow buildings and little squares in Campaniello, the old part of Corfu town, the remains of Venetian forts, and the French arcades on the Esplanade in the style of rue de Rivoli.

The British took over the island in 1814 from Napoleon, at the request of the

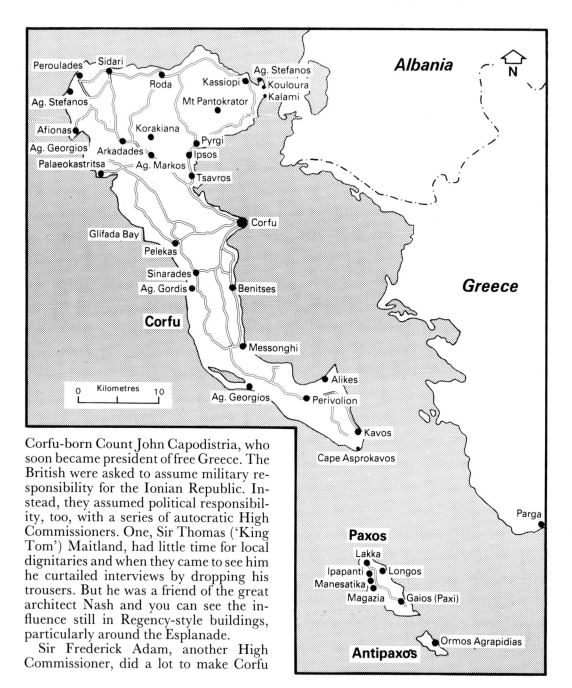

Corfu-born Count John Capodistria, who soon became president of free Greece. The British were asked to assume military responsibility for the Ionian Republic. Instead, they assumed political responsibility, too, with a series of autocratic High Commissioners. One, Sir Thomas ('King Tom') Maitland, had little time for local dignitaries and when they came to see him he curtailed interviews by dropping his trousers. But he was a friend of the great architect Nash and you can see the influence still in Regency-style buildings, particularly around the Esplanade.

Sir Frederick Adam, another High Commissioner, did a lot to make Corfu such a lovely, lush island by bringing water by aqueduct into Corfu town from a spring at Benitses and teaching the local farmers how to drain and water their orchards and fields. The British also bequeathed to Corfu apple chutney (a Christmas delicacy), *kek* (rich fruit cake), *tsintsinbeera* (ginger beer – alas, being replaced by Coke), and cricket. Cricket is still played on the Esplanade, which was a drill ground for troops from Venetian days and a cricket ground for 175 years. Rules vary somewhat from those of Lords. I saw an international team playing against Corfu in 1962 with some formidable players – Wes Hall and Kanhai of the West Indies, Baig and Chandu Borde (the great spinner) from India, Peter Loader and Willie Watson from England, Bill Alley from Australia and Basil D'Oliviera, then still South African. When the Islanders felt that this team had scored enough, they walked off the field and 'declared' for them!

Waiters with ice creams or trays of drinks tend to wander across the pitch as the bowler is running up. But there is nothing like sitting in the sun outside a café with a bottle of cold white wine watching cricket. It beats a beer tent any afternoon. The British left in 1864, but cricket lives on. That is the story of the British Empire.

The Esplanade is one of Europe's largest squares. The Georgian Palace of St Michael and St George beside the cricket pitch was built for Tom Maitland and later became a holiday home of the Kings of Greece. Now it houses a remarkable museum of Far Eastern Art, with 10,000 works from Eastern countries dating back to 1000 BC. But the place for strolling is the west side of the square, where the 'rue de Rivoli' arcades have restaurants, cafés, tea rooms and book shops. And there are some charming little shops and cafés in the streets behind. In high summer they do become crowded. Only important people on a list like *Who's Who* were allowed to walk and sit under the arcades, so they were called The Listons. Now any old tourist is welcome. Sometimes in mid-summer you would think that the British had taken Corfu back. Two nice C-class hotels are here on Kapodistriou – Suisse and Arcadion. Calypso, opposite the Archaeological Museum, is charming.

The old fortress on Cape Sidaro is divided from the Esplanade by a moat. It is a military academy now, but from here you can see over the town down to the little port, Mandraki, where Venetian galleys anchored, and across the water to Albania and the Greek mainland.

On the other side of the Esplanade is the old town, a delightful maze of tall tenements up to eight storeys, separated by narrow lanes, twisting alleys and stepped streets, often with washing strung over-head across the road, adding a touch of Naples to old Venice. Venetian arches and colonnades run down many streets, and the town hall is an ornately impress-ive Venetian loggia, later used as a theatre.

You can hardly miss the tall tower of sixteenth-century St Spyridon's Church, dedicated to a fourth-century bishop from Cyprus whose remains were brought here in 1456. He is patron saint of Corfu, credited with having saved the town from famine, twice from the plague, once from the besieging Turks, and to have sheltered townsfolk safely while much of the town was destroyed by gunfire and bombs when Germans and Italians fought over Corfu in 1944. And he seems to have lent his name to half the male population! His mummified body is housed in a silver coffin with glass top, and you can see his withered feet protruding in embroidered slippers. He is brought out four times a year and paraded round the streets. There may be no peace for the wicked anywhere, but in Greece the righteous are not left undisturbed either!

We were driving into Corfu town at Easter when one of those Greek motor-cycle cops looking like a Michelin man in vast leathers held up his hand to stop us. We were in trouble, it seemed. Greek cops make Parisian cops look like ballet dancers. We wound down the window. With a smile, he presented us with an egg dyed red and wished us a safe journey. It is an Easter custom.

On Saturday we saw St Spyridon car-ried in procession through the streets, led by bands, soldiers, Scouts and Guides, children in best clothes, local bigwigs and many priests. The saint was carried in a sort of sedan-chair with a gold and red canopy – a little figure slumped in the seat. After the procession the streets were cleared and people threw pottery from the balconies. This is a symbol of anger at Judas's betrayal of Jesus. Parades went on all day until at midnight people gathered by the old fortress holding candles and the Bishop shouted to them 'Christos Anesti – Christ is Risen'. Fireworks lit up the night, church bells rang and people kissed each other with the same greeting: 'Christ is Risen!' Then we all went home. What I didn't know was that, as in every house, I was expected to break the coloured egg the policeman had given me repeating 'Christ is Risen', then eat a special Easter soup.

On Sunday after church the whole town smelled deliciously of roasting lamb – another Easter tradition – and we joined the men in a taverna for ouzo as they waited for the family joint to cook in the bakery. When they had gone we ate juicy slices of lamb cut from the vertical spit turning in the corner of the room, with enough wine to have made a second meet-ing with the policeman less pleasant. The lamb was basted with lemon juice mixed with oregano. That night the whole vil-lage, from bent grandmothers to children in arms, turned up at our little hotel for another session of lamb and wine, and the noise would surely have awakened the saint. A truly Greek restaurant in Corfu town is Averof, through an alley beside Hotel Akropolis, two streets back from the ferry quay.

South from the town near the suburb of Anemomilos, with fine villas surrounded by gardens, is the villa Mon Repos in a lovely park. Built for Sir Frederick Adam in 1824, it was given to the Greek royal family and here Prince Philip, Duke of Edinburgh, was born in 1921. Just south is Kanoni, with a gun emplacement from which you have superb views of Chalikiopoulos lagoon, a seventeenth-century monastery on an islet joined by a causeway, and of the whole south-east coast. Alas, the lagoon is bisected by the airport runway, so intermittent thunder of planes can spoil any chance of contemplation, and the beauty spot is colonized by big hotels and apartment blocks.

You can see also Pondikonissi (Mouse Island). According to tradition Mouse Island was the ship which was taking Odysseus from Troy back to his home in Ithaca, as told in Homer's *Odyssey*. Odysseus, who had just escaped from the clutches of the nymph Calypso, was deposited naked on a Corfu beach into the white arms of lovely Nausicaa, daughter of the King of the Phaeacians, who ruled Corfu then. Odysseus seemed to have James Bondian luck in bumping into beautiful women. And she immediately knew he was a prince or a god, even though he wasn't wearing anything. Her father gave him a ship to take him home – possibly a wise move to protect his daughter. Some, including Lawrence Durrell, say that he landed at Paleokastritsa. I prefer to believe the locals.

Corfu was named after Corcyra, mistress of the sea-god Poseidon, enemy of Odysseus. He was so angry at Odysseus's escape that he smote the ship with the palm of his hand and turned it to stone.

The coast southward, a quiet escapist's area until quite recently, is lively with hotels, holiday villas and restaurants past Benitses and as far as Messonghi, where olive trees still grow down to the narrow beach. On the way to Benitses at Kaiser's Bridge is Achilleion, a grandiose, ugly neo-Classical villa built in 1890 for Elizabeth of Austria, the sad, unhappily

married wife of the Hapsburg Emperor Franz Joseph, as her summer retreat. She chose this area just a mile from Benitses for its beauty and peace. In her Italian terraced gardens she put a sculpture of the Dying Achilles. After she was assassinated by an anarchist in Geneva, Kaiser Wilhelm II of Germany bought the villa and came for a month every spring, adding Teutonic touches such as his simple iron bedstead and saddle chair for his desk. He also added to the garden a colossal bronze statue of a war-like Achilles the Victor, with the inscription: 'From the Greatest German to the Greatest Greek'.

There are superb views from the upper

terrace. The house is now a casino, open only in the evenings.

Down the coast you pass some little seaside hamlets which are pleasant.

Kavos beach is very popular, so walk round the cliffs above the beach at the southernmost tip, Cape Asprokavos, among the old olive trees and the bracken.

The south west beaches below Korission lagoon used to be the private hide-away of experienced package tour reps, who rode there on days off and didn't tell their clients. Even now there is only one real road to the sea, at Agios Georgios, where holiday villas and bar-restaurants are spreading but will never take over until access is made easier. However, day visitors from the resort of Paleokastritsa come there by boat. Walk southward along this beach and you will find peace and quiet. From Linia, just inland, is a track running past the Korission lagoon where fishing nets are spread across the water. Keep on to the sea and your reward is a superb beach – miles of golden sand and dunes. I shared it last time with a mobile snack bar and a couple of dozen young people. I could not tell whether they were escaping reps – they were not wearing uniform. In fact, like sensible

youngsters in that glorious sun, they were not wearing anything.

Agios Gordis, which you reach from Sinarades by a delightful mountain road which winds and drops through a narrow defile, is one of those beauty spots which can never really fit into the modern world because nature has revolted against car parking. But it is commercialized, even to some locals letting out their gardens as parking space in high summer. It is a beautiful spot, with vineyards almost to the beach – a mile and half of sands, with rocks at one end, a tall islet on the other. Clamped on the cliff is a concrete, honey-comb hotel – impressive but I would rather they had built it somewhere else.

Glifada beach further north, in a lovely bay of olive groves, has an even bigger, more obtrusive hotel (Olympic), but you can move to the north end where there are a few beach restaurants. Mirtiotissa beach to the north of the bay, far from roads and buses, has been used as an unofficial nudist beach, which has scandalized peasants. Just south of it is Pelekas, with a viewing platform from which you can often get magnificent views.

Ermones beach was where Odysseus landed in the local version of the legend. Now it has straw shelters, a bar-restaurant, and can be reached by road from Vatos or a cliff cable-car from the landscaped chalet hotel (Ermones Beach) on the mountain side.

Paleokastritsa has grown into a popular resort but is still lovely. The best place to see it is near the village of Lakones, a favourite base for walkers in the lovely local scenery. The Paleokastritsa monastery, built in 1228, 300 feet up on a promontory, seems to hang over the sea. Inside is a little museum of ikons but from outside you see the several little odd-shaped coves of Paleokastritsa beneath you. The shoreline of the bay is now lined with hotels and restaurants, behind them are holiday apartments, and even the coves are crowded in high summer with sun-bathers ferried there by a fleet of water taxis. There's a lovely view of Paleo, too, from Bella Vista taverna above the vil-lage, where I used to go for fish meals before the crowds came. Coaches stop now long enough for excursionists to click cameras and sink cold drinks.

After admiring the view of Paleokas-tritsa, go into the mountains behind. Here is the untouched beauty of Corfu – villages and hamlets oblivious to the wave of tour-ism. Between here and Tsavros, as the road climbs and dips steeply, are stunning views to the north coast and south east to the Gulf of Kerkira as far as Corfu town itself. Below southward is the great Ropa plain, the richest agricultural area of this rich island.

The other Agios Georgios – a bay north of Paleokastritsa – is a long sand and pebble beach, little developed, reached by a track down from Afionas, which has some glorious views. This hilly forest of north-west Corfu still has few roads and they are mostly rough, but it is beautiful and worth exploring. Agios Stefanos (the West Coast one) is reached by a winding small road and has a lovely sand beach, shelving gently, church, cottages and a quay for fishing boats, but now a few tavernas, restaurants and villas are appearing. Sidari was a holiday resort long ago but remains a fishing village. It was just the sort of place to attract our grandfathers, with a big beach, often wet from a river running into the sea, bringing lush greenery, and picturesque sandstone cliffs eroded by the wind to make strange shapes and caves. Take the little road

west, lined with big olives, to Peroulades, a delightful village beloved by photo-graphers for its photogenic houses and its women who sit on their doorsteps on Sun-day mornings in their traditional Corfiot dress. One writer described it as a 'beauti-fully squalid Greek village'. Yes, that's just what a lot of them were before many tourists came. And the road from Arkadades to Sidari is just like most roads were, too – attractive but hard work.

Along the north coast from Sidari to Roda are fine sandy beaches all the way, but the real road swings inland. There is a narrow sandy beach at Roda, some useful cafés and para-skiing, which is fun for skiers but hell for people trying to hold a conversation nearby.

Villas and apartments dot the coastline from Roda round the corner to Kassiopi, an historic town which slumped to the level of an insignificant fishing village and is now back in the limelight as a resort and target for tourist excursions from other places, not only because it is attractive but because there is a good road from Corfu town, excellent for coaches, and a spec-tacular corniche road as far as Kouloura, where Lawrence Durrell lived in the 1930s.

Kassiopi flourished as a Roman town, and even Nero visited it in AD 67 for its

shrine to Zeus. The Byzantines built a fort against Turkish pirates but the Venetians destroyed it, leaving the Kassiopians prey to pirates and looters. The ruined fortress stands above the village, full of wild flowers and sheep, while the Kassiopians, like the Venetians, coin money from the tourists.

Before the village of Agnitsini, which has a track to a shingle beach, an unmade road winds to the other Agios Stefanos. Here fishing boats are moored by a stony beach, there are cottages and tavernas, and a view of Albania just across the Straits.

Kouloura is still a charming place, with a little harbour for fishing boats, a taverna, a terrace of cottages and a shingle beach, with a backcloth of hills. Across a headland is Kalami, an enchanting fishing village on a curving bay backed by hillsides dotted with cypresses, but the seaward view is mostly shortened by the Albanian coast.

From the main highway southward the coast to Corfu town has been developed for tourism in recent years, particularly Pyrgi and Ipsos, not so long ago little fishing hamlets. Ipsos had a beachside fish restaurant where people of Corfu town would come by car or boat on Sundays. The fishermen's quay is now jammed with fibreglass pleasure boats, there are hotels of all classes, villas, camp sites and the odd disco. The farms have gone. It is a playground for the young.

Just before Pyrgi is a turning to Agios Markos and Korakiana, a lovely village with more than twenty churches. Markos has a chapel from 1075 and a church with wall paintings from 1576. At Pyrgi you can take a spectacular road of hairpin bends through the mountains to the north coast. The views are magnificent, but then Corfu is one of the most beautiful isles in Greece.

CORFU (KERKYRA)

Most northerly of the Ionian Isles. 229 square miles. The north comes within two miles of the Albanian coast.

Air ...... Charter flights from many UK airports and scheduled services. Three daily flights to Athens.

Ferries ...... To Igoumenitsa on mainland every hour in summer, two hours in winter; to Brindisi in Italy weekly; to isles of Ithaca and Cephalonia and Patras (on the mainland) thrice weekly in summer, once in autumn, none in winter; small car ferry to Paxos daily in summer, twice a week in winter; necessary to stay one night but day excursions run to Paxos in summer.

Coaches ...... Three times daily service from Athens via Igoumenitsa, coach travels on the ferry.

Paxos and Antipaxos

Paxos is a delight. Smallest of the seven main Ionian Isles, just eighteen square miles, it is looked on these days as an excursion from Corfu or even as a bolt-hole from Corfu crowds. But it is three hours' sailing south of Corfu, a lovely trip skirting Corfu's south-east coast and with views too to the Epirot ranges on the Greek mainland, and from the attractive old port of Parga on the Epirus coast the journey is only one and a half hours. That was the way I first reached it in a caique and nearly all the other visitors were Italians. But now there are day trips from Corfu in summer, which can crowd the beguiling little port of Gaios. It is little more than a village, but has quite an important-looking central square opening onto the quay, filled with tables and diners when crowds thin in the evening.

On the quayside boats of many shapes and sizes are packed tight, from sailing dinghies and caiques to private yachts, round to the new port where car ferries dock. Many streets are too narrow for cars.

Though Gaios is sheltered by an islet thick with pines, the olive groves, with huge old gnarled trees, are the symbol and the main source of living of Paxos. You can walk round the island and that is the best way to enjoy its tranquillity. If the day visitors fill Gaios, take a bus or walk five miles to Lakka, a tiny port in a peaceful, almost circular bay. The bay is very pleasant, with nice little tavernas, café-bars and shops. On the way, you could turn right to Longos, smaller, attractive port with only one tall industrial chimney spoiling the effect. By hilly but driveable donkey tracks, there is a very rewarding diversion from the village of Magazia to another village Manesatika and the pretty twin-domed Byzantine church of

Ipapanti, then downhill through groves and past old tumbledown houses to rejoin the Lakka road.

A good road south from Gaios through a corniche reaches Port Spuzo, seemingly a home for geriatric caiques. From along the hillside you can cross a stone causeway to Mogonis Island, a pleasant place, but popular with watersports enthusiasts – sailing, waterskiing, surfboarding. Its restaurant is good. Some stretches of road have been stained black over years with the juice of fallen olives crushed under tyres. In the groves olives are caught in nets hung under branches. You may see large bells strapped to some trees. They are for fire warning. In summer heat, a forest fire could destroy most of the island's livelihood.

Nets pegged below the olive trees to catch the harvest

On Agios Nicholas, the isle in Gaios bay, is a Venetian castle built in the fourteenth century. The Italians still come to Paxos. A weekly boat via Cephalonia comes from Patras, which is linked by big ferries with Venice, Brindisi and Ancona.

Paxos is quiet and undeveloped mostly because of lack of water in summer, though winter rains make it lush. The people try to hoard winter water in cisterns – so precious they are kept locked.

The snag for island hoppers, backpackers or travellers who do not want to plan ahead is a great shortage of beds, especially in summer, when the few hotels are booked by package companies or holiday sailing clubs. So are the available houses and flats and many rooms in private houses, and unofficial camping is strictly banned because of fire risks. So

you will almost certainly be asked to show a room reservation for at least two nights before boarding the ferry in mid-summer. Sometimes there are rooms for rent on offer around the ticket office – at higher rates than on the island. Go in early June or September, find a room near the quay or square and you won't want to leave. The people are very friendly, the atmosphere relaxed.

Paxos is a small-boat sailors' isle. Seas are usually kind, there are many islets to explore or for shelter, and on the west coast, spectacular cliffs and seawater caves. In one cave the Greek Resistance leader hid to waylay Italian shipping. Alas, the Germans thought he had a good idea and used it to hide submarines to prey on allied ships. Homer's legendary golden rooms of the Palace of Poseidon in Ipperandi cave are home to little brown monk seals.

The little isle of Antipaxos has even fewer beds. You might find a village room, but only 126 people live here, so best take a sleeping bag if you intend to stay. It would be frustrating not to.

Antipaxos lives by making soft, pleasant white and red wines and you can drink them in peace and tranquillity.

A mile from the south end of Paxos, it can be reached in a small boat from there in twenty minutes or in forty minutes by caique ferry in June to September. You can hire a boat in other months. Like Paxos, its western coast has tower cliffs diving into the Ionian sea. The east side has little bays backed by gentle hills. The most beautiful, Voutoumi, has a long curving stretch of clean golden sand and superbly clear water – an idyllic spot, except that later in the morning in summer excursion boats arrive from Paxos and drop off escapists come to swim, brown their bodies, picnic, drink and play, sometimes rather heartily. So go early, then move on southward to two more lovely bays with pebbly shores but clear seas and sand bed. Below them is the tiny port and nearest thing to a village – Ormos Agrapidias, with a tiny harbour and a few fishing boats. Try to walk to the west coast for dramatic seascapes, especially of the mountainous little isle between the headlands of Alikes and Rodovani. I was once caught in a storm here. The purple fierce seas, the lightning, the rain, the screaking seagulls seeking shelter, were like a sound and light background for a film of Dante's Inferno.

PAXOS (PAXI, PAXOI)

Nine miles south of Corfu; eight miles west of Parga on mainland. Eighteen square miles.

Ferries ...... Car ferry daily from Corfu in summer, twice weekly in winter; daily summer, thrice weekly winter from Parga on mainland. Boats sometimes cancelled through bad weather. To get a ferry ticket in summer, you must have booked overnight bed. Two hotels often booked solid but village rooms available.

ANTIPAXOS

A mile off the coast of Paxos at Mogonisi (20 minutes – hire a boat), excursion boats from Gaios port on Paxos (50 mins); no accommodation – return same day.

IONIAN ISLES 2

Zakynthos (Zante)

The road from Gyri, a tiny hilltop town in the very centre of Zakynthos, was marked on the map as 'unpaved road'. It wasn't. Maps of Zakynthos are even less reliable than those of other Greek isles. It was a mule track, skirting the edge of the mountain, with fine views but lethal sharp boulders sticking through its dirt surface. Even a mule would have had to tread warily. We had to swerve perilously near the edge to avoid tearing the transmission and sump from our little hired Citroën. But it led us through lovely scenery of wooded hills, long views and thick greenery of olives, orange trees, cypresses and vines to remote farms where light came from oil lamps and water from the well. And it showed me that Zakynthos, which we used to call by its Venetian name of Zante, is still that beautiful Flower of the Levante which the Venetians called it, despite the earthquake of 1953 which destroyed most of the Venetian buildings, and the new airfield which brings in tourists from Athens, Britain and Germany from early April to mid-October, when the rains come almost as regularly as the monsoons.

Zakynthos still casts a magic spell over its visitors. You can simply lie and dream and do nothing happily for days. Or you hire a motor cycle or a car, preferably four-wheel drive, and wander those roads, paved and unpaved, to find a world where the important things in life are sheep, goats and the trees and vines producing the olives and raisins already known to Elizabethan housewives in England.

To the east and south of the island, attractive bathing beaches and pleasant inland villages are linked by metal roads in various states of smoothness and there is little need to use the dirt roads except to reach the remoter beaches or to cut corners. The west coast is rocky and slopes steeply to the sea, with villages inland, uphill and scarce. A road runs inland to the north tip at Korinth (Korythi), joined by a few roads across the island.

The major roads spread like a spider's web from the capital Zakynthos. The port was almost totally destroyed by the '53 earthquake but was rebuilt in its Venetian pattern, with arcades, small squares, narrow streets and little palazzi. Concrete can never recreate the beauty of stone, but with a few years' weathering it begins to look slightly authentic already. But the elegant Venetian houses have gone forever. So, of course, have the smart restaurants, masked balls, burlesques and opera by famous visiting companies which lasted until 1939. They have been replaced by discos, a few summer night-clubs, and tavernas and tourist snack cafés specializing in grilled fish, 'Greek salads, omelettes and souvlaki.

Zakynthos is still a most attractive town because of its lovely position cradled among hills. You find a touch of the old elegance and glory in Plateia Solomou, the gracious main square named after the poet of Greek freedom Dionysos Solomos, who died in 1857. He wrote the Hymn of Liberty, the Greek national anthem, translated into English by Rudyard

Kipling. As with Corfu, the English governed the island from 1809 to 1864.

In a corner of the square is the lovely fifteenth-century church of Agios Nikolaos, one of the few that could be restored after the earthquake. On a long terrace alongside, you can sit outside in summer eating a meal or just drinking coffee and eating the local sweetmeats *pasteli* (biscuits with sesame seeds) and *mandalato* (white nougat with nuts).

Another survivor from the earthquake is the Kastro, the hillside castle, built by the Venetians. It's a pleasant one hour's evening stroll up there for a view of the town, bay and mainland coast. To gauge the elegance of the Venetian buildings that have gone, look at the fine façade of the Church of Our Lady of the Angels (Kiria ton Angelon) behind the Hotel Xenia.

Fine ikons (15th–19th century) saved from wrecked churches are in the Art Museum on Solomou square, with religious paintings of the Ionian School set up by artists who fled from the Turks in Crete.

The most impressive church was re-built. Named for the patron saint of Zakynthos, St Dionyssios, it stands at the opposite end of the harbour from the ferry quay and, with its square white belltower with red roof, looks as prettily effective seen in daylight across the blue water, with a few white clouds puffing across a blue Greek sky, as it does lit and shining in the water on a balmy night. The inside, lit by great chandeliers, is a blend of white and blue, with superbly ornate many-coloured frescos on its curved ceiling.

But all this is a reflection of the past, and today Zakynthos is a buzzing little commercial port, linked by ferry to Kyllini on the mainland, with busy narrow streets and simple very-Greek island shops where goods are displayed and stored in what looks like complete disorder.

Most package tour visitors stay in Laganas, so even those huge sands look very populated in summer. Greeks come over from the Peloponnese on holiday, too. It's a lively place, with animated tavernas and watersports, but for me the use of part of the sands as a road to hotels and a car park spoils it. Don't think that Zante is yet crowded with tourists. They are nearly all in three places. Only a few who take to the smaller roads see very much of the island, so those mule-track bumps are well worth tackling.

The main road by-passing Laganas reaches Lake Keri, where nature pours pitch, a by-product of petrol, from springs. For centuries fishermen have caulked their wooden boats with it. Keri itself, a pretty place on a headland, has some fine old houses and a seventeenth-century church. There's a tantalizing beach below with tavernas. You can reach it by boat – or abseiling.

The second magnet for holidaymakers is Argasi, only four miles from Zakynthos town. It has a narrower beach but nicer countryside, and Mount Skopos behind it. This is the mountain with such splendid sea views that in old times men would climb it twice a day – not for the seascape but to spot if pirate ships were coming!

A few holiday 'villas' have been built in Argasi. There are three pleasant hotels (we like Chryssi Akti), several tavernas, and a few mid-summer discos which can lead to liveliness at night. But it is all on a small scale, and the hilly road leads on to attractive beaches with tavernas – Porto Zorro St Nicholas and Porto Roma, with a fine sweep of sand in a wooded bay – a delightful spot. Through Vassilikos village the road becomes a driveable track, leading to the clean, golden sands of Vas-silikos beach. It is what an estate agent would call 'ripe for development'. But all it has are a taverna at the top, a shack selling cold drinks, nude sunbathers and pedaloes in season. There's good reason. Here giant sea turtles lay their eggs, lumbering in from the sea at dusk to hide the eggs just beneath the sands. They are an endangered species and, sadly, local dogs who do not know any better and visitors who are warned and should know, still steal the eggs. Now, at least, part of the beach is for turtles, people are banned.

Northward from Zakynthos town you pass a lush fertile plain of orange and olive groves, and vines producing grapes for the famous Zante currants. Spring wild flowers are as beautiful as on Corfu, and here they are at their best. Only three miles from town is Tsillivi beach. It has sands as fine as talcum powder, olive trees almost to the beach, and the village is still agricultural. Tourism has started. There is one small hotel, a few tavernas, peda-loes, holiday villas built among the olive groves and one bar called Olive Tree Pub.

Alikes bay has a magnificent stretch of sand backed by dunes and salt lagoons. The little resort of Alikes at the eastern end has tavernas, bars, small hotels, villas and apartments, and souvenir shops, but is still a pleasant quiet family spot.

One road from Zakynthos town west-ward goes to Macherado, which has a church with a delightful interior. Take the road towards Mouzaki and turn right at Romiri to Aghios Nikolaos. Here there is an unsurfaced but widish road weaving through delightful countryside to Agalas. But to see the north of the island carry on to Aghios Leontas and downhill to the quiet village of Kampi. A track winds uphill to one of the most sadly dramatic scenes in Greece. From a sheer clifftop you can look down to an idyllic tiny bay, with almost-violet sea lapping grey rocks. Behind on the peak is a massive concrete cross facing out to sea. It is a memorial to Greek freedom fighters, thrown over the cliff in the 1939–45 war. Alongside is a little bar-taverna where you may well be joined for a drink by a local farm worker.

Back on the road, you reach Maries, where a rough track, marked as a road on some maps, crosses the island. But the real road onwards takes you near to two monasteries – fifteenth-century Anofonitrias, damaged in the 1953 earthquake, and along a track too rough even for a scooter, Aghios Georgiou Krimnou

monastery, where a solitary monk will show you round. Quite interesting but a greater delight was to take the path beyond through wild herbs to a superbly peaceful headland, with wonderful distant views of the isle of Cephalonia.

Back on the main road you reach Volimes, which is joined to Korynth by a new wide road. Beyond a road leads to the sea, where there are two tavernas and a quay from which you can get boats to the Blue Grotto during summer. Go in the afternoon, when the sun shining on the azure sea makes iridescent patterns in several shades of blue on the walls of the cave and under the arches of eroded rock.

ZAKYNTHOS (ZANTE)
157 square miles.

Air ...... Charter flights from many British airports, mid-April to mid-October; daily flights to Athens (30 mins). Three flights weekly to Cephalonia.

Ferries ...... Six each day to Kyllini on the Peloponnese coast (2 hrs); some boats in summer to Argostoli in Cephalonia; speedboat service to Patras in summer.

Coach ...... From Athens via Kyllini (7 hrs).

Cephalonia

I was standing recently at a bus stop in north Cephalonia looking at one of the most dramatically beautiful scenes in the Greek islands. Below me on the hillside, stretching down to the water, were the red-roofed white houses and the white quayside of the little fishing town of Assos. The houses spread onto a strip of land cutting into the near-blinding blue sea to join a tiny peninsula – just a hill rising

from the sea. On this rather rugged hillside opposite were very neatly terraced fields and olive groves and above them, on the peak, a formidable fortress, built by the Venetians in the sixteenth century to protect the people from pirates. Later I climbed to the fortress, now ruined with trees hiding some of its walls, and there the view was as beautiful – the west coast of Erissos with its mountain ridge, Myrtos

Bay, with its tree-speckled cliffs dropping to fine white shingle, and the startling blue Ionian sea. Yet once the fortress was used as a Greek prison!

Down on the quayside, drinking a bottle of the white, flinty Robola wine, I wondered how some travel writers could dismiss Cephalonia as dull and uninteresting. True, it suffered even more than Zakynthos from the 1953 earthquake, few remains are left of its Mycenaean and Classical past and it lives by trade, agriculture and shipping rather than tourism, so that its capital and main port Argostoli has been rebuilt as a working city rather than for the convenience or delight of tourists. But these people can surely have not been to the north. It has some of the most beautiful scenery in the Greek islands.

It is a magnificent climbing drive northwards from Argostoli, with the mountains alongside and superb sea and coast views round each bend. No easy drive, mind you, and you will see a lot more as a passenger than as driver, but the road is good apart from small rock falls. There is a daily bus to Assos.

At the pretty village of Divarata, there is a rather hairy drive down a track to the beach – steep, hairpin bends, loose surface; but the view from the beach makes it well worth doing. There is yet another beautiful, dazzling view just past Divarata where the road reaches the coast. Just look down the high cliffs to the white beach and blue sea of Myrtos Bay. Then the mountain scenery becomes equally dramatic and the sight of goats leaping from one sharp rock to another with a drop of hundreds of feet beneath can be more heart-stopping still.

North from Assos you turn the northern point of the isle past woods of cypress trees and deserted bays and come to the de-lightful fishing village of Fiscardon, undamaged by the earthquake. It is built on the south side of an inlet, with a little harbour looking across the water to a green point of land and mountains beyond. The pension here is sometimes booked well ahead but there are some village rooms. Ask at the shop.

The road from Argostoli to Sami, the small port on the east coast, is as dramatic as any on this island. It climbs through the mountains and across Mount Ainos, and you can on fine days see the sea in some direction wherever you are, and beyond it a variety of distant places – Zakynthos, Kyllini and its Venetian castle, the mainland mountains, the neighbouring isle of Ithaca, and Lefkas. Some claim to have seen Corfu. There are some pretty villages on minor side roads, too. There is a tourist hut at over 4000 feet and the fit and energetic can walk from here through the historic Cephalonian firs to Megalos

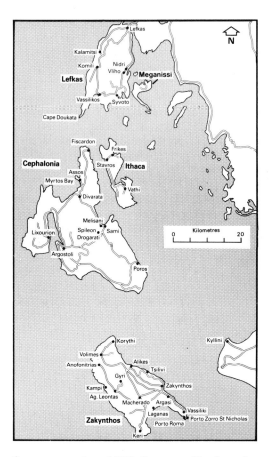

Sorros another 1000 feet up. During the eighteenth century these pines covered the mountain so thickly that the Venetians called it Monte Nero (Black Mountain), but they cut a lot down to make ships and forest fires took toll, too.

The port of Sami, on the site of ancient Same, capital in Homer's days, caught the full brunt of the earthquake and is still somewhat prefabricated and dull. But it is in a most attractive bay, with fine sand beaches nearby, thickly wooded hilly background, and views of Ithaca looking darkly foreboding across the straits.

Sami is the port for Ithaca ferries. But it also has a daily ferry from Patras, which is linked to three Italian ports – Venice, Ancona and Brindisi – so Italian holidaymakers abound. Less frequent boats go to Corfu.

Near to Sami are several strange caves. Spileon Drogarati, with many-coloured stalactites and stalagmites, is impressively lit and concerts are held in it because of its fine acoustics. I am more interested in Limni Melisani, just along the road north to Aghias Evfimia, a charming fishing port with a tiny harbour and occasional ferry services. The Melisani cave ('purple cave') is spectacular and mysterious. At the bottom of a deep circular bowl about 250 feet round is a lake which changes colour from blue to purple and violet according to the light. For long it was thought to be bottomless and there seemed no way to it. In the 1960s an underground cavern, known to the ancient Greeks, was found and opened up so that you can reach the lake. With a guide you can take a boat on the lake. Another strange discovery was made, too. It was known that the sea flowed under the land near Argostoli and the water was used once to drive mills. But no one knew where it went. So they put in some dye and it came out first at Melisani, then in the Gulf of Sami.

The boats from Kyllini on the mainland go to Argostoli and to Poros, south of Sami, another place destroyed by the earthquake. It is not a pretty place, but friendly, with genuine tavernas and a long shingle beach. It's a long drag over a steep hill to and from the ferry and taxi-grabbing is advisable if you have heavyish luggage. Also, Poros's few beds get filled quickly in mid-summer, and it shuts down off-season. But I like it. And the road to Argostoli along the south coast is not quite so dramatic as others but beautiful and must seem quite hairy in a bus. Slopes are thick with olives and cypresses. As you get higher the narrow road has been cut through granite with cliff-face on one side and a sheer drop to a coastal plain. If you can bear to look, there are fine sea views. There are minor roads down to seaside villages and beaches and towards Argostoli you pass through neat modern-looking villages with flat-roofed houses. These were rebuilt after the earthquake.

Argostoli town is a busy place, with a big market, sea trade, shops providing for local people rather than visitors, most cafés, restaurants and tavernas doing the same. Visitors are well outnumbered in most of them. It may not be pretty but it is the commercial face of the 'Real Greece' which many travellers claim to be seeking – the real Greece of today, not of past peasantry and poverty. I find it very interesting. It becomes more attractive when,

their work done, locals join the fairly few tourists in the pavement bars, tavernas and little restaurants around the attractive modern Villanou Metaxa Square.

The British built a causeway across the narrow gulf, with a road, leaving a good fishing lagoon. But beaches are mostly in coves down by the airport, and this is where most package tourists stay, a bus ride from town. Luckily there are not too many aircraft to disturb their peace – not yet, anyway.

The other beaches sought by visitors are across the Gulf on the peninsula, twenty miles round by road or one hour by ferry to the quiet little port of Lixourion. I like this place, too. Divided by a river, it is centred on a pleasant little square with bars and tavernas, and has its own fishing boats, so is a good spot to eat fish. Beaches are along the coast southwards, mostly in little coves.

But it is not for lying on beaches that most people visit Cephalonia. It is for beauty. It is an island for travellers rather than tourists.

CEPHALONIA (KEFALONIA, KEFALLINIA)
297 square miles.

Air ...... Some charters from Britain in summer; daily flights to Athens; thrice weekly to Zakynthos.

Ferries ...... Six ferries daily to Kyllini on Peloponnese, some boats from Argostoli (2 hrs), others from Poros on east coast (1½ hrs); some boats in summer to Zakynthos; daily ferries from Sami port on east coast to Patras on mainland in summer, less often in winter (3½ hrs); speedboat service to Patras in summer; daily boats to Vathi (Ithaca) from Sami; one boat a week from Fiscardon, northern tip of Cephalonia, to Paxos and Corfu, one to Ithaca and Corfu from Sami; the boat to Astakos on mainland from Aghia Evfimia, north of Sami, said to run daily, was not running last time I was there (1987); so check; caique ferry in summer from Fiscardon to the isle of Lefkas.

Ithaca

Few islands a mere seventeen by four miles have achieved such fame as Ithaca. Yet its lure lies in myth as much as reality and unless you read the myth and believe it, then you miss the rocky little island's magic. For this was the home of Odysseus, hero of Homer's *Odyssey*, which describes his ten years of travel, dangers and adventure after leaving the siege of Troy.

Odysseus himself summed up the island's ruggedness as 'impractical for horses, good for goats'. But one modern road at least runs almost down it, another round much of the coast, and the caiques local people used on my first visit because roads were so bad now take visitors so that they can enjoy sea views of the coast. But it is still a simple place, with very friendly people, and often surprisingly few visitors. As Ithaca is only two and a half miles across the strait from Cephalonia at the closest point and the ferry from Sami takes only a half-hour, most visitors come for the day and are gone by around 6 pm.

When the Phaeacians brought Odysseus from Corfu back home after twenty years away, they left him asleep on the coast at Vathi. He missed a beautiful homecoming, for this little port and capital is in a magnificent position, hidden in a deep long inlet off the bay of Dexia. Past a barren mountainous headland the ship aims for a narrow channel. Once you are through, you enter this long U-shaped fjord-like stretch of sea with Vathi at the far end, almost surrounded by green conical hills. Houses cling to their slopes joined by steep steps, which to people returning tired from work must seem to go

on for ever. But being Greeks they take lots of rests to look down at the sea. Its setting is so superb that you hardly notice that the white houses are fairly new (because of that awesome earthquake). Just offshore a tiny isle covered in pines seems to have been put there for photographers.

Ithaca is hour-glass shaped – two bulges joined by a narrow strip about half a mile wide. Just below this is Mount Aetos (Eagle) where eagles still nest. But first, like Odysseus, you must visit the cave of the Nymphs.

The cave, surrounded by cypress trees, has a narrow entrance to a fifty-foot chamber with a hole in the roof cut to let out the

smoke of sacrificial fires, and called 'The Entrance of the Gods'.

A longish but rewarding and sign-posted walk takes you south from Vathi past a clifftop to Arethusa's fountain. Poor Arethusa cried so much when her son Cory was killed that she turned into a fountain.

Classical historians and archaeologists have argued about the exact site of Odysseus's city, which seems fairly pointless. Homer, like all the greatest imaginative story-tellers, was not too worried about facts, which can ruin a great story. It is now said to be near Stavros in the north.

Stavros is more or less just a street with a square half-filled with chairs and tables of a true, simple Greek taverna.

But my favourite place has nothing to do with Homer. The village of Frikes is most attractive – running along a valley between pleasant hills to the sea, with a little fishing port. You can get caiques from here to Vathi, a delightful trip around the rocky coast, and if you are lucky to Vassiliki on Lefkas. I like caiques.

Ithaca's beaches are unexciting – but you don't go there to lounge on beaches. Better to take to the water.

ITHACA (ITHAKI)

Separated from Cephalonia by a strait only 1–2½ miles wide. 38 square miles but isle is only 660 yards wide in one place.

Ferries ...... Daily from Vathi to Sami on Cephalonia; daily to Patras on mainland, where ferries from Italy arrive; every other day to Paxos and Corfu; possibly to Astakos on mainland and Aghia Evfimia (see Cephalonia).

Lefkas (Lefkada)

Before the mid-summer tourist season, I sat drinking wine on the quayside at Vassiliki, a village in the south of Lefkas. The shady tree above me dipped almost into the water, nearly touching a fishing boat. Four fishermen were playing cards at the next table. Suddenly one of them went to the kitchen and produced a plate of little red mullet. I couldn't understand what he said, so another man, who didn't have to tell me that he had learned his English in Australia, explained that the fisherman had caught them, and thought

that I would like them for lunch. I am not such a gannet for red mullet as Barbara is. But it would have been very bad manners to refuse. So the two men sat down beside me and the 'Australian', who was about 5 ft 2 inches tall, thickset and none too handsome but was called Adonis, translated.

Taramosalata appeared, the superb paste of smoked cod's roe, with a garlic dip and bread. They ordered a bottle of the white wine I was drinking – not their own retsina. Fried aubergines and the inevitable village salad followed. Then came the mullet – grilled, tender, delicate in taste, moistened with lemon juice. Perfect! I told my friends so. They promptly each took two off their plates and put them on mine. Red wine came, then grilled steak and a huge pile of chips. Then more wine.

We talked on, still drinking. Around six o'clock they left me to tend their nets. They would not let me pay. Then I knew that Lefkas is indeed a true Greek island, though the bus direct from Athens does not have to board a ferry nor get a tyre wet to reach Lefkas town.

You see, Lefkas was not an island until the Corinthian colonists cut a canal in 540 BC which cut it off from the mainland, and this was widened over centuries by Venetians. Then modern man built a causeway and finally a wide, tarmac road to join it to the mainland again.

Lefkas has always been of importance to conquerors and defenders and they left a series of fortresses on the mainland. Lefkas town faces one of them across the lagoon left by the causeway – the thirteenth-century castle of Santa Maura, after which the island was once called. Flat-bottomed boats are used for fishing in the lagoon, which you can also cross on a chain-ferry.

Lefkas had its earthquake in 1948, when Greece was too poor and devastated after the war for much rebuilding. The upper storeys of some houses have been rebuilt with boarding and corrugated iron. There are still stone Venetian churches and tall houses with Turkish-

style wooden balconies. Perhaps because these are crumbling and not 'renovated' the town has the nostalgic decaying look of some towns in Southern Italy. The big quay is a yacht chartering centre.

Pleasant villages are dotted down the east coast. The attractive fishing port of Nidri, a centre for sailing and port of call for holiday sailing flotillas, is in such a beautiful position that it was bound to develop a few villas and bungalows for letting to tourists but they are five minutes walk from the village. There are bed and breakfast tavernas, too, where you can sit outside seeing stunning views of this lovely bay with delightful little islands. I have marked up Nidri for a longer return visit.

Ferries from here will take you to the little green island of Meganisi and do try to get a room in one of the three villages, for such tranquil places are rare.

Two little places where you could hide even from the yacht flotillas are further south – Vliho, in a fjord-like bay backed by mountains on both sides, topped by Mount Elati, and Syvoto, a sweet little fishing port with shallow water, grass to the water's edge and tavernas with rooms.

Going north, you can reach the best beach on the island, Kalamitsi, but you must be ready to face the boulders, jagged stones and potholes of a steep track with wicked hairpins.

There are two ways at present of reaching Cape Doukata in the south from Vassiliki and you must go, for this is the original Lover's Leap, the white cliff over which Sappho the poetess of love leapt to her death. You can go by caique and see 'the evening star above Leucadia's far-projecting rock of woe', as Childe Harold did in Byron's poem, or drive north to Komili, then down south again on a rough road.

Sappho, the poetess from Lesbos who gave birth to the second meaning of Lesbian by writing love poems to and about her girl friends, in middle age fell for a handsome boatman, Phao, who crossed her. So she fell off the 200-foot cliff and died. But not all the jumpers did. The priests from Apollo's temple made the jump safely as part of their ritual. It was called *katapontismos*. They had a boat waiting below – and it is very heavily rumoured that they used a net to break their fall. It became a fashion among some fashionable young Romans to make the Leap, too. They wore birds' feathers as a form of wings. Some made it.

LEFKAS (LEVKAS, LEUKAS, LEFKADA)

Joined by a causeway to Arkanani on the mainland, and there is a chain ferry. 119 square miles.

Air ...... Possible to fly from Athens to Preveza (northward in the Ambracian Gulf) then take a ferry across to Aktion, then a bus to Lefkas.

Ferries ...... Apart from the chain ferry alongside the causeway, summer caiques go to Fiscardon on northern tip of Cephalonia and to Vathi on Ithaca.

Coaches ...... Direct service from Athens to Aktion, then across the causeway.

SARONIC ISLES 1

Aegina

It was late March but there was snow in Athens, the first for forty years. The only isle which I could reach was nearby Aegina. Ferries to all islands had stopped. Surprisingly the hydrofoil was running. My friend on Aegina, Adonis, language teacher, translator of literature, property owner, scholar and travel agent, had told me over the phone that there were blizzards and that the only hotel open was the simple C-class Avra at Aegina port.

The hydrofoil rocked and rolled its way on the thirty-five-minute journey. It was almost empty. The blizzard on Aegina was what we would call a flurry of snow, but winds were fairly formidable. Little was moving. I was the only guest in the hotel.

Adonis took me to a fish restaurant where we had a superb lunch. This was where all the men were, it seemed – all those who had not gone back to bed to get warm. The weather was impossible, everyone told me. It just couldn't happen here. They urged me to come back later to see their lovely island. No good telling them that I had known it more than twenty years, seen it in glorious spring and hot summer, that I had researched and scripted a TV film here. They were intensely proud of their island. This freak weather was an insult to it.

Adonis drove me to Aghia Marina across the island, a delightful place with an almost-inland shallow bay with huge sands and a rocky cove where boats from Piraeus drop passengers in season. I knew it when it only had one excellent hotel, the Apollo, delightfully sited on high rocks with a swimming pool, a fine sea view and terraces down to the sea, a few villas and pensions along narrow earth lanes, and a tempting row of tavernas on the sands open in summer. Now it grows a little each year, with tiny blocks of holiday apartments creeping up the hillside, more souvenir shops, more mopeds for hire. Adonis was building a small block. His builders were in the coffee bar. After all, you can't work even inside when the temperature is near to freezing. Not on Greek islands, anyway.

Next morning snowflakes hit the window, I had an ice cold shower, shaved in cold water, and haven't shivered so much since having to sleep in a concrete hut with one blanket and no heating in a Polish winter. No one had thought to heat the hotel. Weather like this simply doesn't happen on Aegina, so it would be a waste of money!

Next day the sun came out, the winds dropped, the ferries ran, Aegina town and port sprang into action as if the sun god had pressed a button. Life was 'no problem' again. One thing certainly I have learned in travelling – that the sun does make much of the difference between places and races and human behaviour. Maybe the Ancients were right to worship it.

I love the atmosphere of Aegina, despite its weekend Athenian invasions, its growing band of foreign visitors and its coach tours to the magnificent Temple of Aphaia. It remains an independent island, utterly different from Athens, with a smiling, carefree attitude. It never forgets that in 1826 during the fight for independence from the Turks, Aegina became the first capital of free Greece. Capodistria was elected first president, the first free newspaper was published, and the first drachma minted carrying the phoenix head to show Greece risen from the ashes. Because the Greek fleet and fleets of the Allies (Britain, France and Russia) were at Nauplion in the Peloponnese – just freed – Capodistria moved there. He must have wished he hadn't. Greek political opponents murdered him on the cathedral steps. Incidentally Aegina is pronounced 'Ayina' with a stress on 'A' at the beginning.

Tourism helps, but Aegina still makes its living from fishing and agriculture, though fish scarcities are beginning to bite. Pistachio nuts are a speciality and must be lucrative at the price asked. In Aegina town you can step across the gangplank of a boat to buy your vegetables, fruit and fish, laid out as if in a shop. The boats bring them from the smaller ports around the island – Souvala and Perdika – and from the Peloponnese mainland westward. There are few tourist souvenir or clothes shops for foreigners. The shops,

bars and restaurants are mostly aimed at locals or Athenians.

The austere pink tower of Markellos was the first building of the new Free Government and what is now the public library was the Residence of the President, who worked and slept upstairs while drachmas were minted below. That's one way of balancing the budget. Right on the little fishing-boat harbour, which is still lined with many-coloured boats, is the little fishermen's chapel of Aghios Nikolaos, patron saint of sailors, in which a tall man might hit the roof. The boats catch a lot of *marida* (whitebait), an Aegina delicacy. You can get caiques from this harbour to the isles of Moni and Angistri.

There is another fishing fleet at the charming village of Perdika to the south and a line of excellent fish restaurants where you walk in and choose your fish, then drink your wine on the white terrace above the fishing boats, looking across to little Moni island, seemingly a stone's throw away, while the fish are grilled over charcoal. The smell alone would tempt a vegetarian.

Moni is a delightful little island. Named because it used to belong to a monastery, it now belongs to the Touring Club of Greece and you pay a small entrance fee in your boat fare. What a good idea. It has one of the few, if not the only, camp site in the Saronic Isles. There is a small beach, beautifully clear water, good footpaths through the woods, then rocky scrub pungent with wild herbs, including sage from which the Greeks make a tea for purifying the blood. They don't *all* take ouzo for that.

In spring the hillside is rich in flowering bushes. Nearer the sea white rock roses grow, then purple thyme. In late August skina bushes produce flame-red berries; there are also silvery white woolly plants which I am told are False Dittany, and that their florets are used as wicks for icon lamps and the leaves brewed to make a tea for diabetics. With September rain comes purple cyclamen, thick on the hillside.

If you picnic on Moni's little beach, you will have guests – peacocks. It seems that they are particularly persistent in August, when they bring their chicks. This is when the males shed their spectacular feathers, too, so you might get one to wear in your hat. The kri kri wild goats are, as in other places I have seen them such as Crete and Galloway, wisely shy of humans. I saw some hiding by the look-out post built by the Germans in the '39–'45 war. They are splendid goats, with great long horns.

A lot of vegetables, vines and fruit grow in the north. At Livadi, a walk from Aegina town, a plaque marks the white-washed house in which Nikos Kazantzakis wrote *Zorba the Greek*. Souvala, on the north coast, is a delightful little port and a spa for treating rheumatism and skin diseases. Here you can get away from the intense summer heat when the meltemi

wind blows. Ferries call direct from Piraeus, and fishing boats go out from the harbour in the evenings. After dark, I love to sit drinking wine and eating outside a harbourside taverna and watch in the far distance the mainland lights from Piraeus to Vouliagmes.

The road and bus route to Souvaka goes through Kypseli (meaning beehives) where there is a pleasant little taverna with views down to the port. Kypseli was until recently called Halasmeni (Ruined), after the ruins of a never-completed church. But the village girls took it amiss, just as the ladies of Loose in Kent once wanted their village name changed to avoid being called Loose women.

Just off the road to the south from Aegina town to Aghia Marina is the Monastery of Aghios Nektarios, who was canonized in 1961, most recent Orthodox Church saint. The original chapel is reserved for women. The saint's remains were moved in 1953 to a new chapel. Thanksgiving lamps which cram the church show how many cures are credited to him. Twenty-two nuns live in the monastery. In February the valleys here are filled with pink and white almond blossom. There is also a rough road from Souvala.

On a bare rocky hill above, dotted with tiny churches, are the remains of Palaiochora. Arab pirates operating from Crete were rampaging through the eastern Mediterranean in the ninth century and after a very bloody attack on Aegina town, the people moved up here for safety. But when Aegina was under Venetian rule in 1537, the Turkish pirate-admiral Barbarossa took the town, massacred the men and took away 6000 women and children into slavery. With Independence in 1826, the people moved back to the coast. An American gave most of the money to build their new town. Much of the old town was dismantled to build the new.

Aghia Marina, the little resort across the island, has grown a little too fast and is in danger of losing all its atmosphere, although it is a superb place to take children, for the sands go a long way round the almost-landlocked bay, and the water is shallow and safe. Not being a great lover of sand, which gets in my eyes, ears, nose, toes and navel, I am glad to have such a long row of tavernas and restaurants with tables under umbrellas where I can sit in the cool tasting something more pleasant than seawater.

Cruise ships anchor often off Aghia Marina. Small boats bring their passengers ashore, they are herded into coaches and taken up the hill to see the magnificent Temple of Aphaia, spend a short time souvenir-shopping in Aghia Marina and within two hours are gone.

The Temple is worth a lot more than that, so if cruise ships are due, go in early morning or evening.

Set in a magnificent position on a wooded ridge, from which the sea views on two sides can be bewitching, it is one of the most beautiful and complete classical temples in Greece. It was dedicated to a local goddess Aphaia, believed to have been a moon goddess, and if you see the temple by moonlight with the moonlit sea below, the coast, the rocks, it seems a perfect setting for it. Others say she was a Minoan goddess of wisdom and light from Crete who accidentally provoked a burning passion in King Minos – hardly surprising, in view of what Minos's wife was up to with a bull. She fell in the sea while running away and was picked up by fishermen who landed her on Aegina. Then one of the fishermen tried his luck with her, she fled to the woods and was never seen again.

The temple is in beautiful Doric style, with columns narrowing from the base to the capital almost like the Parthenon. It was built between 410 and 480 BC, and even to someone like myself whose knowledge of Classical architecture is limited, it is as beautiful as any of the other superb old buildings I have seen. Even if you have not the slightest interest in ancient architecture, do see it. I shall not attempt to describe it. For that you must buy a guide on the site. But I was once there as the sun rose and the magic of it gripped me as no plans or technical description could hope to do. It was the magic of being a child again and being aware of dawn for the first time. Perhaps she was not a moon goddess after all. The temple *was* even more beautiful but the British and German archaeologists who excavated the pediment statues in 1811 were allowed to sell them to the eccentric King Ludwig of Bavaria. I have seen them in the

Munich Glyptothek Museum. There is a particularly beautiful sculpture of a dying warrior. They should be in Aegina.

Possibly Aphaia was teasing. After all, these lusty gods and goddesses behaved scandalously. The biggest shocker was Zeus, father of the Gods in more ways than one. He had hundreds of mistresses. It was he who ran off to this island with Aegina, loveliest of twenty daughters of the river Asopos, to avoid the fury of his wife Hera.

Aegina had a son Aiakos. When there was a drought in Greece, envoys were sent to consult the Oracle at Delphi, which advised them to get Aiakos to ask his father Zeus to change the weather. Aiakos went up the highest mountain on Aegina and prayed and the rains came. What a

useful man to have around! In thanks a temple was built on the mountain top to Hellanion Zeus (Zeus of the Greeks) and the mountain became Mount Hellanion. You will find it in the south-east of Aegina, not far from Portes.

Athens regarded Aegina people as pirates. No doubt some were. Piracy became heroic when practised against the Turks and those supplying them in the Greek Independence War last century. Unfortunately habits die hard, and they continued it after the British, French and Russian combined fleet under Admiral Sir Edward Codrington had utterly defeated the Turks at the Battle of Navarino in 1827, virtually ensuring Greek national freedom. The Royal Navy was not putting up with that sort of nonsense. Admiral

Codrington wrote to the new Greek President Capodistria on Aegina: 'The Turkish fleet exists no more. Take care of yours, for we will also destroy it, if need be, to put a stop to a system of robbery on the high seas.'

Anghistri

Caiques take you from Aegina town westward to this little island, landing you either at a newish harbour by the main village, Milo, or at Skala, with a long shady beach backed by tavernas.

It is a very pleasant fertile island, with cornfields and olive, fig and almond trees, and when I was there in spring there were masses of wild flowers. There are a number of cheap hotels at Skala, and village rooms, and it used to be a good place to hide away. I have known of Greeks who have been to Aegina several times who seemed not to know that this island existed. But it has had a lot more publicity lately from Aegina excursion organizers, so it might be more difficult to find a bed in mid-summer.

AEGINA (EGINA)

Biggest isle in the Saronic Gulf and the best served for communications from Piraeus and Athens, 33 square miles.

Ferries ...... Ten a day from Piraeus (1 ½ hrs), mostly to Aegina town but some to Aghia Marina in summer; some call at Souvala on summer weekends; boats also to Poros, Hydra.

Hydrofoil ...... From Zea Marina, Piraeus (35 mins) every hour in summer, less frequently in winter. Some continue to Hydra, Poros. In summer small cruise ships go Piraeus, Aegina, Poros, Hydra, Piraeus.

Salamis (Koulouri)

In the Bay of Salamis in September 480 BC the history of the world was changed as surely as it was by the defeat of the Spanish Armada and by Nelson's victory at Trafalgar.

The great fleet of Xerxes, King of Kings, ruler of the great Persian Empire – 1200 ships – was preparing to deal the death-blow to Greece.

The Northern Greeks had been conquered and were fighting with the Persians. The Athenians and their allies had only 378 ships. So certain was the mighty and all-conquering Xerxes of winning that on a headland near Perama on the mainland he set up a silver throne to watch a battle which could make him master of Greece.

The Greeks were even arguing about whether to give battle here or try to lure the Persian ships to the Peloponnese. The Greek commander Themistocles leaked a rumour that some of his ships were going there. The Persians decided to block the Salamis Straits which are only two miles wide between Perama and Salamis island. The Greek ships, more manoeuvrable, fell back, then turned and drove the bulkier Persian ships into shallows where all but 300 foundered. Xerxes fled without his throne. You can visit the site of it by bus or taxi – two miles from Piraeus. It is called Devil's Tower after an old Venetian watchtower.

The Athenians had sent their women and children to Troezen and their old men to Salamis. Frankly, this old man would not bother to go back to the island. It faces the docks of Piraeus, its own dockyards run down to shallow bays, and the villages are not pretty or interesting.

Athenian families go there, but beaches are gritty or muddy, and the sea is mostly muddy, too. If you want to recreate the scene of the historic battle, you will do it just as well from Xerxes' headland. You can get excursions from Piraeus which tour the bay and call at the island briefly.

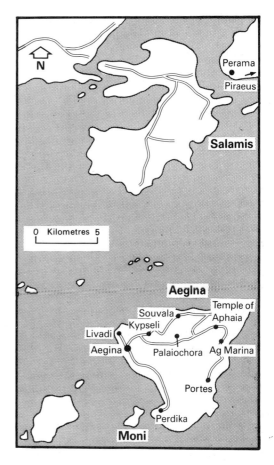

If you hear it called Koulouri, that is because of its shape – croissant.

But it did give birth to the great tragedian Euripides.

SALAMIS (SALAMINA)

Opposite Piraeus in Saronic Gulf and largest Saronic isle, 36 square miles.

Ferry ...... About seventy short crossings daily to Piraeus or Perama, which is 20 mins by bus from Athens.

SARONIC ISLES 2

Poros

The first time I arrived at Poros was aboard a big caique converted with bunks for island touring. I have never forgotten it. Two uneven humps, dark green with lemon groves, grew nearer. Then we saw Poros town, with houses like white cubes piled up the sides of a cone. We sailed through a narrow, almost secretive entrance and the bay opened up before us. Then, as we reached the town, the neck of water narrowed until we were nudging the town quay alongside and the village of Galatas on the mainland seemed just a stride across the water. Such an apt name, Poros. It means ford or passage. And in those days the little ferry caiques used white sails as well as engine power to cross and criss-cross the water, so that a fleet of gulls seemed to be skimming across the straits.

The arrival in Poros has been described by many great writers and painted by hundreds of artists. In *The Colossus of Maroussi*, Henry Miller compared it to sailing through the streets of Venice. Lawrence Durrell, in his book on the Greek Islands, wrote of those white houses up the hillside as 'a child's box of bricks that has been rapidly and fluently set up against a small shoulder of head-land which holds the winds in thrall'. He wrote, too, of the illusion that you could lean over the rail and order an ouzo.

Alas, you do not get the same feeling of intimate closeness from the decks of the big ferries which takes tourists from Athens on a day cruise popping off at Aegina, Poros, Hydra and Spetses, and lunching on board to save time, or when you arrive on the 'Flying Dolphin' hydrofoil. I have only recaptured it once, when I arrived aboard a little motor yacht on an island tour. But I still adore Poros. It is a place to *absorb* yourself in a Greek island.

The Venetian effect is heightened by the ferries – not so much the official car carriers but the little benzinas (water taxis) which pop back and forth.

Durrell talked of the charm of Poros and the elation it brings. 'It is the happiest place I have ever known.' Many more day visitors come now, many more cruise boats and ferries unload more quick in-and-out tourists. More visitors find villas or rooms, too, or arrive on package tours to the bays on the bigger 'hump', Kalavria, but the number of them is paltry compared with many other isles. And for me Poros still keeps its happy atmosphere, as if every day is a holiday or even a fête.

One reason is that the harbour quay is a market, with stalls selling not only to the tourists but to locals.

Mind you, when I arrived very recently on a cold March day with rain in the wind blowing across the harbour, the shops were shut for the day at twelve o'clock, the few market stalls on the quay were bare, and there wasn't even a sailor around from the naval school at the end of the bay. Suddenly a ship's siren sounded and through the narrow gap into the harbour came the luxury island cruise ship from Piraeus. Within three or four minutes the shops were open, vans pulled up noisily and unloaded cargoes of tourist-style dresses, shirts, sweaters, sandals, handbags, belts, copies of ancient vases, and soon every inch of the stalls was covered in souvenirs, every other shop was hung outside with clothes like multi-coloured flags.

The passengers poured ashore and started their buying sprees. Past me came bunches of Japanese high-school girls 'doing Europe'. They had four days in Greece to see the Acropolis, with trips to Olympia, the temple of Poseidon on the clifftop at Sounion, and this cruise round

the islands. Then they would fly to Rome, Paris and London.

The ship's siren sounded a warning. The passengers all hurried back to her, and before the ship had got through the gap the shops were closed, the stalls stripped, the vans gone. Down the quay one solitary, empty yacht banged against a quayside fender. Nearly all the bars and restaurants were closed. The boats across to Galatas were almost empty. Even the joie-de-vivre of happy Poros can be dampened by the sort of weather you get in England or France.

In the sunshine of spring or summer, housewives buy their vegetables, fruit and fish from those quayside stalls, which share the space with the tables and chairs of bars, tavernas, and restaurants, full of drinkers and lunch-eaters, and the noise of talk, laughter and waiters calling would fill the quay. Yachts line along the quay further along, and come and go through the gap as holiday yachtsmen arrive from Piraeus. That is the scene which artists still love to paint.

Poros Hotel (B-class) has lovely sweeping views. Seven Brothers taverna near the ferry is run by seven brothers. Lagoudera on the waterfront serves superb fish.

You can walk round Sferia, the 'hump' on which Poros port is sited, in about an hour. Cross the causeway to the bigger 'hump', Kalavria, where there is a short stretch of tarmac road, and you are in a greener, quieter land, with several coves of shingle shaded by pines. Most of the hotels are here. So is the attractive-looking eighteenth-century monastery in deep woods overlooking Askelli Bay. There are no monks left and you can visit it.

Alas, only a few stone walls remain of

the great temple of Poseidon, built in 500 BC and once as magnificent as the temple on Aegina. In the eighteenth century the marble blocks from which it was made were systematically plundered, being cut into sizes a mule could carry, taken to the shore and shipped to Hydra to build a monastery. There they are covered in plaster and whitewashed.

The temple was a sanctuary. Any fugitive, any shipwreck victim, was safe within its walls. Demosthenes, who roused the Athenians disastrously to fight the conquering power of Macedonia under Philip and Alexander the Great, fled here from arrest by the Macedonians. The Macedonian soldiers called him a coward and dared him to come out. He pleaded for time to write a last letter, bit the end of the pen where he had hidden poison and died on the temple threshold.

The Greek Navy school for petty officers is descended from the naval arsenal set up in the War of Independence. After the victory of the British, French and Russian fleets over the Turks at Navarino in 1827, the ambassadors of these three countries deemed it wise to leave Constantinople and set up shop in

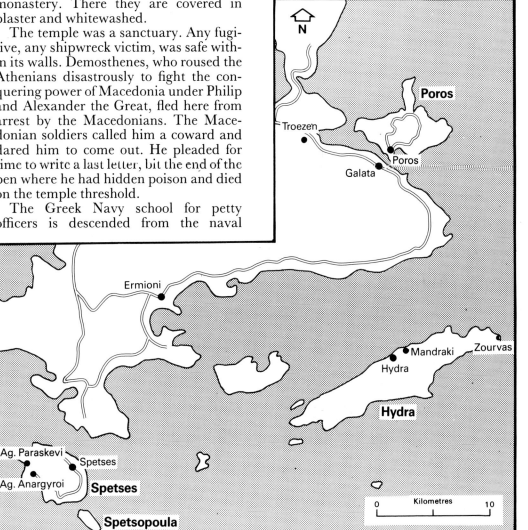

Poros, where they made an agreement on the terms by which the Free Greek State was to be introduced, the Protocols of Poros. Poros harbour was the home port for several ships of the Free Greek forces, including a steam gunboat *Karteria* (which means Perseverance), commanded by the Englishman Frank Hastings, which was the scourge of the Turks on land and sea. Captain Hastings was killed in a raid on a Turkish garrison near Missolonghi in May 1828 and his grave is west of Poros town on the coast at Little Neorion, with an obelisk marked 'Astinx'.

Hydra and Spetses, nearby isles, did not like having their affairs controlled by the new President, the Corfiot Capodistria, who in exile had been foreign minister to the Czar of Russia and was very pro-Russian. The Greek ships in Poros were ordered to sea under a Russian admiral, Ricord, and the sailors of Hydra believed they were going to be used to attack their ally, the isle of Spetses. So they sent Admiral Andreas Miaoulis and fifty men across to Poros to seize the arsenal and Greek ships in harbour.

Capodistria sent Admiral Ricord and his fleet, with soldiers. The Poriots gave in – but not Admiral Miaoulis, who told the Russians that unless they withdrew, he would blow up his ships. They didn't, so he blew up the frigate *Hellas* and the corvette *Hydra* and escaped to Hydra. And Capodistria was murdered three months later. Free Greece got off to a bad start.

The first ship launched in the new Greece in 1833 was from Poros and was called the *Miaoulis*.

The arsenal is now the naval college; the battleship *Askeroff* is anchored permanently alongside in honour of her rout of the Turkish fleet in the Dardanelles in the Greco-Turkish War in 1912.

Poros makes its living now from fishing, tourism and agriculture – mainly olives, lemons and flowers, such as gladioli, carnations and hyacinths. I wondered at first where they grew all these crops. Then I found that most of the farmers also owned land across the straits at Galatas, five minutes away by boat. Here is Lemonodassos (the 'Lemon Forest') with 30 000 lemon trees. Nearby is historic Troezen, where the Athenians sent their women and children in times of danger, known now for its Devil's Gorge, where the stream runs cold all the year and you can cool off in potholes. It has a bridge said to have been built by the devil overnight. A busy little engineer was Satan!

If the view of Poros as you arrive has inspired great writers, the view as you leave can be awesome. I have caught the five o'clock ferry in winter from Poros to Aegina as the sun went down. The colours were made for a Turner painting – a flurry of white snow, the silver sea gradually tarnishing to black, the blue-black hills of the Peloponnese, the sun setting behind them in a halo of gold and orange. Then a black curtain of darkness. No wonder the Ancients worshipped the sun.

POROS

Strait between island and the Peloponnese mainland is only 280 yards wide. 11½ square miles.

Ferries ...... Car ferry from Piraeus, Aegina, Mathana on mainland several times a day (2½ hrs) going on to Hydra; regular ferries to Galata on mainland; benzina (water taxis) to Galata on demand.

Hydrofoils ...... From Zea, Piraeus (1 hr).

Hydra

Hydra (pronounced and sometimes spelt 'Idra') is bare, rocky, hilly, with inhospitable shores, is often short of water, has no good beaches, bans motor cars, so that you must risk your neck on a scooter on rough tracks or cycle or walk in the hot sun to see anything outside the port, and it is desperately short of accommodation, so that rooms are pricey and it is hopeless to find a room without a reservation in midsummer. Most visitors come for only a few hours.

Yet Hydra has such passionate devotees that until very recently it was with Mykonos the fashionable island of Greece, haunt of the rich and of poseurs. It has been called 'the Greek St Tropez'. Yachtsmen love it, artists still come, and it is a lure for happy, lazy layabouts who just want to sit outside the tavernas of the port drinking, talking, eating, and watching the boats come and go.

The port is truly photogenic and it was inevitable that the film-makers would discover it after the artists. They did, in the 1960s. Many films have been made here, including *Boy on a Dolphin*. With tracks for roads, old farms and cottages repaired and painted up by Athenians and foreigners for holiday homes, and the Venetian-style mansions of the old rich sea captains built of heavy local stone with beautiful interiors decorated often by Italians, it is rich in film settings. Old wrecks of houses have been rebuilt strictly in their original style and local laws have forbidden building square concrete boxes which have spoiled the look of much of Greece. This accounts for the bed shortage.

In summer, with many visiting yachts, from little flotilla boats to the luxury yachts of the rich, Hydra port has a truly cosmopolitan atmosphere. Lobsters are everyday fare, the shops quote you prices in US dollars, and the four or five discos keep open until all hours. I find it great fun and expensive. My memory, too, is of the heat of burning rock as I have tried unwisely to explore inland in summer. In June, July and August, the island can be very hot and very crowded.

If you get to know the right person in a bar or taverna, you might see inside one of those splendid old villas. Two can sometimes be visited. Ask at the door. They are the old home of the Tombazis family, now a School of Fine Art to which genuine professional artists are especially welcomed, and the Tsamados family home, now the Merchant Marine School. Though the furnishings in this marine school are necessarily practical, many old features survive, such as the Italianate chequer-board black and white marble floors and the intricate ceilings of wood in geometric patterns. For a pre-dinner

ouzo, there is a good bar on the ground floor (To Laikon). For dinner, try Xeri Elia Douskos, under trees in the square, or Three Brothers taverna near the cathedral.

It is a long haul by lanes then paths up to the twin Monastery of Profitis Elias and Convent of Aghia Efpraxia. It takes a good two hours on foot. When I went up there you could hire a mule (you could – I couldn't; muleteers always say I am too fat). But these mule saddles are flat and uncomfortable, which is why the Greeks ride side-saddle, and prices asked were outrageous. The monastery, founded by refugees from Mount Athos after the monastery there was raided in 1770, has one monk left and, as at Athos, no women are admitted. A few nuns still weave and embroider at the convent and you can buy their work – mostly shawls. Some other items are imported.

There are four monasteries in the north, but only one is thriving – the Convent of the Birth of the Virgin at Zourvas, on the eastern tip of the island. It takes four hours to reach on foot. The nuns weave and tend their gardens and animals. On the forbidding north coast, where bare, jagged rocks stab the water, you come suddenly to the old deep harbour of Mandraki, with a deserted nineteenth-century boatyard. Along a concrete path here is the only sandy beach on Hydra, and a very modest resort is growing up. You can reach it along a coast path from Hydra town in about forty minutes.

In summer a small boat makes daily excursions round the island which gives you a clear view of some of its inhospitable rocks.

Men of Hydra are famous for seamanship as they have been for centuries. Even the Turks gave them much freedom in return for providing much-prized Hydriot sailors for their navy. To augment fishing and sea trade, the Hydriots took to a little piracy. Then they made fortunes running the British blockade in the Napoleonic Wars, particularly running wheat to Corfu, which was in French hands and being blockaded by the Royal Navy. One captain named Skourtis, wanted by the British, who circulated a drawing of his ship, altered the profile of the ship's poop and bow and carried on blockade-busting.

All Hydra grew rich and was doing so well under Turkish privileges that it was not so keen on the idea of a revolution for Greek independence. But the boom ceased. The Napoleonic Wars were over. Grain prices collapsed.

Sailors were idle, poorer and discontented. So, under a sea captain, they forced their Hydriot leaders to join the Revolution. And Hydra then played a leading part in the Independence War. Miaoulis, their admiral, a superb sailor who could not read or write, and could not even write his name until he became an admiral, commanded the Greek fleet. He had had an adventurous sea life and when blockade-running had been captured by Nelson, but turned on the Greek charm and got away with it. Another case of Nelson turning the blind eye.

Hopelessly out-numbered and out-gunned, the Greeks relied on superior seamanship, light fast ships and fireboats to harass the Turks. Under cannon-fire, they sailed boats full of sulphur, tar, kindling and gunpowder right up to Turkish boats, lit a fuse and jumped into a launch. The Turks tended to jump into the sea long before their arrival.

The Hydriots resented the autocratic rule of the first Greek President Capodistria and when the Greek fleet was ordered to sea under the Russian admiral Ricord,

Miaoulis went to Poros, took over the fleet and tried to resist (see Poros). Before retreating to Hydra, he blew up two Greek warships rather than surrender them to the Russian.

But the Independence fight had left Hydra poor and short of ships, and their sailors were prominent among those whom Admiral Codrington accused of continuing their piratical habits on British, French and Russian ships after Independence had been won. When steam came, Hydra had no money to replace its sailing ships and it sank in decline. Some sailors took to dangerous sponge fishing, others emigrated to join other fleets. By 1950 Hydra was half empty, its shuttered houses succumbing gradually to the weather. It was like a ghost island left over from another century, with no roads or cars, while Spetses, its rival, boomed as a tourist centre and weekending hideaway for Athenians. But now Hydra is successful – mainly because it does have no cars or roads and because it has charming old houses which could be bought cheaply and restored.

HYDRA (IDRA)

Separated from the Argolid peninsula by a narrow strait. 21 square miles. Some water has to be imported from mainland by tanker because too many pine trees were cut down for ship-building and the huge underground cisterns became low. No cars allowed.

Ferries ...... Regular from Piraeus, either express (2½ hrs) or calling at Aegina, Methana (on mainland) and Poros (3½ hrs). Boats run regularly to Ermoni on mainland (½ hr).

Hydrofoil ...... From Zea, Piraeus (2 hrs) or calling first at Aegina, Poros.

Spetses (Spetsai)

Some time ago a taverna owner in the sloping square by the quay in Dapias, the port and capital of Spetses, almost refused to serve me. I had refused a bottle of retsina. I *loathe* retsina. I insisted upon drinking a dry white wine. Two thirds of Spetses is covered in pine trees, and they are used for the resin in retsina all over Greece. It was like refusing porridge in Scotland.

The pines give the island a dark secret atmosphere which is not quite Greek – a touch of Southern France or Ischia. The horse-drawn fiacres, the clomp of their horses' hoofs outside your window at night, give the place an air of unreality. Like Hydra, Spetses bans private cars, although it does allow an island bus and a couple of taxis. The fiacres are the main means of transport. Those and the water taxis which will take you to the beaches. For some crazy reason, mopeds are allowed for hire to tourists, and they are smellier, noisier and more lethal than any car. On the partly-tarmac road that encircles the island they can spoil the whole stately clip-clopping effect of travelling by fiacre.

There is another reason why the island looks 'less Greek' than most as you approach it from the sea. Dapias port is built on the level. There is no hillside backcloth dappled with white houses – the hallmark of most Greek island ports.

Spetses is a charming island and it is small wonder that it has been popular with Athenians for so long. Its first tourist hotel was built as long ago as 1914, the grand old Possidonion, still open, and, with a casino operating between the wars, it was *the* fashionable place to go in Greece until at least the 1960s. A good C-class hotel is Myrtoon, with roof garden and bar.

You could walk round the island in a day – it is only about fourteen square miles in area. And all round the coast are little coves you can reach if you wear reasonable shoes and are not trying to live in Ancient Greek sandals. Some have a taverna, some can get a little polluted with rubbish left by picnickers. Don't blame

fellow tourists. Greek families are notorious litterbugs.

Most developed of the coves is Aghios Anargyroi, where a village has built up around holiday homes. Small boats call, the island bus stops at the taverna in summer, but anyway it is not a difficult walk either round the road or by path across the island. Right round the south of the island you see the little wooded islet of Spetsopoula, privately owned by shipping millionaire Stavros Niarchos, guarded and 'forbidden' to anyone but local people working there. Placing the island's rubbish dump opposite it might well have been a silent comment.

High on a promontory between Aghios Anargyroi and the little beach of Aghia Paraskevi, which has a church with a bell hung in pine trees, is an imposing villa seen best from the sea. It is called Villa Yasemia (Jasmine) but is now known as 'House of the Magus'. To readers of John Fowles's novel *The Magus*, it is Bourani. It is difficult to reconcile Spetses, a tourist island since before World War I, with the seemingly wild island Fowles describes, but he was telling a story, not writing a guide book.

Fowles taught at the imposing Anargyrios and Korgialenios School on the outskirts of Dapias, founded in 1927 on the model of an English public school.

Although almost everyone calls the port Dapias, its real name is Spetses Town, and the Dapia is the square near the harbour, packed with the more fashionable restaurants and bars, lit at night with coloured lights and still protected by cannon left from the War of Independence. The less fashionable bars and tavernas are round by the fish market.

The sailors and ships of Spetses played as big a part in the freedom fight as those of Hydra and were equally rumbustious, if not to say ferocious. The Spetses 'navy' had the first victory over the Turks, before Hydra joined in. On 4 April 1821, the Spetses ships captured two Ottoman ships near Milos. On 8 September 1822, a Turkish force came to invade Spetses but was repelled by the locals using fireships. The scene is re-enacted each year in the old harbour, with fireworks taking the place of gunfire, and a regatta. When another Turkish fleet came to invade, the Spetsiots created dolls with red fezes and Turkish style uniforms propped up around the harbour. The Turkish commander thought that the island was already occupied and sailed on.

Spetses had the only woman admiral in the war. Lascarina Bouboulina was a rich widow, with nine children, a shipyard and ships and she continued her father's business of building ships and making money – so much that the Turks suspected that she was up to no good. This was undoubtedly true, for her ships not only indulged in piracy but were armed on the excuse of fighting against Algerian pirates, but really in preparation for the Greek revolt. The Turks were going to confiscate her shipyard and fortune, and she was called to Constantinople but talked her way into keeping both.

In the Revolution she commanded her flagship at the head of her squadron. Dressed in the striped costume of Spetses, carrying a cutlass, she led her ships in two big naval engagements, played a very major part in the blockade of Nauplion, often landing to lead her forces, and in between she supplemented her income with patriotic piracy, preying on neutral ships supplying the Turks. She obviously liked money, for she let the girls of a Turkish leader's harem escape from a siege in return for jewellery. She had a lusty sexual appetite, too, making off with other women's husbands to satisfy it. If the men seemed at all unwilling, she persuaded them with a pistol.

Unfortunately one of her sons followed in mother's wake and seduced a girl from the powerful Koustis family. In the vendetta that followed, the Admiral was shot through the head when looking out of the window of her house just behind the Dapia. Her remains are in the Mexis museum, with other mementoes of the revolution and of island history. The museum is in the home of the Mexis family and its interest to me is to see how these powerful ship-owning families lived. Built in 1795, the house, half Venetian, half Moorish in style, was almost a fortress, surrounded by high walls. This was not for privacy but defence. The rivalry between the rich shipping families was intense, and the Mexis family, backed by the rich islanders, and the Botassis family, backed by the popular vote, were always fighting for power, right up until the institution of parliamentary elections in this century. Their quarrel once became so fierce that the Turks sent an official to mediate.

Ferries now arrive in a new harbour. The old harbour is for yachts and fishing boats. Restaurant meals are above the average for most islands and the speciality is inevitably fish – *Psari Spetsiotiko* (sea bream in a very spicy sauce). Try it at Mandelena's taverna on the new harbour waterfront.

SPETSES (SPETSE, SPETSAI)
Most southerly of Saronic Gulf isles. 8½ square miles. No cars allowed.

Ferries ...... Frequent boats from Piraeus (4½ hrs).

Hydrofoils ...... Daily from Zea, Piraeus (2 hrs).

CYCLADES 1

Andros

Andros is an easy island to reach. Buses leave every hour from Athens on a fifty-minute journey through the Attica wine country to the scruffy port of Rafina from which an old and sometimes crowded boat drops you in a dull port called Gavrion. Because of a huge lorry park, the row of uninviting cafés and tourist shops, and some shanty bungalows, it has the temporary-look of a place grown up around a wartime naval base. But don't be misled. A short bus journey in any direction will soon convince you that this big mountainous island, wooded, well watered and rich in olives and vines, is most attractive, has an undeveloped coastline and is prosperous.

On my first visit I could not understand how such an isle so conveniently placed could have escaped development for tourism. The reason, I was told, was that it was too rich to bother with tourists and that its prosperity meant unattractive prices. The people were shipowners, shipbuilders and sailors and the vineyards were prosperous, too. Certainly, the expensive villas, old and new, seemed to back this story. How was it then that many I met had been to America or Australia to work or had sons over in these countries?

I learned the real reason from Yiannis, farmer, restaurant and bar owner and car hirer. Everyone gets to know Yiannis sooner or later. The island was a hide-out for well-heeled Athenians. They came for weekends, for holidays in July and August and some retired here. Local shipowners had built the earlier grand villas. Now that shipping was in the doldrums, Athenians were building their dream homes.

This also accounts for Andros being so different from the rest of the Cyclades. It does not have the same 'away from it all' feeling as most others, the relaxed contempt for time, nor the picturesque poverty. You do not feel as if you are living in another world in another era, as on isles such as Seriphos or Lipsos. But I soon grew to like Andros, partly because of the friendliness and helpfulness of the people I met.

We stayed at Batsi, sometimes spelt Vatsi, on a bus route 8 km from Gavrion. Most foreign visitors do, because it is the easiest place to find a bed. It is in a horseshoe bay, with a fishing harbour at one end and a grass covered sand dune, with a little beach, at the other, and it has interesting little local shops, including one of those wonderful old Greek general

Octopuses drying in the sun

stores where you buy everything from food and wine in bottles or casks to clothes pegs, books, buckets and towels. It has

tavernas with tables under vines, a few small hotels, a long sand beach with shading trees and *two* banks – a miracle for such a small place. In most such places in the Greek isles you would have to change money at a ferry-ticket agency or in a grocer's shop. It is backed by tiers of red-roofed white houses, reached by steps, and hills with terraced farms. If you stay in a village house you will almost certainly have to climb steps. There are steps, too, to the little square above the harbour where you have a choice of four good tavernas, all specializing in fish. We have had some happy long evening meals here. Yianni's taverna is below the steps on the esplanade. He keeps farm animals and serves good meat.

Three very small two-storey apartment blocks have been built near the sand dunes, and when we were there last one British villa package company was filling a handful of apartments, a few rooms in a hotel, and some village family rooms. A droplet in the sea of tourism.

We stayed last time at one of the new apartments. The balcony view of the bay, the harbour, the sands and hills beyond was a delight. But my wounded leg was biting badly and the walk up the hill when I could not get a taxi was long and painful.

One night we were drinking and talking at a table outside a taverna and the last taxi had gone home. The young owner said: 'No problem', the Greek national catchphrase, and spoke to the garage owner at the next table. He fetched a car and they both drove back with us. We sat drinking wine on the balcony, watching the bobbing lights of the fishing boats for a long time. Next day the garage man called and drove us up the steep road to the village of Kato Katakilos, where there are three tavernas, two of which offer music, dancing and sometimes Greek dancers in mid-summer. But this was May, and there were only four other customers. We sat outside drinking ouzo. The owner

showed us a superb fish. After salads and wine, he brought the fish, grilled, tender, delightful and far too big for us. Then he himself joined us for more and more wine. He would not let us pay. We were his guests. In high summer the place is crammed, which shows once more how much more fun these islands are in May, early June and September. And there are winds here in July and August, too.

I rarely had to walk up that steep hill again and rarely paid a taxi fare. I had the feeling that many people of Andros were rather embarrassed to take money from visitors. Even if you ask a Greek out to dinner in Greece, you will find that he has paid the bill behind your back. It is traditional hospitality.

The road north from Gavrion turns into one of those rugged tracks but that is the way to get right away from other visitors. A track to the coast from Vassamia goes to a cove at Fellos, and with a little fairly rugged walking you can, I am told, reach other coves here. You will still find those posher villas hidden in these hills. What a splendid place to retreat from the business world of Athens.

I like the capital and port, Andros Town, on the east coast. It is not pretty but pleasant and interesting. Only the square where the buses stop is tatty. The town's changing levels make it a bit bewildering, for it is built partly on a finger of land above two good sandy beaches with remains of a castle on the end. The main street, paved with marble, is for pedestrians only. It ends in a charming little square (Kairis) where you can drink coffee or wine or have a meal outside or in, with fine sea views.

I have heard the people of Andros Town described as 'indifferent' to visitors.

But it is a working town, still heavily involved in shipping ('real Greece', if you like), and visitors are traditionally other Greeks, so it is no good expecting to be cosseted. People are still polite and helpful.

A right branch on the road from Batsi to Andros leads over Mount Gerakonas to Ormos Korthion – a fishing port with a small hotel, rooms and restaurants in lanes off the main street, tavernas offering fish and a sand beach south of the village. The Athenians don't seem to come here. Perhaps it is a bit down-market for them.

It is ironic that Athenians like Andros so much, for throughout history they have thoroughly disliked the island. The feud started with the naval battle of Salamis when Athens broke the power of the mighty Persian Empire. Andros supported Xerxes of Persia. The Athenians tried to fine Andros, which refused to pay, so Themistocles besieged the island. But the siege failed. The Athenians seem to have won in the end.

ANDROS

Best to book rooms ahead on weekends because of Athenian weekenders. Vatsi (Batsi) is the best place to stay.

Ferry ...... There is no direct ferry from Piraeus; bus from Athens to Rafina, then ferry to Andros (3 hrs). Some Rafina ferries call at Tinos, Syros; others call at Tinos, Mykonos. Almost daily ferries Andros–Tilos (2 hrs) with connections to Syros and Mykonos.

Tinos

Tinos is called the 'Aegean Lourdes', which may surprise you in an Orthodox-church country. But the Venetians ruled Tinos from 1207 until 1714, when the Turks took it nearly 200 years after they took much of Greece, and anything from a third to a half of the islanders are said to be Catholics. However, it is an Orthodox 'Lourdes' to which pilgrims come to pray on two Feast days of the Virgin, 25 March (Feast of the Annunciation) and 15 August (Feast of the Assumption), hoping for spiritual help, relief from their afflictions and, who knows?, perhaps a miracle cure.

It all started in July 1822 at the Convent of Kechrovouvio when an eighty-year-old nun Sister Palagia (now a saint) had a dream or vision in which the Virgin Mary revealed where an icon showing her and the Archangel could be found in a field. Excavations began and next year the treasure was found near the ruins of a church. The Greek fight for freedom from the Turks had just begun. The finding of the icon was hailed as a sign from God.

That year they started to build the neo-classical Church of Panaghia Evangelistria (Annunciation). That, of course, is the centre of pilgrimage.

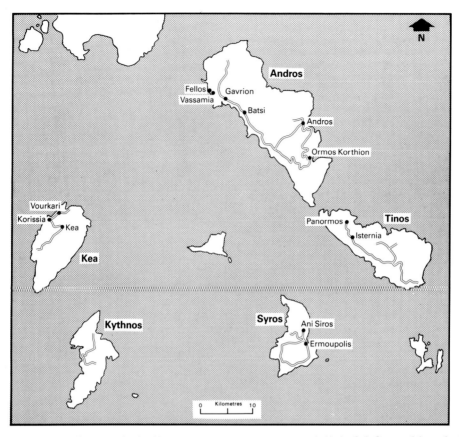

The street leading to it is lined with stalls selling anything from icons, candles and incense to plastic bottles for holy water and games like Monopoly. The church is hung with hundreds of votive offerings and lamps in silver and even gold, given in thanks by the faithful. A red carpet now covers the grand marble stair leading to the church, which is helpful to those who go up on their knees, and people queue to kiss the icon itself, which is decked in gold, diamond and pearls. I don't know what dear old Sister Palagia would have made of it all.

Because of the richer pilgrims, Tinos has some delightful fine, old-style hotels which you find on few islands. And more modern hotels line the seafront, so finding a bed is not difficult except during Holy Feasts. More secular visitors are arriving.

The Colonels, the South-American-style dictators who grabbed power in 1967, did tourism no good at all. Devout bigots who preached 'moral cleansing', they were still not above torturing people who disagreed with them, and fixing bank loans for their friends to build hotels in prime positions. They declared that poor Tinos was a Holy Isle and that all women must wear long skirts in the name of decency and behave at all times as if they were in church. Even many religious young people stopped going there. But dictators were ever thus, and the Greeks who invented the word and concept of democracy have suffered more than their fair share of democracy's enemies.

Another dictator made a costly mistake on Tinos. When the religious festival was at its height on 15 August 1940, an Italian submarine sneaked into Tinos harbour and sank the cruiser *Elli*. The countries were not even at war. Mussolini was trying to bully the Greeks into letting him use their country as a corridor for his army. Lawrence Durrell, who was there the next day, describes in his *Greek Islands* how it vitalized Greek anger and determination, which lasted until their country was freed in 1945. It did the same for the Greeks in the United States, a powerful voting lobby, when the US was wavering about entering the war.

Once Tinos nearly went to war with neighbouring Andros. Andros had a pelican mascot which flew across to Tinos. The men of Tinos clipped its wings to stop it going back. Such a row developed that the Greek Prime Minister ordered Tinos to return it. So Tinos bought its own bird.

My memory of Tinos is of villages high above the sea on the west coast, with some steep tracks to the sea and some gritty beaches, and of Panormas, called Pyrgos locally, where artists work in green marble. There is a museum, a school of Fine Art where a famous sculptor teaches students from all over Greece, and in an attractive shaded square are shops selling students' work. From Istenia, just south, you can drive down a steep paved road to Aghios Nikitas beach – pebbly, but there is a little sandy cove over a hill to the south. There is little more than an hotel, some tavernas and rooms. A big old quay is left from the days of marble exporting.

My other memory is of Venetian art. All over the island you see fountains, statues, carvings on buildings left by the Venetians and inland, where roads and mule tracks are surprisingly plentiful, the terraces are dotted with beautiful dovecots, like tiny houses of stone embroidery, many whitewashed and kept in good repair. And, as well as the domes of Orthodox churches, you will see in many villages the bell towers of Catholic churches.

It is a most pleasant isle to explore. But remember that there are few trees in many areas and from the end of May the sun parches the terraces to a look of desolation.

TINOS

Rooms including hotels plentiful but booked way ahead during religious festivals (see text).

Ferry ...... Daily to Piraeus (5 hrs). Almost daily to Andros, Rafina (4 hrs), Mykonos. Less frequently to Syros. Summer ferries to Paros, Naxos.

Syros

Even the local people call Syros 'The Rock', and its barren, dry image hits you as you sail into its capital Ermoupolis, an industrial city. To the north, the island is high and barren with few roads, but southward are some greenery on the hills and beaches with summer villas. But Ermoupolis has been an important port and city since the beginning of the nineteenth century. After the War of Independence, it nearly became capital of Greece although the local people had not taken part in the Independence struggle. They had been lightly treated by the Turks because they were nearly all Catholics and had been under the protection of France since Francis I in the sixteenth century. It was even called 'The Pope's Island'.

During the Independence war refugees from Chios and other Aegean isles settled on the uninhabited shores of Syra Bay and built Ermoupolis, named after Hermes, god of trade. Other islanders later pointed out that he was also god of thieves, for successful traders are usually regarded as thieves by the unsuccessful and this port was certainly successful, building up sea trade, coal bunker yards, repair yards, and manufactures, especially wrought iron. Architects from France and Germany came to design public buildings, elegant houses with balconies of wrought iron, splendid churches, and villas for the shipowners and merchants. Its greatest splendour was the Apollo theatre, a copy of La Scala at Milan. Once it presented a regular Italian opera season. It is now derelict.

The town's elegance is now faded but still there, even to the marble-paved main square shaded by trees. It is a monument of nineteenth-century neo-Classicism, and has a nostalgic charm. But many houses are shuttered and decaying, due to the Greek inheritance laws which share legacies among all children, causing family feuds and farms and buildings to remain neglected while lawyers cash in.

The cutting of the Corinth canal started the decline of Ermoupolis. Piraeus, port of Athens, became the great port of Greece. And when oil replaced coal for firing ships, the port really declined. But newer

manufactures, including those cotton shirts and dresses which tourists love and *loukoumia* (Turkish – or Greek – delight) which comes in many colours and flavours, including ouzo, plus tanneries and iron foundries, have given it a fresh prosperity and it is the centre for many Cyclades ferry routes, so that its shipyards still keep fairly busy.

Ferries come here from Piraeus, Tinos, Mykonos, Paros and Naxos, Ios, Sykinos, Folegandros, Santorini, Syphos, Seriphos and Kithnos. Many travellers change ferries here, staying overnight, so there are hotels, rooms, tavernas and some good restaurants. It's a busy place and interesting enough for one or two nights, but not for a longer stay. Do see the old Roman Catholic town, Ani Siros, high above the port. It takes three quarters of an hour to walk up the steps and you need a bottle of wine or ouzo or two to recover. Go by taxi. It is a criss-cross of winding, steep, narrow streets with many chapels (Carmelite) and a Jesuit convent. In the square at the top of the hill are St George's cathedral and the Bishop's palace. Interesting, but – dare I say it? – hardly Greek.

SYROS

Accommodation has improved enormously, but it is regarded by most people as a place where you spend an interesting overnight or perhaps two whilst changing ferries, which are plentiful. Alas, water is not plentiful in high summer.

Ferries ......Daily sailings to Piraeus (4½ hrs), Tinos (1 hr), Mykonos (2 hrs). Mykonos route useful as there are frequent sailings from there to Tinos, Andros and Rafina. Paros, Andros and Rafina four times weekly. Less frequent boats to Naxos, Ios, Santorini, Sikinos, Folegrandos, Milos, Syphnos, Serifos, Kithnos, Ikaria, Samos, Iraklion (Crete), Amorgos, Donoussa, Astipalaia. Also seasonal small ferry boats to various islands and express catamaran between Santorini and Crete calls in mid-summer.

Kea

Closest island of the Cyclades to the mainland at Lavrio, Kea has been largely taken over by Athenians for weekends or holidays, rooms are booked by them on weekends well in advance or even on a regular basis in summer, and in winter much of it shuts down. Many of its hotel-, restaurant- and shop-keepers winter in Athens, where they have other businesses. Some restaurants, bars and shops shut down during the week even in summer. Prices, too, are a bit Athenian.

Despite all this, it is an attractive wooded island, with historic interest, and worth driving round if you don't mind braving some unmetalled roads, or even walking round. There is quite a good bus service, too, but only to a few villages.

The ferry from Lavrio is the old Merseyside ferry *Royal Daffodil*, renamed

Ioulis Keas II. I was disappointed that the graffiti urging on Liverpool have been removed. It docks at the port of Korissia, also called Livadi, which is not exciting, and faces a derelict coal mine. Along the quay is a taverna called United Nations which is *very* Greek: noisy, chaotic, pleasant.

Around the bay at Vourkari, a fishing village, a Minoan colony was excavated in 1960, revealing a palace, temple and road. Vourkari now lures private yachts and converted caiques so it has several tavernas and restaurants.

The old town of Kea (Oukis or Hora) is really a village. Three miles from Korissia by tarmac road, it is in a fold in the hills and its houses are in tiers, joined by steps and cobbled paths. In the square, where shops sell local wine and honey, is the town hall in a pink Venetian mansion with statues on its old rooftop balcony. It is a working village, centre for local agriculture, and was built on the ancient town of Ioulis. The Venetians built a fort on the old temple to Apollo, using some of the stones in their walls. The view from here of the red roofs and white domes and houses is charming, and at night, when the village lights are on, it is impressive, too. There's a rather incongruous modern hotel in the castle grounds.

On the way to Chora you pass the Lion of Kea, a haunchy beast, either growling or grinning, cut from solid rock. He is a big fellow – thirty feet high.

Although even official publications claim a ferry connection between Kea and Kithnos, I have never found it. I once got a lift on an old caique which had brought vegetables from Kea. In high summer, however, there are some boats from both isles to Rafina on the mainland, so you could go the long way round.

Kea's agriculture thrives, with cattle farming, producing beef and dairy products, vegetables, nuts and honey and a fair wine, so with the mainland so near, meals tend to be more varied and better than on remoter isles.

KEA

You must book rooms on weekends, when Athenians flood in. Expensive, attractive island.

Ferries ...... Bus from Athens to Lavrio port (1½ hrs), ferry to Kea (1½ hrs). One, two or three boats daily according to season. Despite constant forecasting of a service to Kithnos, none was running in May 1987.

CYCLADES 2

Mykonos

A bare, rocky island where the wind blows so hard quite often that visitors by sea cannot land, and which was for long just a jumping board to the little isle of Delos, sacred isle of Ancient Greece – how did it become the most fashionable isle in Greece, a place where the rich and the fashionable of Athens loved to say that they owned a house, and then a Greek headquarters of the pre-jet set? Its main asset seemed to be those very Greek, delicate windmills, which were appearing in watercolours and on calendars a hundred years ago. Despite its barrenness, it was also very pretty, with little cube white houses, pretty dovecots and 365 little churches built as votive offerings for favours received from heaven. As for long the inhabitants were pirates one wonders what the favours were. And it had a lot of good small sand beaches.

But I think that the success of Mykonos was due to the farsightedness of its people. It was the first smaller isle to swallow its Greek pride and make a living out of willing, smiling service to tourists – something which some Greek islanders still cannot bring themselves to do. With hotels, shops, good restaurants, dance floors, bars, nightlife, it set out to persuade those who intended to stay one night to visit Delos to stay on and enjoy Mykonos. Its bigwigs built an airfield and persuaded Athens into setting up the first air route from the capital to a small island. That made it a weekending island for well-heeled Athenians, and many bought houses as second homes.

Furthermore, in a country tending to be very old-fashioned, and often prudish about sex, the people running Mykonos took a very broadminded view long ago. They tolerated homosexuals in a world which not only did not tolerate them but sent them to prison, so that it became a haven, like Cannes, for rich homosexuals. Some of my very prudish friends in Greece actually called it 'Sodom and Gomorrah', and some Athenians I knew always insisted that they were only going there on business. Permissive is a better word, for Mykonos was the first island to tolerate the fashion for bare bosoms on beaches and its police turned a very blind eye to nudism on two beaches – Paradise and Super Paradise, the very names of which seem to have been borrowed from St Tropez.

The popularity of Mykonos has driven away the international jet-setters, but the

Athenians still go. Tourism has run riot in mid-summer, the beaches are over-crowded, the charming little narrow streets of the port, made that way to keep out wind and too much sun, can be hell to walk along because of crowds coming the other way. There are too many shops selling gold, expensive jewellery and furs. The shops and streets are especially tiresome when the crowds are augmented by hundreds of people from the frequent cruise ships which arrive. Restaurants and bars overcharge. Buses and banks are un-necessarily overcrowded, too. They could surely provide more of each in season.

It is an ostentatious island. The night-life is 'casual-sophisticated', with the best and most fashionable casual clothes worn, and some of the slim young men do rather overdo the jewellery, even on the beach. But there are good unfashionable beaches which can be almost empty, even in mid-summer, at Elia, Anna Bay, and two coves between Paradise beach and Platy Gialos. Buses, if you can get on them and stand the heat and intimacy of sixty people on a bus built for thirty, and caiques from the harbour will take you in season to any of the sand beaches around the coast.

Inland the barrenness of Mykonos shows, and rock can make it white-hot in summer. Furthermore the newer square

houses built for Athenian refugees from crowds in the port do not have the same architectural charm as the older cubes in town, often with outside steps to the upper floors and with flowers growing up the walls. It is very easy to get lost in the labyrinth of little streets, which the locals tell you with tongue in cheek were built like this to confuse pirates. The houses, lanes and steps are whitewashed afresh every year.

In spite of all I have said, I think Mykonos is great fun for two or three days – or especially two or three nights. I just like to watch the scene. Take your best beach and casual clothes, even if you are not going to the night clubs or discos. You will need them for the nightly parade of walking from bar to bar. No one with self respect would be seen dead in the backpacker's bare-kneed jeans on Mykonos. The evenings and nights are happy and, for some, gay, and the white houses which can almost blind you in mid-day sun take on a beautiful ghostly look by moonlight.

I do wish that Mykonos would curb its garish advertising, which makes it unlike a Greek island. There's too much neon, too many advertising notices for rooms and cars and mopeds to rent, for bars and restaurants. There is even an airline advertisement on the windmill you see as you land. Shades of Majorca! And the touts who meet ferries to offer rooms come at you like Moroccan salesmen in a souk. But at least there are no high-rise hotels or apartment blocks.

Beware those winds, especially the midsummer *meltemi*. You can avoid it by picking the right beach but you could be stuck on Mykonos for several days more than you intended. The first time I saw it in the 1950s I got a fine view of the windmills but could not land. It served me right for arriving on a round-the-islands cruise ship, even if it was a small one. The caiques were getting in and out.

MYKONOS

Still the fashionable Greek island, with full quota of pricey restaurants and night life. You will love it or hate it. Dressier than the rest. The wind blows on the south coast and the wind can stop you landing or leaving. Athenians come in by air. In 1987 the single fare was about £12. You can fly on to other islands.

Air ...... Charters from Britain. Athens (50 mins) seven to eleven flights a day. Iraklion (Crete) daily (1 hr 10 mins). Rhodes daily (2 hrs). Santorini daily (1 hr 40 mins). Kos service in summer.

Ferries ...... Daily to Piraeus (5¼ hrs), Tinos (1 hr). Also to Andros, Naxos, Rafina (5 hrs) four times a week. Less frequently to Syros, Paros, Ios, Santorini. High summer express catamaran to Santorini, Syros, Iraklion (Crete).

Caique ...... Daily to Delos (weather permitting – 45 mins – no overnights).

Delos (Dilos)

Zeus, father of the gods, was up to his old tricks. This time it was Leto, daughter of the Titans Kronos and Phoebe, he was chasing, and when she turned herself into a quail he did the same and caught her. Hera, Zeus's wife, was so cross that she swore that Leto would find no place on earth to have her child. Delos was floating around under the sea at the time so the sea-god Poseidon anchored it to give her sanctuary. Here under a date palm she gave birth to Artemis, virgin huntress and goddess of chastity, and Apollo, symbol of manly beauty and god of a variety of matters, including truth, light, music, prophecy, medicine, archery, and the tending of flocks and herds. It was as the sanctuary of Apollo that Delos be-

came sacred, becoming a religous centre for the Greek Classical world and a rich port.

This all started around 1000 BC. A temple was built to Apollo, a massive marble statue was provided by the isle of Naxos. With Delphi, Delos became the most important sanctuary in the Greek world. It was made capital of a sort of United Nations of the Aegean nations, and the treasure contributed by the member states and cities of this Delian League was kept in the Apollo sanctuary. But Athens had become a member of the League and Athens was in no mood to allow a little island to become so powerful. So the Athenian ruler, Pericles, who did a lot of good for Athens but not the rest of

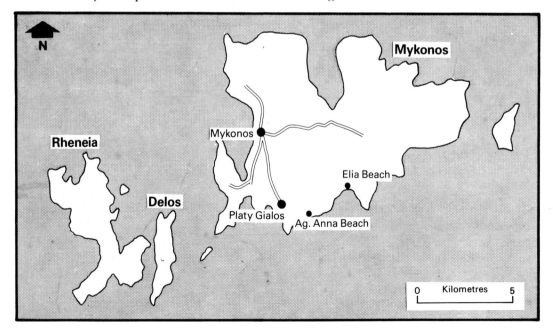

Greece, had the treasure moved to 'safe keeping' in the Acropolis. It was used to repair damage from the Persian Wars (in Athens only, of course) and to improve the city.

Athens also announced that Delos must be 'purified'. No births or deaths were allowed on the island. If you felt a baby or a heart-attack coming on, you had to rush across to the neighbouring isle of Rheneia. Then a second 'purification' came and all tombs on the island and their contents were removed to Rheneia and dumped in a big pit. The Delians appealed for help to Sparta, Athens deported all the islanders in 422 BC and murdered their leaders, but Sparta was winning the Peloponnesian Wars, so Athens was forced to let the islanders back.

After Sparta had won, Delos prospered in independence, and its four-yearly May festival, once religious, became a mixture of religious rites, a sports meeting, and a commercial fair where each day 10 000 slaves were sold.

When the Romans took over the Aegean, they made Delos a free port, in order to curb the power of Rhodes. Merchants, bankers, shipping magnates moved in from Italy, Greece, Syria and Egypt. But Mithridates, King of Pontus, warring against Rome, sacked the island in 88 BC, killing the people or taking them into slavery. Delos was finished. Pirates used it as a base, and frightened off pilgrims to the Temple. Shipping ceased. Athens tried to sell it but could find no takers. Builders from Tinos, Mykonos and Syros looted blocks of marble from the sanctuary and buildings, the Venetians removed statues and works of art to Venice and Rome. They tried to remove the huge marble statue of Apollo, but didn't get it very far, so now poor Apollo's torso is on the ground, one hand in the Delos museum and one jumbo-sized foot in the British Museum.

Every passing sea captain seems to have stopped off at Delos to see what he could loot, including the English. In 1628 Sir Kenelm Digby, a privateer, spent the

day on the isle 'in search of antiquities', and took back fragments from the temple for Charles I's collection.

Since 1872 the French School of Archaeology has carried out excavations, and some buildings have been reconstructed. There are sixteen inhabitants of Delos – archaeologists and catering staff serving food and drink to visitors.

Try to visit Delos in spring, when wild flowers deck the rock and grow out of crevices in ruined walls. In summer heat, with no vegetation or trees except a replacement sacred palm, it is rather de-

pressing, especially when a cruise ship is in, swelling the crowds of sightseers, and guides are droning in several languages.

The caiques leave Mykonos around nine am, take forty-five minutes to reach Delos, and return sharp at twelve-thirty pm. The wind usually blows, the seas are often rough, and the *meltemi* winds of July and August can turn the sea white like boiling milk. Then you may have to wait up to a day or two on Mykonos for the wind to die or wait on Delos to return. You might even be lucky enough to wait overnight on Delos, which is forbidden in better weather unless you are a professional archaeologist, for whom the only hotel is reserved.

Three hours might be enough for visitors with only a passing interest in the far-distant past, but were not enough for me. You just have to go back. So much has been looted that it is very difficult for a layman without a deep knowledge of classical Greek buildings to imagine it as it was. Even the sacred lake where Apollo's swans swam was filled in in 1926 for fear of malaria. But there are still some wonderful things to see, including superb mosaics and fine wall paintings.

Even if you are not a dedicated classicist, I suggest that you read the excellent and easily understood descriptions in *Greece, a Phaidon Cultural Guide* (Phaidon Press) which was translated from German and is a valuable guide to buildings, statues and remains all over Greece.

I was particularly impressed by the processional road, the Sacred Way, lined by votive monuments given in thanks to Apollo for favours received, and with the Terrace of Lions with five long slim crouching beasts in marble of Naxos. Originally there were nine lions. One was taken by the Venetians and stands at the entrance to the arsenal in Venice but with a new head. The theatre, which sat 5000 spectators, with marble walls, is quite well preserved and there are splendid views from it. The House of the Comedians was so called because of a painted frieze showing actors in a comedy.

There were three temples to Apollo – the first temple of the sixth century BC, financed by the island of Poros, which was the place where the Delian League funds were kept, the Athenian Temple of 425 BC, and the Doric Great Temple of the Delians, started about 417 BC but not finished until the third century BC because the Athenians had made off with the cash.

I think it worth visiting Delos just for Mount Kynthos. It is 370 feet high, has traces of a sanctuary to Zeus and Athena and gives you the most gorgeous panoramic view of Delos and many isles of the Cyclades.

Nearby Rheneia (Rinia), where the pregnant and dying were banished from Delos, is uninhabited and I know of no one who has been there. *There's* a challenge for the adventurous and for lovers of solitude.

DELOS

No overnights except for professional archaeologists (Xenia Hotel) or those held up by weather. Daily caique from Mykonos (45 mins) gives morning visit. Some excursions from other islands in summer.

CYCLADES 3

Siphnos (Sifnos)

Siphnos hides its fertile beauty from the sea. As the ferry from Piraeus rounds the north-west coast you see little but brown rock slopes dotted with scrub. The neat white houses and tavernas of Kamares harbour are encased on three sides by arid hills. But as the bus to the inland capital of Apollonia, three and a half miles away, climbs steeply and turns inland, you see immediately a fertile valley, richly green in spring and still unscorched in mid-summer. The terraced fields are still care-fully cultivated, their walls neat and re-paired, farmhouses are freshly whitened, superb castellated dovecots survive un-crumbling, millions of wild flowers colour the valleys, especially in April and May when poppies, crown daisies in yellow and white and dark purple, and Venus's-looking-glass flourish in fields and along walls. River gorges are rich in oleanders in summer.

Apollonia, the old Chora, is a hilltop town so neat, clean and fresh-whitened that it looks spanking new, from its tree-shaded museum square to the narrow lanes and donkey steps of the older town. From the terrace in front of the telephone office and patisserie are lovely views over farmland to the sea, a view shared from the balconies of the little modern Anthoussa Hotel, and from the taverna run by a good chef.

The hilltop is capped by a white church with a big blue dome and a smaller dome atop its bell tower. More, older churches hide in the alleys among the well-kept houses, some of which have not only ornamented gardens but grow orange and lemon trees just for show. Gardens in Greece usually are for food. Apollonia has some good taverna restaurants and even a bank these days. Restaurant Cyprus is formal but very good. The best is Kreva-tina in a lane uphill from the police sta-tion.

The secret of such prosperity is that Apollonia is a holiday resort. But you would not know it. There are none of the usual 'Rent Rooms' notices everywhere – just a big board shouting 'Disco' below the church. The Cyclades are the isles of the colour magazine travel articles and Greek calendars, and Apollonia gives rich photographic material.

Holidaymakers here are nearly all Greeks. Island-hopping foreigners find rooms easier to get in the port of Kamares, which has more souvenir shops and tavernas which are used also by the fishermen and are simple and cheaper. Hired yachts from Piraeus arrive, too.

A good sand beach stretches right round the bay but you have to walk far out before the water reaches your waist and you share the sands with ducks.

From Apollonia is a bus route passing through farming villages growing corn, olives and figs, to near the Monastery of Vrissi at Exambella, founded in 1614 and possessing precious icons and a little museum of religious art. You pass watch towers built by Byzantine and Venetian occupiers and a squat windmill. The left fork of the road winds down to the charming little fishing village of Pharos (Faros) where you can stay in rooms – some very simple. There are two taverna-restaurants.

Two small sandy beaches lie beyond the quay and a path along the hillside, looking more rugged than it is, takes you with pleasant sea views to the Monastery of Panagia Chryssopighi, built on a rocky cape after fishermen had found a glowing icon in the sea. Nearby is a little beach, Apokofto, with some villas and a taverna known all over Siphnos for fish.

Another bus from Apollonia takes the right fork through stony hills and dives down to Platy Gialos, a tiny seaside 'resort' with a long beach lined with tavernas and bars. It has a quite good B-class hotel called Platy Gialos, which opens only in summer, a small two-storey D-class hotel called Panorama, a number of cottage rooms to rent and the only official camp site on Siphnos. Fishermen's cottages are beside the beach, too, and their caiques bob in the bay. On the beach is the usual notice: 'Do not swim naked in the crowded beaches. Withdraw to isolated places.' It's a great concession in Greece to suggest nude bathing *anywhere*. The

rugged hills behind this beach are popular with walkers.

On the road back to Apollonia is a steep path down to Panagia Chryssopighi monastery. Then the road loops past a convent, Panagia tou Vounou. The nuns left last century, so now you can rent a cell, and the Aegean views are superb. Further along you can see white on a distant hillside the glorious mediaeval town of Kastro. It is three miles from Apollonia. Buses will take you but most people walk to see three windmills on the way, though it is a steep walk back.

Kastro is a mediaeval fortified town, clamped dramatically to a hillside on a headland which falls sharply to the sea on two sides. It captivated me.

There are no souvenir shops, no notices in its steep alleys or steps except one marked 'taverna'. There is a drinks and snack bar with a garden with fine views and the village shop doubles as a taverna in the old Greek style.

You sit at one of the old wooden tables among a chaotic jumble of vegetables, groceries, cartons of detergent and

cigarettes, and faded family portraits. You are served with whatever happens to be cooking in the kitchen upstairs. For me it was a salad of lettuce and onion, spaghetti with a thin meaty tomato sauce and Demestica wine, then cheese. No choice – just an old taverna meal served with genuine smiles.

Narrow whitewashed streets and alleys climbing the steep hillside pass under arches of overhead houses and in places form bridges leading to upper floors. Pieces of ancient columns and headless busts of ancient heroes have been used in making walls and houses, some of which bear Venetian coats of arms.

Kastro was capital of Siphnos until 1833. It has survived, and often flourished, through classical years, when Herodotus called it a city, and through foreign occupations by the Byzantines, Venetians, the Franks who were here from 1307 to 1617, and the Turkish occupation from 1617 to 1834. The town as it is today was built mainly as a defensive capital by the Koronia family from Corunna in Spain, who ousted the Venetians. They held the island from 1407 until 1463, when it passed by marriage to a Bologna family, the Cozzadini, who governed Kythnos for 200 years by backing both sides. They paid taxes to Turks and Venetians.

In classical times, Siphnos grew rich from its gold and silver mines, so that it was one of the biggest contributors to Delphi, where it had its own marble treasury. Siphnos sent its annual tribute in the shape of a gold egg. The islanders got fed up with paying this tithe to the gods and one year sent a stone wrapped in gold leaf. But you cannot fool an oracle and the gods showed their wrath by making the mines sink beneath the sea. Later, the island was known for pottery and

there are still potters at work in the port of Kamares, Vathy and in Apollonia.

On the other side of the mountain from Kastro, overlooking Seralias Bay, is yet another monastery, Chrysostomou, founded in 1550. This was the illegal centre of opposition to the Turks, with a secret school where men risked torture and death to teach the forbidden Greek cultures.

Just before you reach Kastro is a steep drop on the right to a small stony cove. A winding track leads down to a narrow strip of beach where a little group of buildings includes a church and restaurant.

Siphnos is very short of roads or even driveable mule tracks. On the west coast are several little bays which can be reached only by very hard walking over mountains or by sea. The most popular is Vathy, which has a harbour used by fishing boats, a sand beach in a horseshoe bay, a 16th-century church, two tavernas, a pottery and rooms in village houses. Caiques go there in summer from Kamares and drop sun worshippers for the day. At other times the port police might be able to tell you if a supply boat is going.

I love Siphnos. It is big enough to have interesting things to see and has variety in its little towns and villages. It is not big enough to be commercialized and to lose its undoubted charm. The port of Kamares is great fun for watching boats and people, and for its lively little taverns with their tables and chairs crowding the quayside. They are informal but offer a variety of dishes, and when the fishing boats come in their owners wander down the quay and take the pick of the fish before the foreigners from hired yachts get at it. I saw one buy a dozen lobsters, each carefully weighed on the quayside, so I knew where to go for my evening meal and what to order for freshness.

Stavros Hotel, over the family's food store, is simple and friendly.

SIPHNOS

A green island which grows on you very fast. No big hotels, most small ones are very simple, and few tourists go.

Ferries ...... Important small excursion boats (no cars) to Paros, where you can pick up boats to other islands. Daily June–September; two or three times a week in spring and autumn.

Car ferries ...... Piraeus five days a week (5–6 hrs). Seriphos and Kythnos four days a week. Milos four days a week. Kimolos twice a week. Ios and Santorini three days a week. Syros weekly.

Seriphos (Serifos)

My favourite taverna-owner in Livadi, the port of Seriphos, had cooked a superb moussaka, with lots of aubergine, and so I had eaten much more lunch than usual. I knew better than to wait until the evening. The local fishermen love his moussaka and they would have scoffed the lot by seven o'clock. Even patriotic Greek islanders appreciate Swiss cooking.

Contented but immobilized by food and wine, I sat on the harbourside looking at the fishermen clearing and drying their nets, some French men on a hired yacht getting slowly more boisterous on wine, the sheep eating their way across the hillside opposite where I remembered only goats feeding years ago.

It was May, the wind blew a little, the sun shone, the sea was as blue as the seas of Greece in travel brochures. From up the steep hillside towards the old town came the thuds of a man building new houses in stone.

A superb big caique, converted to a yacht, sailed into the bay and swung on its anchor. I looked at the sky, blue with white patterns of horses' tails, mackerels and puffy lumps of cumulo-nimbus, with a firm layer of strato-cumulus covering the horizon sky. Samples of every kind of cloud.

Then the caique began to sway faster until it was almost spinning on its rope. A little fishing caique hurried for harbour. The taverna owner battened down his paper table covers with metal clips. A straw hat went past me. The clouds seemed suddenly to merge in a war against the sun. The rain came down in great droplets. The quay, the esplanade, the road round the bay were clear of people in seconds.

The Greeks are a brave people. They were not cowed by Turks, pirates, Nazis nor Mussolini's Fascist thugs. But the pitter-patter of raindrops sends them running as if they are under deadly ray-fire.

Strange, because to their grandfathers rain was pennies from heaven, especially on a mountainous, rocky island like this with towering cliffs and just two fertile valleys – an island whose name means 'dry' or 'barren'. The greatest crime of the various occupiers of Greek islands was cutting down trees without replacing them.

Life is hard on Seriphos. That young man was building little houses up the mountain on his terraced farm because his father, grandfather and theirs before them had grown hunched and prematurely old trying to scrape a living from those terraces. Now the sea view from them was their greatest asset and the young farmer would make more money letting rooms to tourists for five months at what to us are very low rates than his father could make in years of killing toil. As in so many of these Greek isles, some rockier terraces high up mountains have been abandoned.

Yet Seriphos is not really a tourist isle and may never be. The centre is a mountain and it would need very expensive roads to reach the beaches sprinkled round the island and make it worthwhile building near them. And I am not sure that the locals want to look after tourists. They are polite and helpful but I get a feeling that they don't want actually to *serve* you. That may account for the Swiss taverna owner, the bright couple from Chios who run the boutique and high-class souvenir shop in summer, a jeweller from Athens and a young Austrian couple running the newest little hotel, Seriphos Beach. But Greeks run another good taverna, International, on the quayside.

Traditionally the local men were miners and farmers. Iron ore and copper were mined from antiquity until the last mine was exhausted in 1960. Although at one time mining made the owners rich and so the island was called rich, the miners themselves were very badly paid. The population fell dramatically to under 1000 as the young left to make a living elsewhere, but with the trickle of tourists many have come back – older, more knowledgeable and prepared to run small businesses. Nearly all the tourists are Greek.

I do find Seriphos alluring. The slow pace, the lack of any hustle, give you time for the important things like thinking, dreaming, talking, reading books – or even writing them. A young Swiss who works hard in Zurich just to allow him three months holiday to spend in his own little house here told me: 'It changes my whole attitude to life and even my personality to be here.'

Beaches are not difficult to find if you don't mind walking. There is one round the bay from the harbour and although it has boats and often taverna tables on it at the harbour end, there's room further along.

Ormos Livadakia is reached by a sign-posted track over a hill behind the ferry quay. Narrow, sandy, tree-lined, it has a windsurfing school in mid-summer. Walk on along a path for another thirty minutes and you reach Karavi beach, fairly empty with holiday homes on the slope behind it. You follow the stony river bed, dry in mid-summer, from the port beach, then a

rough track over a hill to Psili Amos beach, a lovely sandy cove backed by a sand dune. My favourite. It has a taverna. In another fifteen minutes you reach Aghios Giannis, larger but coarser sand.

A paved zig-zag road up the mountain takes you spectacularly to the old capital, the Chora, which itself looks spectacular from down in the port. You have to climb steps from the bus stop square and beware on sharp, narrow corners, for I have twice nearly been run over by a relentless mule with panniers laden with rubble. The mules of Seriphos are well-fed, strong and know their rights of way. The steps take you to a marble-paved square with a charming church and large important town hall of 1908, painted a rather nasty ochre and with a roof balcony with iron railings of sculpted swans. Any mayor would be proud to address the peasants from it.

Steps spiral upwards to a crumbling Venetian fortress where the whole population could take refuge from raiding Turks and pirates.

The view from the top is magnificent. You will notice lumps of fortress built into houses and cube-shaped houses built into the fortress walls. If the sun is not too hot, there is a pleasant hour's walk down to the port by wide 'donkey' steps that cut across the zig-zagging road. I noticed that the mules now prefer the longer route by road!

A mile after the Chora, the road divides into two. The right-hand branch goes to Sikamia Bay, climbing steeply at first to a ridge from which are glorious views to the sea. The road is rough but driveable. After you pass the village of Panayia, a big village with a tenth-century church, it divides into two tracks which are very rough and especially dangerous for mopeds. It is really mule country. Your reward for braving the left track is the super unspoilt sandy beach of Sikamia, with clean, clear sea, backed by dunes where bamboo grows. A few new and old buildings, no taverna so far, but I heard of plans for one. The right hand turn at this last branch takes a very rough track to the Taxiarchon Monastery, built in 1600, fortified, now painted white with a red dome and red-roofed chapel. It contains some Byzantine manuscripts and fine eighteenth-century frescoes. Past the monastery on a track is a pretty village, Kallistos, with a restaurant.

The left-hand turn on the road from the Chora is another driveable track masquerading as a road. It forks later. The right fork leads to the old mining town of Mega Livadi, where ruins of buildings and a ship-loader, and a derelict mansion tell of its former importance. A broad sandy strip is backed by scrub, trees and a hamlet with a taverna.

The left fork leads to Koutalas with shingle shore in a big bay. A few houses dot the hillside and there are fishing boats. I joined the fishermen for lunch in the fairly primitive taverna and had superb fresh fish of a variety I did not know, at a very low price indeed. There is a cave with signs that prehistoric people lived here. I am told that a mule path round the coast leads to Livadi.

Some visitors to Seriphos hardly leave the port of Livadi and find the island relaxing but dull. Transport is a problem. The only two buses run between Livadi and the Chora, the only two taxis I have found are usually busy doing the same journey. You can hire scooters but, again, some roads are really too dangerous for them. Hire cars are few; the fit walk. Distances are not that great, but the hills are.

Livadi port to the Chora is little over a mile, but I wouldn't walk up there in mid-summer sun, which bounces off the rocks. From Chora to the other seaside hamlets I mentioned is around 4 miles, with a steep walk back. It is well worth going early morning and returning in the evening. Then you will have tasted a little solitude, perhaps, had a swim and beach-lounge and worked up an appetite and thirst for a meal on the portside.

There are a few rooms in the Chora but the port is the place to stay, with several little hotels, pensions and rooms.

Oh, yes – I forgot those rocks. They were people. Some soothsayer told King Acrisius that he would be killed by the son of his daughter Danaë, so he shut her in a tower to keep the boys away. Zeus was not going to pass up a challenge like that, so he slipped in on a shower of golden rain and laid the lady. Her son Perseus was born. The frightened king put Danaë and her baby in a box and set them adrift.

They drifted to Seriphos where Perseus was brought up in the court of King Polydectes who really fancied Danaë. She fended him off but the King, thinking that his chances would be better if her son was out of the way, tricked Perseus into promising to get for him the head of the gorgon Medusa, only mortal of three horrible sisters, who had hair of living snakes, fangs for teeth and bulging eyes which could turn anyone who looked into them to stone.

But the goddess Athena gave Perseus a mirror-like shield, winged shoes for quick escape and a most useful cloak of invisibility. He returned with Medusa's awful head in a sack to find his mother hiding from the lecherous King in the hut of the fisherman who had saved them originally. Perseus was so put out that he walked into the royal banquet, opened the sack, said: 'There's your head!' and turned them all to stone.

SERIPHOS

For connoisseurs of quiet, relaxed Greek isles. Transport difficult but good walkers will find lovely walks.

Ferries ...... Piraeus five days a week (5–6 hrs). Five days a week to Siphnos, Milos. Three days a week to Kythnos. Twice a week to Ios, Santorini. Once a week to Kimolos and Syros. Some seasonal boats to Paros, but otherwise go to Siphnos and change boats to Paros.

Kythnos (Kithnos)

The people of Kythnos are very friendly and are not in any way trying to screw drachmas out of tourists. Last time I was there the lady in the little Kythnos Hotel overlooking the quay in Merchias port where the fishermen land their fish and sell them from baskets, charged me only half the official price for my double room with bath, loo and a balcony. Her daughter explained that I was alone and had only used one bed. The young man running the Byzantio café-bar had run out of non-retsina dry white wine, so he went to the nearby supermarket and bought me a bottle, then refused payment.

Like most Greeks not addicted to money making, they show little interest in time or clocks. Buses can go five minutes early or half an hour late. I was waiting in the port square for a bus to the old town of Kythnos (called locally Chora, of course) when another bus arrived. The driver leaned out. 'I am going to Driopis,' he said. 'You will like it. It's a lovely drive. Jump in.' Round the corner a truck was blocking the road, with men unloading stone slabs. Our driver waited patiently until they had finished. The unloaders were in no hurry, either.

Driopis is a white hilltop town in the centre of the island and it *was* a lovely drive to it, if only for the views. The driver dropped me on a terrace with more spectacular views and told me he would be returning at twelve-thirty to get home to lunch.

I wandered happily in the narrow, weaving streets and up and down the donkey steps, with sudden views appearing round corners and old windmills at the top of the town until, tired, I went into a shady taverna with a neat terrace where eating in the cool of the evening must have been delightful. The old taverna owner had one of those old Greek drooping moustaches. He was a retired soldier, still upright, well into his seventies, and was learning English. He brought me his exercise book and asked me to read aloud sentences he had written and to write others.

The bus-driver came in. 'We go,' he said. He was twenty minutes early. He must have got hungry. A pity that he was going back. Some buses continue to Kanala, a well-groomed little modernish holiday resort with pines and firs in the hillside, a public garden giving shade from the noonday sun, and trees and flowers, especially roses, in the private gardens. Beyond a fishing boat quay, a path over a hillside takes you to a bay with a narrow sand and gritty shingle beach, a pension, café-bar and a taverna serving pleasant if not imaginative meals.

There are rooms in Kanala and it would be a pleasant place to relax completely away from other visitors. Not that there are many on Kythnos – certainly not many foreigners.

I think that it is a charming island. One reason why people do not bother to go is that guide books nearly all dismiss it as a dry, arid island, which is not true. I wonder just how far from the port and Chora some writers have explored. There are arid areas and water can be short at the end of summer, so that your shower may be off except for morning and evening. But there are wide fertile valleys surrounding the two main roads, pine trees behind some beaches, and less than ten minutes' walk from the port is a very fertile valley leading to a long narrow cove like a miniature fjord, with greyish coarse sand. It has a taverna. Unfortunately there is some unofficial camping, which can make beaches untidy and noisy, but the beach looked clean enough to me, and you can cross a strip of sand to a tiny island. You can go there by water taxi.

I find Kythnos town, the Chora, less attractive than Driopis. It is set in a high plain among farming country of the less-fertile sort, but it has useful shops, post office and a restaurant. This is mainly donkey country, and on the winding road down to Loutra you will meet farmers riding side-on using a brightly coloured blanket instead of a saddle.

Use the shared taxis to get around. I asked one driver to take me to Loutra. It was lunch time so I went straight to one of the tavernas, by the beach, eating outside under the trees. The taxi driver had agreed to pick me up early evening. He came in and had lunch with a jolly man who seemed to know everyone. When I had finished eating the jolly man called

me over and gave me a glass of wine. It was like battery acid. It was his own wine, he said, so I made the mistake of lying and telling him I liked it. It seemed safe. The bottle was empty. But he went home and brought another.

The jolly Greek man was having a hotel built behind the taverna. We all went to inspect it. The workers were very busy, said the taverna owner, which was why I had not been able to have Greek salad with my lunch. The only tomatoes on the island were in the builder's lorry. They had brought them over that morning from the mainland port of Lavrio, but were too busy to unload them.

I explored the town. At one end was a quay with a walled church, a small castle which is someone's summer home and rusting iron-mining gear above it. Fishing boats were alongside, nets spread over the quayside and around bollards, and round the edge were tiny hut houses which contained fishing gear and rooms where people obviously ate and slept. Streets led past a mini-market, bars and little shops to a biggish new apartment block. Stone was being dug out for more building.

At the other end was the bungalow style Xenia Hotel with twin streams of water, brown from iron deposits, running each side of it. One, it seems, runs constantly at exactly 37°C (used for drinking) the other at precisely 52°C (for bathing). The spring is under a church which is next to the baths. The waters alleviate rheumatism and promote fertility. At my age, both would be welcome.

I like Loutra. I am not quite sure why, but it has simple charm. It was early evening when I found the taxi driver in the taverna waiting to take me back to the port. I hope no one else was waiting for a taxi. Still, it was May – not the tourist season, and the big hotel in the port of Merchias was not yet open. It fills later with Dutch and Austrian package tourists.

Merchias is a very pleasant little port, with a fair choice of tavernas and bars where you meet as many locals as visitors, even Greek, and quite a lot of rooms.

Tavernas have tables on the esplanade above the beach which, although tree-lined, is not very attractive – greyish, coarse sand and shingle. The esplanade itself runs out of concrete and becomes a dirt track before it reaches the hotel. No one can say that Kythnos has been 'spoiled' by tourism.

KYTHNOS

Not yet a tourist island and delightful. Few foreign tourists know it. Most visitors are Greek. Still cheap. Ferry to Lavrio on mainland is useful.

Ferries ...... Piraeus four days weekly (4 hrs). Lavrio on mainland three days weekly. Seriphos and Siphnos four days weekly. Milos three days weekly. Kimolos, Syros and Ios once weekly.

Milos (Milo, Melos)

Many Greek islands look bare and inhospitable as you approach from the sea, but hide their beauty and fertility inland. Milos has a superb approach into a great bay, but once you are ashore it looks like a great painting which has been slashed and gashed. The gashes are made by mining and quarrying which have made Milos rich since antiquity. Minerals torn from the volcanic rock are barium, sulphur and alum plus, it seems, obsidian and bensonite, and I have not a clue what these two are used for except that obsidian was once used to make knives. Many have said that Milos flatters to deceive. Lawrence Durrell called it 'a damnedly dull hole of a place'.

Coming in as I did a few years back on a small yacht, I thought that I had found another Greek paradise. We sailed into the vast Bay of Adamas, big enough to have held the whole Allied fleets of this area in the Crimean and First World Wars. We passed the uninhabited isle of Anti Milos, a sanctuary for chamois, then we cut between the inshore islets of Akradies and the shore of Milos.

Already we had seen some of the bizarre rock formations, such as the Arkoudes – the bears – which look as if they are wrestling. Then we passed the little fishing hamlets Phoukovouni, Areti, Klima and Skinopi, with their houses right down by the shore. The fishermen leave them in winter for higher ground. They certainly look as if they would be awash from the first big wave of winter seas.

We swept round an inviting sandy headland and turned for the quay of Adamas village. That looked a pleasant enough place, too. But there was no wind, we had come in on engine, and the little port, in a ring of hills, was stifling and sticky. And it was dusty, too, from the mineral ores brought here for shipment. I was told that the streets have to be watered down every day.

You see a good variety of different national and yacht club flags and boat registrations around the Greek isles. I was surprised to see on Milos a boat registered in Berlin. Lake sailors, I suppose. In appalling weather, I have seen little boats come in, crewed by fine fit blonde boys and girls, flying the Finnish flag. But I suppose Finnish sailors have to learn to conquer all weathers, like their rally drivers.

Adamas received some other rugged visitors, too, in 1836. They were Cretans, escaping from Turkish reprisals. They stayed and founded the modern port.

The modern capital where most coastal people live in winter is Plaka, a short bus ride up the hill. But summer tourists stay mainly in Adamas, which has several package hotels along Lagada beach.

Buses also go from Plaka along the coast eastwards, then inland to Zephiria, but walk the three miles if you fancy a bathe for there are several places for a swim along the narrow shore, though inland the mines and their machinery have taken over and produced scenery fit for a *Dr Who* set. You turn left for Zephiria at the big electric power station.

Zephiria was the island's capital from the eighth century until 1793 and once sheltered 5000 people, seventeen churches, two bishops and assorted pirates whose loot brought wealth to it. It was abandoned because of pestilence and sulphur fumes from mines, but there are a few inhabited houses, a church and taverna. A track from there which is amazingly used by buses leads over the hills to Paliochori beach of grey volcanic sand and pebbles, deeply shelving. It is clean, but the country behind is littered with quarry works. There are several tavernas, one smartish restaurant. Round-the-island boat trips, which take nine hours, call here for lunch.

If you follow the coast from the power station, you find Hivaolimnis, with a good sandy beach. From near here you can take a track to two sandy beaches on the south coast, among farming country (Provata and Aghios Sosti). The road itself climbs steeply up to Aghios Marina Monastery on the side of Mount Profitis Elias.

North of here but, because of extremely steep cliffs, reached only by boat from Adamas, are two pleasant beaches, Phatourena, near a lagoon, and Ebourio, with a few houses and two tavernas. They are good places to escape from the heat and dust of the port.

The Plaka and the villages around it are a bit of a mess but have some interest. Plaka has two museums. The Folklore Museum is the more interesting, with relics of island life including an old kitchen and wine press.

On a steep mountain peak above Plaka is a Frankish castle with a thirteenth-century church within its ruined walls. Plaka is believed to have been built on the ancient Acropolis of Melos. During the Peloponnesian Wars between Athens and Sparta, Milos sided with Sparta. Both peoples were Dorian. In 410 BC the Athenians besieged Melos which surrendered unconditionally. The Athenians killed all the men of military age, enslaved the women and children, and replaced them with Athenian colonists. Going round the Greek islands, I get strong reservations about the civilization of the ancient Athenians.

The Turks took over in 1580 but did not garrison the isle and pirates moved in so completely that one, John Kapsis, declared himself King of Milos. He got away with it for three years until tricked by the Turks to Constantinople and killed. A hundred years later people from Milos escaping from the Turks emigrated to London and James, Duke of York, granted them land to build a Greek church – the origin of Greek Street in Soho.

The most interesting village near Plaka is Tripiti. Near here, in 1890, British archaeologists unearthed the catacombs dating from the island's conversion to Christianity in the first century AD. The arched tombs were full of bones when discovered, but the air turned them to dust, so now the catacombs are closed to avoid further damage. There are also remains of a Roman theatre, some of it unexcavated. Spectators could look out over the sea.

Near here, too, is the spot where, in 1820, a local farmer, George Kentrotis, found a cave with a statue of the goddess of love and fertility, Aphrodite, inside – the Venus de Milo. Venus is Aphrodite's Roman name. The masterpiece was from the second century BC.

George was warned that the Turks would take her from him and was persuaded to offer her to the French consul in Constantinople. The Greeks say that he lent her to the French for safe keeping. The French say they bought her. Anyway, when the French Navy came to take her away, there was a lot of ill-feeling among locals, and in a scuffle poor Aphrodite lost her pedestal and her arms, one of which

was said to have been proffering an apple, in the manner of Eve. She was presented to Louis XVIII of France, who put her in the Louvre museum in Paris, where she still stands, armless – the most visited beauty in the world. It is amusing to read Greek versions of the Venus de Milo story and the French version in the Michelin green guide to Greece. If only her arms were intact, we could have avoided the most appalling lines, even by standards of American pop songs: 'Strictly between us, you're cuter than Venus, and what's more you've got arms.'

The third bus route from Plaka passes Phylokope (Filakopi), an archaeological site dug by the British in 1890, revealing the remains of three prehistoric cities, one believed to have been of the Minoans who were on Crete. Most finds are in the Plaka archaeological museum. Alas, the site when I saw it was overgrown and meaningless to an ordinary visitor.

The bus reaches Pollonia, an attractive little port in a bay, with a sandy beach, tavernas and restaurants, rooms to rent and quite a few villas and Greek holiday homes.

From here you can catch a caique to the isle of Kimolos, which people who can get a room there regard as a delightful haven of peace. The problem when I visited it was that the caique went from Milos very early and returned at two pm, leaving little time to explore. The journey only takes a half-hour, so it should be possible to join with others in hiring a boat to stay at least a few hours longer.

Kimolos used to be called the Silver Island because of the sun shining on its white cliffs or possibly because of the colour of the fullers' earth dug and exported.

The caique passes some lovely sandy coves on Kimolos, but when you arrive the only way to reach them is by boat or a stiff twenty-minute walk up the hill to the Chora and an even stiffer walk to the beaches, taking a good hour more. The hired boat becomes a better bet the more you learn.

There are no rooms in the port but there is a taverna-kafeneion nearby which serves good meals.

The Chora up the hill looks pretty and brilliantly white against the blue sky, but is crumbling somewhat in its winding maze of lanes and alleys through which donkeys weave, and tend to despoil, attracting flies. But that is old-time Greece. You cannot have photogenic donkeys without manure. There are some nice old churches, rooms, and tavernas specializing in fish.

On the way up you can look down on a very lovely fishing village, Oupa. You can get down to it from the Chora. It is cut and built into a rocky hillside, its houses built over boatsheds and fishing net stores, and joined by primitive bridges over gaps in the cliff. There is a stony beach below, extremely peaceful, but no taverna when I was there, for tasting the lovely fresh fish which the boats land.

MILOS

Of interest for its historical and archaeological associations rather than its looks. But its airport, with Athens planes, is useful for catching ferries to Siphnos, Seriphos and Kythnos.

Air ...... Athens daily (¾ hr).

Ferries ...... Piraeus three days weekly (5½ hrs). Siphnos (2 hrs), Seriphos, Kythnos three days weekly. Kimolos twice weekly. Ios, Santorini once weekly. Caique to Paros July–August.

CYCLADES 4

Paros and Antiparos

Paros was for long my favourite Greek island, a beautiful, friendly, light-hearted place where I always feel happy and well. Now it is called 'everybody's favourite', and the growth of its popularity over the last ten years shows that to be true.

It has changed. There are four or five big package hotels, an airfield linked with Athens and Crete, more frequent ferries from Piraeus, many more souvenir shops, more piped music and night life. Inevitably, there are many more visitors, too many in the port of Paroikias and the lovely fishing port of Naoussa in July and August. But commercialized as Mykonos? Ruinously overcrowded? Already spoiled? Not yet, certainly, and never, I hope and pray.

Paros is big enough to absorb a lot of people, has enough good roads so that they can travel around and disperse. It has built more holiday and retirement villas than package hotels with swimming pools.

Paros never was one of those quiet, primitive Greek isles, sleeping time away. It has too important a shipping port for that, always a centre for inter-island trading caiques and haven for fishing boats. Paroikias was a busy little port when I first knew it in the early 1960s. It

had the relaxed vigour of a place where boats come and go – people are arriving and departing if only to change boats – the quayside spread with nets and baskets of fish, the bars filled with as many sailors and fishermen as landlubbers.

They all used to meet at a big taverna on the corner at the end of the ferry quay. Here you could watch the comings and goings on sea and land while just drinking an ouzo or coffee, or you could eat a full meal with superb fresh fish landed that morning and wine from the vineyards in the central valleys known since classical times. You could sleep there, too, but you were liable to find octopus hanging outside your window to dry in the morning sun.

That taverna is still there, but the octopus have gone. It is a bar and snack bar, serving hamburgers and cheese pies. The fishermen drink in a little bar nearby.

I dreamed once of spending a few years on Paros. I had never found anywhere so relaxed yet lively. But I did not know enough then about the winter gales of the Cyclades which can tie you to an island while everyone hides indoors.

There are so many ferry connections here that in high season passengers waiting for a boat on the quay are kept caged in pens until those getting off have cleared the end of the jetty. A wise precaution – Greeks are not trained to queue and if you have seen them scrummaging to get onto a ferry – especially the older Greeks – then you will be reminded of the New Zealand All Blacks rugby pack in full cry. But these cages do spoil the quayside scene rather.

The more photogenic fishing boats are further down the quayside or beached where the sands begin. But this is a working waterfront, not a quaint, almost-dead fishing quay to photograph for a calendar, and it is not pretty. There is a caique repair yard, and bits and pieces of boat and tools lie around.

The beach at the end, with trees behind, attracts back-packers who cannot find a bed or do not want one. Behind this is the new development of Paroikias, including villas and some small, neat hotels run by families. There are very, very few bigger hotels on Paros. The beaches are obviously the lure for many of Paros's converts, although it seems a long journey to fly to Athens, then take an eight-hour boat journey to do little else but lie on a beach.

Round the corner from the old taverna is Plateia Mavrogenous, with flowers, trees, fountains and pavement taverna tables. This is today's centre of Paroikias. Here are the banks, a good travel agency and the office of the helpful Tourist Police, transferred from the old, now-deserted windmill on the end of the ferry quay. There are real shops, seasonal tourist shops selling 'everything you need for the beach', postcards and souvenirs, and three little hotels, as well as a fair choice of tavernas and bars.

We have stayed at the little Argonauta on the far right corner, with a café and bar

downstairs and half its rooms over a bank. It is modern, clean, simple, with little sun terraces on each floor and our room had a clean loo and shower and a balcony overlooking the square. It could be noisy with revellers or late taverna eaters at night but I don't mind sitting on a balcony watching others enjoy themselves so long as I have a bottle of wine. It was good value. In the morning there was a gorgeous smell from the baker's opposite the bank. Nearby is restaurant To Tamarisko where you dine deliciously in a garden.

Between the bank and baker's begins Lochagou Kortianou, the High Street, a narrow white road with shops of all sorts. True, more are hung with dresses, shirts, beach mats and sandals aimed at the tourist these days, but there are still the fruiterers, cleaners, butchers, cake shops, wine shops, clothes and shoe shops aimed at locals, and higgledy-piggledy old-fashioned grocers with food in the windows, an assortment of buckets, witches' brooms and such outside, and cheese, cooked meats and wine counters inside.

From this little High Street runs a maze of white-painted lanes, donkey steps and alleys, with flower boxes and well-fed cats on window sills of the houses, old churches, a few open workshops with men making shoes, furniture and clothes, and the occasional bar or restaurant, so hidden away that you wonder that customers can find them. You pass, on a hillock, the ruins of Kastro, a Venetian fort built in 1260 using parts of an old Greek temple, including drums of Doric columns. Then you can emerge from the maze onto the sea front among tavernas and cafés. A little further down is a tree-lined beach of mixed sand and shingle where many back-packers sleep.

Only in the Archaeological Museum and the great Katapoliani Church have I seen any of the Parian marble which made Paros rich centuries ago. It was used by Pericles to build the Acropolis in Athens, and for the Temple of Solomon in Jerusalem, and the Venus de Milo is made of it. The old marble quarries became uneconomic but were revived once in 1844 to supply marble for Napoleon's tomb.

You can visit the ancient quarries at Marathi, three miles out of Paroikias, on the Lefkes bus route. It's fun to poke

around them but you must take a light and a sweater because they are completely underground and very cold and damp. You go down the centre of three shafts and the tunnel below is 300 feet long. There is a relief of the Parian Nymphs carved in the wall around the fourth century BC and vandalized since. The marble was always very expensive. Near Lefkes is another village, Marmara (meaning 'marble'), where the very streets are paved with it.

The marble fragments in the museum in Paroikias are from the great Parian Chronicles, a history of Greece in stone from about 1500 BC to 264 BC discovered in the seventeenth century. Much more of it is in the Ashmolean in Oxford and Greek scholars would like it back, together with the Elgin Marbles, Venus de Milo and other treasures of Ancient Greece acquired by the British and French. The author of the Chronicles is unknown but he gets the censure of some writers and the approval of many for writing mostly about festivals, music and poetry and almost ignoring politicians and wars!

And in the museum is a short biography and frieze of the satirical poet Archilochos, a man after my own heart. A Spartan and a soldier, he did not believe the Spartan teaching that a man must come back from battle bearing his shield or borne upon it, dead. He wrote a poem telling how he left his behind a bush to escape the Thracians:

'To hell with it! I got away.
I'll get another just as good.'

Not surprisingly, he had to leave Sparta. But the Parians loved him, and his philosophy of 'live to fight another day'. He invented the iambic pentameter as the best way of delivering his witty, wicked blasts at authority. He did fight another day, against Naxos, and was killed by a man called Korax (crow). Apollo, god of poetry, was so angry that he excommunicated Korax until he did penance. Wasps were said to hover over the satirist's grave, which bore the warning: 'Move on, stranger, lest you rouse the hornets.' I think of Hilaire Belloc.

The Parians practised his philosophy. Paros sent some warships to help the Athenians against Xerxes of Persia at the Battle of Salamis but prudently had them delayed at Kythnos until they knew the result of the battle.

Parians were so well known for switching sides for gain that other Greeks called faithlessness or equivocation *anapariazo* (to behave like a Parian).

The Romans came and cut down Paros's trees to make ships and took over the marble quarries. Three times up to 1197 Paros was reported barren and uninhabited, its people killed or taken as slaves by pirates, mostly Arabs. The Venetians took over and Paros was ruled by the Italian Dukes of Naxos. Then in 1536, the pirate Turks complained about Paros pirates and the cruel Ottoman pirate-Admiral Barbarossa invaded, and took off 6000 Parians to be slaves and the young boys to be trained as janissaries in the Turkish army. He made the young women dance on the sands and personally picked out the most attractive.

Later, the Parians took to the hills to avoid pirates, making Lefkes the new capital. Now Lefkes is a lovely old hillside farming village with a big Xenia hotel and the marble quarries nearby. Take the bus to Lefkes, walk downhill to the coast at Piso Livadi.

The Turkish fleet used to invade, loot the churches and commit rape and murder, too. One Turkish fleet stayed at Dryos in 1690 during the wine grape harvest and ate the lot as they were picked, so it was a dry and dull winter for Parians.

A Parian born in 1738, Nikolaos Mavroghennis, emigrated to Constantinople and rose high in the Ottoman Empire. Before being beheaded for losing Bucharest, he made gifts of three lovely marble fountains to Paros, all still in use.

Very near to the museum, in a shady park, is the real pride of Paros, the Ekatontapyliani – 'the church of a hundred doors'. It was designed in the sixth century by Ignatius, apprentice of the master architect of St Sophia's Cathedral in Constantinople (Istanbul now, of course), Isadore of Miletus. It was so lovely that when he saw it the master was jealous and pushed his pupil off the roof, but Ignatius grabbed his foot and pulled him down to his death, too. They can be found now kneeling at the column bases across the courtyard, the master pulling his beard in anguish, the pupil holding his broken head.

The church has suffered several restorations since the sixth century. It was severely damaged in an earthquake in 1773 and not restored until the 1960s. The idea was to return it to its original Byzantine appearance. It is built in the form of a Greek cross and has been described aptly as three churches joined into one. Its bell tower was destroyed in the earthquake and its new 'tower' is a huge cypress tree from which the bell dangles and sways. I wouldn't stand under it in a storm.

It is said that ninety-nine doors have been found, and that when the hundredth is found the Greeks will recover Constantinople. But spoilsport scholars, as usual, say that the name is really a corruption of 'on lower ground'.

Roads are good on Paros, with a most useful coast road round the island, though it becomes a dirt track between Alyki and Dryos. Bus services are fairly good, but buses do get crowded in summer, so car hire is worthwhile at least for a few days. A lot of places can be reached without too much effort by bike, too.

You can walk or get a water-taxi from the ferry quay to Krios Bay, two miles round the coast to the north. It is an attractive sweeping bay of sand and clear, clean sea, divided by a bar and café-bar which, alas, becomes a disco on summer evenings. Otherwise it would be an almost idyllic tranquil spot.

Naoussa, the fishing port seven miles north of Paroikia, is absolutely charming and very crowded in summer, although it clears a bit in the latter part of the evening. New little hotels and small low apartment blocks have been built recently but they have not intruded on the little working port where brightly coloured caiques are jammed gunwale to gunwale against the sea wall, and you can watch fish being landed then eat it in the tavernas right alongside. The harbour is formed of large rocks and spreads round a headland with a half-submerged ruined Venetian castle, yachts and bigger boats one side of the headland, caiques on the other side. Through an archway from the main square you can wander through a network of little streets of typical Cycladic houses. Hotel Aliprantis, on the square, is good value.

Ambelas, a fishing village very near to Naoussa, has become a small resort with hotels. So has Piso Livadi, thirteen miles across the island from Paroikias, a fishing port which was once used to ship marble and is now lively with hotels, villas and rented rooms. It is almost deserted in winter.

You can walk along the water's edge from here to Dryos on five beaches. Or you can catch the bus if you can squeeze on it. The first beach is Logaros, with beautiful sands, shading trees at one end and tavernas.

I go to the last beach, Chrysi Atki, best

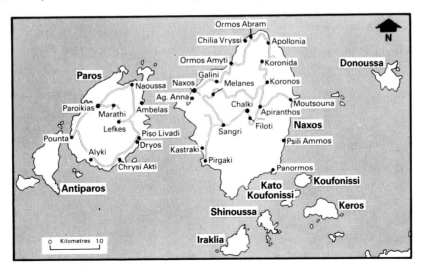

on the island, with long hard golden sands. Here Barbara can swim or sunbathe while I sit in the bamboo shade of a taverna in the backshore writing and reading. I have sat here with my mid-morning glass of white local Kavarnis wine, wandered into the taverna to choose my lunch, eaten it with more wine, gone back to writing and realized as Barbara wandered back and sat beside me, thirsty and dopey from the sun, that it was time for aperitifs before dinner. That is the sort of relaxed day's work I like. And Paros is one of the best places for it.

A little further down the road, where the bus turns to go back to Piso Livadi and Paroikias, is Dryos, which I have seen grow from a fruit-farming village to a posh little resort where Athenians have built summer villas. Its secret is plenty of water, and in times of shortage tankers take it from here to other parts of the island. Half an hour's walk and more south of Dryos are beaches with excellent swimming which are often deserted.

Alyki, seven miles from Paroikias on a paved road, has changed twice in twenty years. When I first knew it, it was a fishing village where the fishermen augmented their incomes by panning for salt. Its fish tavernas were excellent. The tree-lined sandy beach was deserted. Then, around 1980, with news of a little airport being built nearby for flights to Athens, Athenians started to build summer houses of cement blocks. Several restaurants, café-bars and a disco followed. When I saw it again in 1987, the airfield was being extended, with strong rumours that charter flights would be coming in, which would be very convenient for tourists and profitable for Parians but would almost certainly mean that package tour hotels and apartment blocks would be built on

those near-deserted beaches I mentioned. Paros would be like Mykonos. I don't think it can absorb any more visitors without changing almost completely.

Pounta, half way between Alyki and Paroikias, is still a little village with one good hotel, bars and tavernas and a big quay. It is the port for the little ferries which shuttle between here and the small isle of Antiparos, a ten-minute journey, but not always a safe one for small sailing boats as currents are strong and winds can be tricky. An English tourist trying to improve her surf sailing technique went out too far, got caught in the currents and was carried right across to Antiparos. Luckily she had enough sense to hang on and not to try to put the board about to get back to Paros. But Antiparos is only seven miles long, so she could have missed it. No one thought to rescue her. She could not let go to wave for help and the locals thought that she was just another mad Englishwoman winning a bet.

In the hills behind Pounta is the lush valley Petaloudes, thickly wooded, with a constantly running stream. This is the Valley of Butterflies. In July and August they swarm around you as you walk. But so do people from coach excursions and buses. At other times, there are no butterflies but it is cool and tranquil.

Antiparos is to me a perplexing little island. I think that I should have enjoyed it more in my camping days or if I loved swimming, for its swimming is said to be a delight. So is the fresh fish in the restaurants.

In Byzantine days the isle was reported to have been inhabited only by wild asses. Now the youngish Athenians who have moved into summer houses here since Paros built an airfield have brought with them the disco beat.

A cave has lured tourists for centuries. Boat excursions run there in summer from Kastro, Paroikias and Pounta. Take rubber shoes and a torch. From the landing stage you have a half-hour's walk up Mount Aghios Ilias, less if you hire a donkey. The entrance is by a church.

Once, visitors went down and up again by rope but now there are 400 cement steps which descend about 230 feet. The cave is dripping, dark, cold and spooky. Stalactites and stalagmites, some nearly ten feet long, make it particularly eerie, and through centuries people have written on them – a strange form of graffiti.

One inscription in Latin reports the Christmas mass celebrated here in 1673 by Count Nouantelle, the French ambassador to Constantinople, who paid 500 Parians and Antiparians to attend. Ever non-conforming, he had his Christmas dinner aboard the pirate ship of Daniel of Malta. They say that Byron carved his name on a stalactite, but he was known for graffiti in Greece.

Refugees have hidden in the cave since men fled here from the unpredictable wrath of Alexander the Great. Greek Resistance fighters hid here in 1941–45 and Nazis did no good to the icicles by throwing in hand grenades to flush out the Greeks.

An American study said that Parians can expect to live longer than others because they are happy with their work, the island and within themselves. That is how I have always felt on Paros.

PAROS

A delightful island, attractive in its own right and a pivotal springboard for seeing other isles. Old Paros-lovers like me tend to get cross when we can't get in our favourite taverna in mid-summer and crowds throng the two ports of Paroikias and Naoussa, and say that Paros is 'spoiled'. But outside July and August and even then outside Paroikias, it can absorb its visitors and lose them.

Air ...... Two flights daily to Athens, more in July–August (50 mins – fare £15 1987). To Iraklion (Crete) 1 May–Sept three days weekly (45 mins). Rhodes four days weekly (1 hr 10 mins).

Ferries ...... Piraeus one to three daily May–Sept, five days weekly in winter (7 hrs). 'No-car' ferry to Siphnos daily, useful also for changing ferries to Seriphos, Kythnos and other isles.

Daily ferries to Ios, Santorini, Naxos. Other ferries to Amorgos (five days weekly), Astypalaia, Ikara, Iraklia, Shinoussa, Koufonissi, Mykonos (all three days weekly) Folegandros, Sikinos, Kalimnos, Kos, Nisiros, Tilos, Symi, Rhodes, Crete, Karpathos, Kasos, Syros and Donoussa (once weekly). Also many excursion boats in summer. To Antiparos – summer excursion boats from Paroikias port (¾ hr). Taxi-ferry from Pounta to Antiparos (10 mins). At one time if the boat was not there, you opened the chapel door and the skipper on Antiparos came across to fetch you. It might still work, out of season.

Naxos

Naxos and Paros, which look like twins from way out at sea, squabbled and warred through centuries. Even among visitors, each still has its ardent devotees.

But Naxos devotees can point to the mountainous beauty of Naxos, greener and more colourful than the rugged, majestic mountains of Crete. Even when the mountain rivers and waterfalls are dry in summer, they run riot with oleander flowers. Between are the green fertile plains with an abundance of lemons, olives and grapes, vegetables, nuts and flowers. Peoples of more arid isles always thought of Naxos jealously as a garden land of plenty. And the beaches are superb. The west coast is one series of fine beaches, almost worthy of Corsica.

Naxos has mystery and romance, too, inspired by the beautiful story of Ariadne. Byron loved Naxos. He had intended to return there to live. Richard Strauss was inspired here to write his opera *Ariadne auf Naxos*.

Yet the port of Naxia, with its vestiges of Venetian houses, doorways and coats of arms within the walls of the old Chora, has the ambience of an Italian port. An Italian freebooter, Marco Sanuda, took the isle in 1207, became Duke of Naxos and ruler of several Cycladian isles.

The narrow streets of the mediaeval town of Naxia up the hill from the harbour are dark and almost sinister, like some of the backstreets of Naples. There is less whitewash than in other old Cycladian towns. And the ruins at the hilltop are of a Venetian kastro, the Ducal Palace and other Italian palazzi. But it is a working

town still, and the people of Naxos put tourists second to commerce.

There is nothing Italian about the big marble doorway, twenty feet high, on the islet of Palatia, all that remains of a Temple of Apollo, begun in 522 BC and never finished – a gateway to nowhere. A Christian basilica built inside in the fifth century AD has gone, too. The islet is joined to the mainland by a causeway.

Though Naxia is still very much a working port, there are plenty of tavernas, bars, restaurants and shops along the harbour to lure tourists. Like Paros, Naxos became rich on marble. Then lemons were exported to the world, but the competition became tough and many lemon groves have sadly been grubbed and ploughed to grow grain. Now they export wine, olive oil, grain and figs. But they make a liqueur called Kitrou from lemon leaves, in four varieties – white, green, yellow (very sweet) and white special (less sugar, more kick). It is pleasantly sweet and sour and if I were a Naxian I should make more to export and sell to tourists, and save those superb old lemon groves. In mid-August a festival of folk music and dance, wine and souvlaki is held in the main square – dedicated to Dionysus (Bacchus, god of wine). Who else? He was Ariadne's second lover and brought wine to the island.

Not long ago, Naxos was a hideout for travellers avoiding crowds on Mykonos. But with those superb beaches and its beauty, it was bound to lure more people,

Marble blocks from an ancient temple have been reused to build this Naxian house

which it has. And with the opening of the airport with flights from Athens, there will be more bodies cooking on the beaches. At present, Naxos is mainly cheaper than other Cycladian islands. In May or September, when there are few visitors, it is at its best, and not so hot, either.

A good means of transport to hire is a mini-moke. Closed cars can be too hot, scooters too dodgy on the dirt roads of the south and north-west and dangerous with two-up in the mountains. But bus services are not bad.

A new suburb has grown around the popular Aghios Georgios beach – hotels, bars, disco, including a café disco in a fake windmill, pedaloes. Greeks have a habit of driving on the beach. It is long, with dunes where some bedless back-packers sleep at night. Taverna Meltemi is excellent value.

Aghia Anna beach is becoming very popular because you can reach it by bus or caique from Naxia. Alas, it tends to get a lot of litter. You can find rooms here. So you can at Aghios Prokopios, a fifteen-minute walk further north along the sandy shore and much quieter. There are more rooms at Kastraki, further south along this unpaved but driveable road. A hamlet is by the beach, a taverna on it.

From here you join the paved road which runs inland from Naxia and has a bus service. And you arrive at something surprising and quite different. At Pirgaki is a fine sand beach with clean sea. A smart bungalow holiday complex has been cut into the rocky hillside where, in 1985, they were charging all of 200 drachmas a night (£10 or US$16) for a bungalow with full plumbing sleeping three people. Blessedly there is a fairly primitive taverna by the sea. An hour's walk inland is the Byzantine fortress of Tapaliru which Marco Sanuda took in 1204 after a two months siege and so grabbed Naxos.

Among the mountains in the centre of the island are many villages with varied interest, from old Byzantine churches to Venetian towers where the most important men like the Dukes lived in summer, ruins of fortified Venetian villas (they deemed it wise to be protected not only from pirates but the Naxian populace) and old emery-mine workings, as well as lovely views and pretty fertile valleys.

My favourite spot on Naxos is the delightful little fishing port of Apollonia in the north-east corner. There are two routes from Naxia port – the interesting road through the centre, paved except in very short stretches which can catch you unawares, and the lovely unpaved track-road north from Naxia round the coast.

The paved way goes to Sangri, passing close to Aghios Mamos, an eighth-century cathedral, recently restored, with fascinating icons. Earlier you can make a diversion by left fork to Melanes and the marble quarries of ancient times. By the quarry at Flerio, two miles east of Melanes, you can see two of Naxos's statues called Kouroi, which means 'young men'. They were sculpted in the seventh century BC, are fifteen feet tall and may have been Zeus's guardians. They are marching stiffly with arms straight down their sides.

Sangri is the name of three hamlets of little courtyards and cobbled streets, encircled by castles, windmills and ruined Byzantine and Venetian villas. There are three monasteries round here.

The road dips into the delightful Tragea valley with some superb old olive trees. Then you climb to Chalki (or Khalki), with Byzantine and Venetian towers. The route becomes spectacular with gorgeous views as you climb into the rocky mountains and on to Filoti, the largest village on the island, on the slopes of Mount Zas. Some people stay here in rooms for walks over hills and in olive groves. One path follows the mountainside to the Tower of Chimarou, built by King Ptolemy of Egypt who ruled Naxos in the Hellenistic period around 100 BC.

The road zig-zags to high villages such as Apiranthos, where the Dukes built a tower-home, now rather run-down looking. You can take a dreadfully rough snaking road to the old port of Moutsouna, where the emery from the old mines was loaded on ships and where now are abandoned sheds, a shingle beach and two tavernas. I have never followed the track south along the coast, but I am told that it is very rough, passes several pleasant coves, and comes to Psili Ammos, which has a few houses and a big sand beach with dunes but no taverna. Then the road gets worse until it runs out in a small beach cove of Panormos with a church, a house and sometimes fishing boats. Sounds like a real hideaway spot if you have tent or sleeping bag and provisions.

The main road continues through the mountains to Koronos, stepped up the mountainside, then to Koronida (or

Komiabi), highest of the villages and pretty with lovely views of fertile country with mountain streams and glades of trees as the mountain drops down among vineyards to Apollonia.

When I first saw this little fishing port of Apollonia I wanted to stay for weeks. It *was* the Greek Islands – a small quay, fishing caiques slapping gently against it or against each other, tavernas and tavernas posing as restaurants on the quay road, with houses and a few simple hotels on the bigger shingle beach beyond the rocks. All the women seemed to have time for a long relaxed chat with whoever they met and the men had plenty of time for an ouzo or a bottle of wine in a taverna at any time of the day or evening. I could spend hours drinking, reading, just watching hardly-anything happening, almost too relaxed to pick up my wine and sip it, until the smell of cooking had me wandering inside to see what was for supper. There was one bus a day from Naxia and its arrival was a main event. If you felt the urge to move, you could walk to nearby sandy coves or go and look in the old marble quarries at the Kouros, over thirty feet high, so much bigger than those at Flerio, but abandoned uncompleted around 650 BC. A pity, for the Naxians were responsible for much of Delos and its masterpieces.

Now Apollonia is visited by excursion coaches from Naxia in high summer and has more hotels and tavernas. I don't worry too much about day excursionists on Greek islands. They go long before the evening's first ouzo and the serious business of taverna eating, drinking and talking begins.

You could return to Naxia by the rougher, coastal route – a most rewarding journey with spectacular scenery which has made Naxos so loved. Ormos Abram is a real farming village by a pebble beach, a small chapel and a pension already known to a few regulars who spend much of their holiday there dozing to the sound of goat bells. The road hugs the coast to Chilia Vryssi, where a track takes you to a delightful cove at the end of a valley, and a larger cove where the cultivated fields go right down to the rocks on the shore.

Just after Chilia Vryssi is a monastery, Faneromeni, built in 1606 but which the monks have left. More coves follow.

You reach Galini and join a paved road to Naxia. There is a pretty valley path from Galini down to another attractive cove.

I have never discovered on which Naxian beach the Cretan princess Ariadne slept so innocently while her lover, the hero Theseus, set sail sneakily for Athens, abandoning her. Odd behaviour after she had helped him slay the Minotaur.

Anyway, Ariadne did not cry for long. Sailing towards that beach was Dionysus, god of wine, who fell for the sunbathing Ariadne and soon seduced her. Perhaps she was under the influence of wine. He taught the Naxians how to make wine and she soon forgot about Theseus. After all, a god *and* wine maker was a good catch even for a princess.

East of Naxos is the isle of *Donoussa* (Dhonoussa), a truly remote hideaway where a few people live by making wine and fishing, and there are no more than half a dozen rooms for visitors. There's a mountain in the middle and the north coast is uninhabited. And you will often find more fishing boats than people on the beach, too. There's a taverna near the quay.

A ferry from Piraeus arrives twice a week in summer, once a week in winter, but in rough weather you can be cut off. The ferry stays off-shore and you land from little boats. In summer small boats and caiques go from Naxos, Paros and Amorgos (see page 103).

There's a string of little isles between Naxos and Amorgos, served by boats from Naxos and Paros, except for Keros which is served from Amorgos.

Largest is *Iraklia* (Heraklia), ten square miles with a population under 100. There is a taverna in the tiny port, which is an hour's walk from the Chora inland – just a hamlet. A twenty-minute walk takes you to Livadi beach. Excursion boats come here in summer from Amorgos, and boats from Naxos connect with the next island – *Shinoussa* (Skhinoussa). Here ferries dock in a lovely bay, almost landlocked by gentle hills. The taverna-restaurant here has rooms. A hillside track leads to the little old town, seemingly unchanged for centuries, with a mediaeval fortress, church, taverna and a few rooms to let. Shinoussa has plentiful water from fresh springs.

Koufonissi is a collective name for a chain of islets, all uninhabited except *Kato (Lower) Koufonissi*, with a few houses, and Koufonissi itself is where everything happens. Its port with a big quay is actually expanding and the adjacent village has two tavernas, a pension and rooms to let. Two beaches, too, and a notice banning nudity and camping in four languages.

You can sometimes get caiques to *Keros* from Koufonissi, but there are more frequent caique links with Amorgos. As I have never been to Keros, I can tell you only that it has a 1500-foot mountain in the middle, the remains of a mediaeval castle, a little port, two shingle beaches and its name was used by Alistair Maclean as the island where British troops were marooned in *The Guns of Navarone*.

These little islands are true hideaways from the world. But if you don't speak Greek they can become boring unless you take a very interesting companion or two and a Greek phrase book. The food may become boring, too, if the fishermen cannot get to sea and the supply boat does not arrive. They sometimes run out of such Greek basics as the ingredients of a village salad.

NAXOS

Superb scenery with good sands. Some roads very rough. Reasonable bus service, good mid-summer.

Ferries ...... Piraeus six days a week (8 hrs). Paros daily. Ios, Santorini six days a week. Mykonos (non-car vessel) four days a week. Other ferries on various days to Iraklia, Shinoussa, Koufonissi, Donoussa, Amorgos, Syros, Astypalaia. Little motor vessel (no cars) twice a week to Crete, Donoussa and Amorgos.

CYCLADES 5

Ios

Alas, poor Ios, I knew her well. She was the idyllic, peaceful Greek isle, the place where a man or woman could rest, think, walk, swim in near-perfect tranquillity. Gialos, the port, hardly rebuilt after destruction by a tidal wave during an earthquake, slept until a ferry came in. Fishing caiques and a few small private yachts wandered in and out seemingly unnoticed.

The startlingly white old Chora up the hill, with as many tiny domed churches as houses, was empty of people except priests, shopkeepers and a few old ladies hobbling up and down its steps until the rest of the people came back from the fields and vineyards in the evening, when the loudest noise would be of talk and laughter from the bars and tavernas.

Now the isle rocks throughout summer to disco noise until dawn. It has changed from a haven of peace to a heaven of energy, frenzied music and freedom for the young. The revolution took local people completely by surprise. They were bemused, then overwhelmed. Now they have cheerfully joined in the profitable tourist boom, opening bars, discos, snackbars, souvlaki bars and pensions not only cheek-by-jowl with the Chora's churches

but, inevitably, on Milopotamos beach, perhaps the finest stretch of sand in the Cyclades. It was literally deserted when I first saw it, now it is so crammed with bodies between mid-day and early evening that it must be difficult to find room to walk to the sea.

Apart from the older local fishermen, the peace-lovers and the few yachtsmen who thought this was their private hideaway, everyone seems happy.

But why, in the name of Zeus, did they have to pick this fairly remote, idyllically peaceful, attractive and fertile Greek island for their playground of sand, sun, sex, souvlaki and sound?

That wonderful beach had a lot to do with it. So did the tolerance of the local people, who pretended not to notice their illegal camping on the beaches or their nudity.

I arrived there first by yacht around mid-day and no one noticed. I saw a few men drinking inside a taverna and two old chaps, in the embroidered waistcoats rarely seen now in Greece, talking on a quayside seat. I followed the new concrete road winding up to the Chora and it was hard going in the noonday heat. People in the fields were resting, mostly asleep. The windmills which were still used in those days were still.

I reached the Chora by the square outside the town hall. The bus was standing in the shade, unattended. No vehicles moved. Up the hill in the narrow streets and white-painted steps one old lady walked down the steps nervously, tapping her stick. A priest came out of a little church, locked it and, keys jangling, walked confidently to a house higher up, like a man whose ouzo and moussaka were waiting.

In a small field behind white walls a frail old man in a faded check shirt and big-brimmed straw hat was rhythmically scything a field of ripe corn, never resting nor straightening his back. It was like a Van Gogh painting of Provence transposed to the Cyclades.

I took the old overgrown mule track back to the port. It was a dangerous journey. Three times, runaway mules with huge loads rushed past, sending me scampering into the heavy rough. One carried bricks, another a high load of hay which threatened to topple and the third had a car engine strapped across its back. The only man awake in the port, it seemed, was a taverna owner who served me salad, bread, moussaka and wine at an outside table, then closed the taverna door and went to sleep.

In the few days I was on Ios, I made a three-mile walk down a track to that beautiful beach at Milopotamos and was mesmerized. How could a beach like this have been missed by the growing tourist trade? After all, Ios was already served by a ferry twice weekly and the island bus did drive down there sometimes. I went to another superb sandy beach, Aghios Theodoti, but I hired a caique because the yacht on which I had come had sailed on and I was not in the mood for a three-hour walk on a rough path and three hours back.

There someone had tried to set up a tourist complex. There were stone huts like the old-style Club Mediterranées. But they were as abandoned as the ruined Venetian castle nearby. I took a caique, too, to Manganari beach because that is the only way to get there. Here, too, someone had just started a holiday complex.

The one significant historic monument of Ios, I have not seen. Many Greek towns claim to be Homer's birthplace. Ios claims his tomb. It is said that he came here to die, and why not? A Dutchman dug up his grave in the 1770s and although the inscription he claimed to have found disappeared, a commemorative stone has been erected at Plakatos, on the slopes of Mount Erimitis in the north of Ios. Most scholars scoff. But it would seem an inspired place for a poet to die, and there was an ancient city here, destroyed by another tidal wave.

When I returned to Ios in the sixties the flower children had found it. They were sweet young people, happy, polite, smiling, believing that the world could be beautiful if people would behave as gently as they did. They were broke, and many slept on the beach, but because they were kind and charming and gave no trouble the local people liked them.

There was one disco in mid-summer in a derelict windmill in the Chora and a few more bars up there. But most evenings there was a classical music recital using an ancient gramophone and there were jazz recitals and guitar playings on the sands by those who had brought their own in-

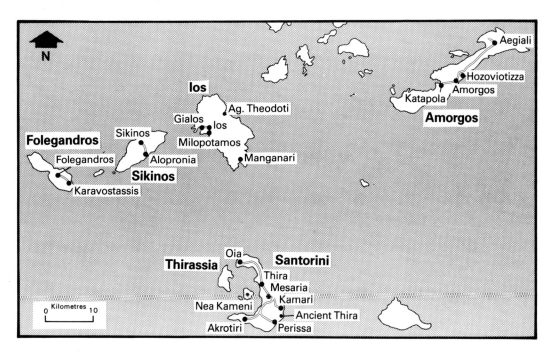

struments. And the boys and girls cleared up their litter. One entrepreneur had a chair on the beach and a cardboard notice saying 'hair cuts'.

When I returned in the seventies the bad, sad days of Ios had come. You could smell the 'pot' as you landed – a sickly smell. The island was over-run with youngsters; far too many of them unwashed and smelling of it. Beaches were fouled, litter piled up, mosquitoes and flies became a menace. The Ios water supply, always very dodgy in summer, simply could not cope. After the smell of 'pot' came the unsavoury smell of loos. The music and disco bars arrived in the Chora – Electric Bar, Nick's Musik, a dozen others, competing in loud, monotonous rhythm and no melody into the night. With drugs came thieving and thuggery. The local police force, much reinforced, not unnaturally got fed up with the scene, particularly with the beach sleeping, and turned nasty.

Of course, the majority of kids were not like this. They were just broke, and thoroughly enjoying companionship, freedom and an almost innocent permissiveness.

The unwashed hippies gradually dispersed. Now, most visitors have enough money to afford rooms or even beds in pensions or small simple hotels. A few still sleep on the beach but the police have 'persuaded' most of the campers into camp sites. You even have to pay for those huts on Aghios Theodotis Bay. Anyway, there is a bus down that track in season. And there are two tavernas, a disco and quite a posh hotel complex at Manganari

Bay, which you reach by a posher tourist boat now.

Behind Milopotamo are restaurants, cafés, bars, two camp sites, several small hotels and a supermarket. It is on this beach that most of the young spend their days until early evening, when they make for the tavernas and then the discos, which have run riot on Ios. They dance until dawn, fall into bed or onto a beach, then start the same round next day.

Even the Ios Club, which still supplies the classical concerts, gives them early evening so that it can switch to disco beat.

The youngsters are pleasant and well behaved. But the water-shortage is as acute as ever, the loos in the port smell no better, and, oh, that disco noise!

Ironic that many tourists were first lured to Ios by the beautiful description of

the isle by Lawrence Durrell in *The Greek Islands*. Ios, he wrote, was full of calm poetry. 'Taste the felicity of its silences, fractured only by some distant church bell or the braying of a mule. Even the wind seems lulled, and in Ios one sleeps the full sleep of early childhood.'

There are three ferries a week each way calling at Ios and Sikinos, so you can travel between the two, but I read recently that there are no longer any caique trips for tourists to Sikinos. I find it bewildering. The people of the two islands used to regard each other as thieves and pirates, but the boatmen of Ios always welcome the chance to earn a few drachmas.

The ferries cannot reach the harbour quayside on Sikinos. The cove is not deep enough, the quay too small. So there is a performance rather like abandoning a sinking ship every time a ferry arrives. Two 'rescue' boats (or 'bum boats', as our grandfathers called them) come out from the quay, and the jostle of passengers waiting to disembark with their suitcases tied with string, their huge boxes and tied-up bundles, their children, their sticks, is a live Greek play. Even slightly-laden back-packers have a problem.

The fairly easy way onto the harbour boat is when the ferry lowers its car ramp. Then the only real problem is the swell, the impatient scrum, the big boxes and oil drums, and sometimes reluctant sheep or goats to be coaxed across. I am glad that I have never landed from a side-door boat. These, it seems, necessitate a climb down a rope ladder, which can be very tricky with a big suitcase or bulky back-pack.

Sikinos has changed very little since I arrived on a caique all those years ago and became a 'member' of taverna society. There are about six assorted tavernas now instead of two and more rooms to let. Down in the port there is even a pension and a ferry ticket office where you can change travellers' cheques, both run by a friendly man called Peter (or Panayotis by the Greeks). His pension has a taverna attached, he appears to make his own retsina and own a farm.

But it is still a simple Greek island, living from the land and sea, with mules and donkeys doing most of the fetching and carrying because no cars are allowed and there is just one narrow stone road from the port, Alopronia, to the village Chora. Vines still cover most of the cultivated area.

There is a broad sandy beach at the port (also called Skala). But the wind blows down here, and most simple comforts are up in the Chora. There is no bus to it – just an hour's hot uphill walk. But they were widening the road in 1986 and that surely means some sort of wheeled transport. The loaded donkeys and trains of mules are prolifically photographed by Sikinos's few visitors.

The Chora is a delight to connoisseurs of old Greece. If only the windmills were still working! It is still charming and quiet, with many dilapidated houses where mules or chickens are kept. A long flight of steps takes you from the lower town to the main square with a large rather tired-looking town hall. In a narrow vine-covered close is the posher of the two tavernas I have found in Chora.

It is not a white-painted, colour magazine village but a living town for men who work on the land. I noticed that a few old houses seemed to have been 'restored' and was told that they had been bought by 'foreigners'. I did not meet any. Athenians perhaps.

There are two walks, each taking well over an hour. A path to the north-east leads to very scant remains of a classical fort. South-west at Episkopi is a Roman temple converted into a Byzantine church.

You can, I am told, walk to beaches round the south-east coast from Alopronia. They must be very peaceful.

IOS

Don't go if you are seeking peace.

Ferries ...... Almost daily from Piraeus in summer, two to three times a week in winter (11 hrs). Daily to Santorini, Naxos, Paros. Thrice weekly to Sikinos, Folegandros, Siphnos. Twice weekly to Seriphos, Syros. Once weekly Tinos, Milos. Small boats to Sikinos.

SIKINOS

Plenty of water but you cannot drink the local wine – *too* resinated. See page 120 about arrival by ferry.

Ferries ...... Piraeus thrice weekly. Ios, Santorini, Folegandros, Paros, Syros thrice weekly. Naxos twice weekly.

Folegandros

Folegandros is an arid, rocky isle with terraces up the mountainside and much of its coastline barren high rock, rising 1000 feet sheer from the sea. Its name means 'rocky and arid'.

The Folegandros I knew was totally unprepared for tourists. The people seemed as dour, stern and suspicious as some I used to meet on Scottish isles, but underneath just as welcoming, friendly and generous. People turned out from cottages, hamlets and even in the Chora to greet foreigners and the forty-five minute walk from port to Chora took anything up to two hours because the hospitable local people still practised the old Greek welcome. They came out to offer you a glass of water and some bread, or, if richer, ouzo or wine and a sweetmeat. Water was precious then. It all came from wells and by the end of summer was distinctly thick and sticky.

But tourism has now arrived; a Danish organization runs holiday courses there. There are *two* buses from the port to the Chora and even on to Ano Meria, a village spread on terraces across a mountain top with herds of donkeys, goats and cows and one taverna. Folegandros now has piped water, though only turned on between nine-thirty and eleven-thirty am, so there must be a good trade in mineral water. There are also many more rooms to rent but they are needed since the Danish invasion and you may end up in the one camp site.

The ferry comes into an almost enclosed bay at Karovostassis, where there used to be just one taverna. Now there are several tavernas, bars, and at least one good restaurant called Remezzo, spread round the bay. I remember going in the old taverna for lunch and the owner asked me if I would like a crab. I was delighted. So he rushed down the old small quay to a fishing boat, found the fishermen mending nets, came back with a crab and kept me topped up with wine while he boiled it, cooled and dressed it. Now most visitors walk down to the port from the Chora for their evening meal.

The Chora is a jewel, the sort of Cycladian village you would choose to paint or photograph, as many do, but yet an unselfconscious working village. It has several pretty squares with fountains, lined with shops, tavernas and cafés and filled with flowers and trees. Lanes and alleys lined with houses join them.

The old town is behind the walls of a mediaeval kastro – two streets with charming old houses, many with external stone staircases to their upper storey. You can reach it up steps leading also to a general store selling anything from shoes

and pins to bedding and underwear.

The Chora roads come to a sudden halt at the clifftop, with lovely views down very steep walled terraces to the sea. A second hotel has appeared – a modernized old building on the Ano Meria road. I knew only the Danassis in the old town.

There are several beaches you can reach along the coast from the port or by crossing the island. Livadi, sand backed by pines, is most popular, probably because the camp site is here.

I persuaded a fisherman to take me to a beach called Katergo on the south tip because the route to it was so circuitous round the foothills that it would have taken me about one and a half hours to walk. The fisherman took fish, bread and wine, he cooked the fish on the beach and we lunched in a desert-island scene looking across to a tiny island. Now I am told caiques from the port will take you and fetch you a few hours later for around 500 drachmas. But it is still often deserted.

FOLEGANDROS

Desolate, arid, with one road. Friendly people. For walkers.

Ferries ...... Piraeus thrice a week in summer, once off-season. Thrice weekly Santorini, Paros, Syros. Twice weekly Sikinos, Ios, Naxos. Summer caiques to Ios, Sikinos.

Amorgos

Even Greek islands can go in and out of fashion. A few years ago there was such a rush of visitors to Amorgos seeking the quiet idyllic life that rooms were extremely difficult to find and people were sleeping on benches beside the main square. Now it is one of those few islands being promoted by the government Tourist Office with free ferry fares off-season.

I don't know why it lost some of its appeal. Perhaps because its people seem mainly uninterested in visitors though they are friendly if you can get to them. Mind you, it is crammed still in July and August with mainland Greeks, Germans and Scandinavians, and maybe that is enough for the locals. Or maybe they are

just choosey about whom they accept in their rooms, for it is mostly the young who have problems and some young travellers, with their torn clothes and unkempt look, do not appeal to the formal, old-fashioned Greeks on small islands.

It is a rugged island and looks from some angles like a fortress isle to which dictators would send political prisoners. Cliff scenery can be dramatic rather than beautiful. But the entrance to the main harbour, Katapola, is gentle enough. In a bowl-shaped bay between hillsides, the port appears to be three villages linked by a tree-lined promenade, with none of the dramatic effect of those white island ports backed by houses climbing a hillside. It has pensions, small hotels, tavernas, shops and a dominating silver-domed church looking out to sea. The fishing boats and old fishermen's houses make up the most attractive scene. There is also a yacht supply station, and holiday yacht flotillas come in here.

The road to the capital Chora Amorgos is only five miles but it's a hot dusty walk on a summer's day. A battered Dodge school bus goes up there about four times a day, but the timetable is strictly Greek-island – variable, though you can be fairly sure that it will meet ferries. As these are often hours late, you have another old-time Greek island situation. If you are lucky you can get a taxi.

For me the Chora Amorgos is the best reason for visiting Amorgos. It is very simple, very white, very Cycladic with narrow cobbled streets and alleys, empty of cars, with little chapels or intriguing houses round each corner. It stands 1000 feet up, perched on a plateau, with terraced slopes to the sea on one side, windmills no longer in use on the other. You often see a row of windmills in the Cyclades – at Ios, for instance. Each farming family had their own. A well-preserved Venetian castle of the Dukes of Naxos in the town centre has panoramic views of the whole island.

The Chora has a few shops, a post office and a few rooms. A little hotel was due to be started recently. You can get toasted sandwiches and light snacks at the café, run by an Athenian, but nearly all the tavernas are in the port of Katapola, though half of those open only in July and August. The only registered hotel is in the other port of Aegiali (Egiali).

There's a donkey path from Chora along the rocky edge of the mountainside, then zig-zagging down the mountain to Hozoviotizza Monastery, founded in 1088. The building is starkly beautiful – a white fortress built into the brown rock, reached by a steep stepped path. Inside is yet another magic icon – many island monasteries have them. The walk to the monastery is hard and takes half an hour. The walk back to Chora is much harder.

It is a very hard walk along donkey tracks, too, to the northern port of Aegiali and most people use the ferries which call at both ports, in different order according to which ferry you catch. There are sometimes caique excursions between them in summer.

Aegiali is a friendly little port where the people seem more outgoing, and most back-packers, island-hoppers or more-relaxed visitors stay. It is the home port, too, for ferries to the little isles – Keros, Koufonissi, Shinoussa and Iraklia (see pages 114–15).

It is a pleasant little place in a large bay, with fishing boats inside the rocky ferry quay, where their nets are spread to dry. Tucked under the cliffs are attractive houses with bright balconies, pensions, one hotel (Mibe, by the sandy beach nearby) with spacious rooms, very few shops, some cafés, bars. A shop selling mostly souvenirs offers donkeys to rent. To my mind, you need more experience to ride a donkey than a scooter in Greece, and donkeys are much more expensive these days. Scooters are useless on Amorgos. Up the hillside is the upper village, Potamos.

I am sure that you could grow to love this island if you could make friends here, and the place to do it is Aegiali, where the tavernas are friendly and pleasant.

AMORGOS

Best outside July, August. Ferries nearly all arrive and leave very early morning or late at night. In 1987, boats direct to Piraeus left only Friday and Sunday.

Ferries ...... Piraeus twice weekly. Four days a week to Koufonissi. Thrice to Astipalaia, Shinoussi, Iraklia, Naxos, Paros. Twice to Donoussa, Kalymnos, Nisiros, Tilos, Symi, Syros. Once weekly to Kos, Rhodes, Crete.

Santorini (Thira, Thera)

I cannot love Santorini. I know that it is one of the most dramatic of Greek isles, that its capital Thira, standing above the cliffs, is attractive, with white domes contrasting with dark volcanic rocks. But it seems to have spawned some of the most grabbing, nastiest people in the Greek isles – and I prefer trees to bare rock. The saving graces for me are some attractive countryside, the violent history and the interesting archaeological discoveries.

I think that the trouble with Santorini is that for forty years or more it has received well-heeled trippers off cruise ships with credit cards burning their wallets and a limited time to use them. This has encouraged the most vicious, blackmailing donkey drivers in Greece and shopkeepers and restaurant touts who harry and annoy you as you pass in a way which would even make the souk salesmen of Morocco blush. And prices are ridiculous. One British travel writer who knows Greece well described the donkeymen and shopkeepers as 'mercenary maniacs'.

Santorini has an airport, with international charter flights and flights from Athens bringing in a wave of tourists with which the island does not seem able to cope.

I admit that I got off to a bad start. I arrived in a little boat under the cliffs, at Skala Thira after the rebuilding of the 1956 earthquake damage but before the very recent and much-needed cable car. It may have been traditional and quaint to go up those 600 steps 900 feet up the cliffside on a donkey but one look at the vicious way the donkeys were beaten, especially round the legs, with heavy sticks, and hurried so that their drivers could make as many journeys as possible persuaded me to walk up.

The donkey drivers swore at me. They drove their donkeys at me, crashing me against walls. They knocked down two ladies and injured the arm of an old man. All that on one journey. Determined not to give in, I walked down again, this time using the footwork of a bullfighter. But I still got one bad wall-crashing. The donkeys hurrying upwards in the heat looked almost on their knees. I never saw one watered or given a minute's rest.

On the little quay I went into a bar for a glass of wine. A bunch of German tourists were drinking ouzo enthusiastically and the bar owner brought in a donkey and tried to make it dance on a tiny table for their 'entertainment'. It struggled and slipped and looked likely to break its leg. The tourists cheered the show. A young Briton put a stop to it.

Our attempt to explore the town was made almost impossible by the shop touts, who were not even very good humoured, and the little restaurant hurried us through a meal, as if they wanted our table. Perhaps they thought that we had to rush back to a cruise ship. But it was all such a contrast to the other Greek isles. And later visits have done little to change my views, alas. Happily, since those days, a bigger harbour has been built at Athinios, and with the cable car up the cliff, too, you can miss those donkeys.

The cable car was a gift from ship owner Evangelos Nomikos and the donkeymen fought very hard to prevent it, finally settling for a cut from each ticket. One year their payment was late so they occupied the lift control until they got their money.

In timetables Santorini is almost always called Thera – its official name since independence in 1821. It was formed by volcanoes about 20 000 years ago and theorists believe it was part of Plato's 'Lost City of Atlantis'. There are lots of those about. Earthquakes have changed its history and its shape. Around 1500 BC an explosion of pent-up gases made a huge central crater which filled with sea water through a gap. Whole cities were buried under ashes, the island split in two, forming what is now Thirasia isle, and a gigantic tidal wave destroyed most of the Minoan civilization on Crete 128 miles away. Only Knossos itself could be rebuilt.

Christianity came early to the island. St Irene of Thessalonika died there about 304 AD and a shrine was dedicated to her, so Italian sailors called it Santa Irini, which became Santorini. An earthquake in 1650 lasted on and off for weeks, flooding Ios and Sikinos and causing havoc on the Cretan coast.

In 1925 another earthquake brought to the surface an islet which enlarged the size of the isle of Nea Kameni. Nea and its neighbour Palea Kameni are still active. You can take a boat trip to them from Skala Thira, make a thirty-minute climb to the crater and inhale the pungent sulphurous fumes which can only be expelled by a bottle or two of the strong Santorini wines which tourists buy as far away as Athens to take home – the sweet white Vinsanto for irregular wine drinkers, the dry white Nichteri for regulars. To me, Nea Kameni is a slag heap. But beware of it. People of Santorini have believed for centuries that it harbours vampires.

The last earthquake was in 1956 and the town of Thira had to be rebuilt after it. Once the shops have shut, you can admire Thira – a white cubist town built on terraces, with pretty churches between houses. The pleasure of Thira is its position and its views, and you can see some of the best from restaurants, which is convenient and civilized. Leschis has excellent food and superb views. The cruise ships stop in October. Then Thira shuts down, for the winter weather is gruesome and Santorini can be cut off by fierce seas and gales.

The museum by the cable car has some most interesting sculptures and ceramics from many periods, including the sixth century BC, though some of the greatest Santorini finds, such as the famed frescoes, are in Athens.

Though there are many hotels and pensions in Thira, there is a local rule against letting rooms in private houses except in July and August, so you should book ahead. There are more hotels with hot showers here and though restaurants are more expensive than on most other islands, the food is also better.

On the way to the important and interesting archaeological site at Akrotiri are more hotels and pensions. At Karterados, among vineyards on a rough side road, are several hotels, pensions, rooms to let, tavernas and a path to the beach. As this is only just over a mile from Thira, on a bus route with about ten buses a day in season, it is quite a good place for island-hoppers to stay. Bus routes are fairly good on Santorini but timetables can be Greek-island. Scooter, car and mini-moke hire is a bit pricier here than on most islands.

Two miles from Thira at Mesaria are some posher hotels, some with bathrooms en suite. A road east leads to the beach at Monolithos on the east coast. Not very exciting. It has two tavernas of sorts, that grey volcanic sand called 'black', and a tomato canning factory used, obviously, in high summer.

The road from Thira divides at the hillside village of Exginia, one road going to the port-resort of Kamari, the other on to Akrotiri in the south-west, still only nine miles from Thira.

Professor Marinatos, a Greek, started the excavations at Akrotiri in 1967. He was killed in 1974 when a wall on the site collapsed on him, and is buried here. If you want to make a deeper study of the site read the book by his son, Dr Nanno Marinatos, *Art and Religion in Thera – Reconstructing a Bronze Age Society*. If not, translate into English the English versions of the guide books you can buy on the spot.

Marinatos unearthed a Minoan town, not quite so impressive as Knossos in Crete, but with buildings up to three storeys preserved under the larva, even to

Sacks of olives

doors, fireplaces, window frames and water systems.

Walking round in the silence of footsteps muted by a carpet of volcanic dust amid those ancient houses is eerie, especially when you are told of vivid local stories of ghosts seen by locals over centuries. Ghosts are so real to some farmers here that they will not work certain fields.

Below the site is a bay of pebbles and black boulders, with an hotel and taverna, and in the village above some bars and rooms, all surrounded by vineyards. Eastward across the isle is Perissa, another 'black' sandy beach in a big bay, with many small hotels, rooms, tavernas, minimarket, pedaloes and a lot of people in summer, but there is room at the far end from the village, with tamarisk trees for shade. The big modern church is on the site of the Byzantine church to St Irene. Do beware of walking bare-footed or lying without protection on these 'black' sands. They absorb heat and you can be badly burned.

Perissa is divided from its rival beach of Kamari by a mountainous headland, Mesa Vouna, with the remains of the ancient city of Thira, and from either you can reach it by tackling a steep mountain path – easier from Kamari because a road goes nearer. It is 1000 feet up, and you can sometimes see Crete from the summit.

The ruins, spread over terraces, were excavated in 1867 and the remains included temples to Egyptian gods, Isis, Seraphis and Anubis, Dionysus, god of wine, Apollo and the Ptolemies, as well as a theatre, mosaics in houses, and inscriptions from around 800 BC recording names of competitors and dancers at the *gymnopaidia*, a festival at which young men doing military service took part in athletic contests, exercises and dancing, all in the nude. The view from the theatre, with a sheer drop to the sea, is frightening. Locals say that in 1890 a uniformed band tackled the mountain track to give a concert!

The city dates from the ninth century BC and once had 5000 people. It became very important under the Egyptians (300–150 BC) when they built a naval base at Kamari.

You reach Kamari from the turning off the Thira road at Exginia. Kamari used to be a charming fishing village with a few hotels and tavernas and big 'black' beach. Now there are dozens and dozens of pensions and villas devoted almost entirely to young package holidaymakers, waterskiing and surfing, pedaloes, dancing until dawn in nightspots and even in the streets, music bars with names like Banana Moon, Yellow Donkey, Sail Inn, and a Pizza Parlour. But at least a few fishing boats still catch fish for the tavernas.

A stiff path up the mountain from Kamari takes you to the 1712 Monastery of Profitis Ilias at 1857 feet. It has a museum of icons, paintings and relics. But it is disconcerting to hear fatalistic locals say that when Santorini disappears under the sea after an earthquake, only this will remain above the waves!

The zig-zagging road west from Exginia leads to the port of Athinios where most of the big ferries come in now, and awaiting them are usually rows and rows of buses, including buses from hotels. When arriving in summer, get off the boat early, because the island buses get very crammed. And beware if you arrive in the night. Sometimes island buses don't come at all. Then you must catch a hotel bus or you may have to sleep on the adjacent sands. And book your ticket ahead and get on a ferry quickly in high summer as far as that is possible against the competition of old Greek ladies. This is one of the few islands where police sometimes count heads and at this season the ferries are nearly always over-booked. Two of my friends were not allowed aboard. There is little at the port except a big concrete quay, and a row of concrete cafés and restaurants.

The road north from Thira town leads to Oia (Ia), the third port, half ruined by the last earthquake, so that among the white houses piled up the steep slope are many leaning drunkenly or with tipsy roofs. It still has nearly as many churches as Ios town. On the shore below you can pick up pummice-stones to take to your friends for souvenirs. There are rooms and simple hotels, but the little town can be crowded in daytime with people from day-trip boats. Just before you reach it at Foinikia some old houses have been con-verted into holiday apartments, with su-perb views to Thirasia island across the bay – expensive by Greek standards.

Beyond Oia is a path leading round the northern coast and down the middle of the island to Thira – about ten miles of fairly hard walking.

Oia is the best place to pick up an excursion boat to *Thirasia* island. It is bigger than you think – twenty-eight square miles – but mostly it is very arid and rocky. It was joined to Santorini until an earthquake of around 1500 BC. There are a number of sandy beaches to which you can walk. But you must be fit. You must walk up 300 steps from the quay to the port village. Up there are several tavernas, shops and houses where you could get a room. A very steep path leads to the Chora, with fewer tavernas and other paths to two inland hamlets from which you can walk to beaches.

It could be your haven of peace, away from civilization, for a few days. But the days might drag on, for I am told that the ferries stop at any suggestion of nasty weather. And there is a water shortage. Take plenty of wine.

SANTORINI

Water shortage but water boats bring it at intervals. Plenty of transport in summer but ferries can be cancelled because of seas and wind, so check. Check which port. Island almost shuts down from October until early May.

Air ...... International charters and package tours. Athens two or three times daily in summer (45 mins). Crete four times weekly (40 mins). Mykonos daily (40 mins). Rhodes thrice weekly (1 hr).

Ferries ...... Piraeus (12 hrs) six days weekly, often twice a day in summer. Daily, often two boats, to Ios, Paros, Naxos. Crete five days weekly. Mykonos four days weekly. Three days to Sikinos, Syros, Folegandros. Twice a week to Ios, Siphnos, Seriphos. Once a week to Tinos, Kimolos, Milos, Kythnos.

SOUTH AEGEAN

Crete

The man on the plane who knew it all said: 'Tourists have ruined Crete. It's impossible to get lost there any more.'

Well, we have known the rugged, harsh and lovely isle for thirty-eight years and within two days we were comprehensively lost. After crossing Crete on a bumpy mountain road to the tiny port of Aghia Galini we followed a map road round the coast. At dusk we ran out of road. Dirt tracks took us through farmyards, fields and silent dark hamlets. Then we were on a narrow track in the mountains. We saw no lights, people or cars. At last lights flickered below us. We hit the main Heraklion road at about three am. The problem had been that the main road marked on our map had not yet been built.

True, Crete now has a concrete road laughingly called a 'motorway', a few Costa-style hotels with swimming pools on beaches where goats used to roam, and the romantic little port of Aghios Nikolaos used as the scene for TV's *The Lotus Eaters* is jammed now with ice-cream eaters. But tourism is still a thin veneer on this wild, beautiful, courageous and utterly individualistic island. There is nowhere on

Beehives line this stony Cretan track

earth like Crete and no invasion of package tour companies will alter it much, any more than such invaders as Saracens and Venetians, Turks and Nazis could. The people of Crete are Cretans first, Greeks second. Their philosophy is of carefree courage. They sing little rhymes called mantinades and one goes: 'Man's courage is the only real wealth, so eat, drink and make the most of this world.'

Of the many courageous acts of the Cretans in the Second World War, the one which appealed to their senses of humour, courage and revenge was the stealing of the Nazi General Kreipe, governing the island, by the Cretan Resistance with the poet Stanley Moss and the writer Patrick Leigh Fermor, who smuggled him back to England. Stanley Moss told the story in *Ill Met By Moonlight*, which was later made into a film. To understand Cretans better, read the Resistance side of this story – *The Cretan Runner* by George Psychoundakis.

It is on or just off the coastal road sweeping round from Heraklion to Hersonissos (Chersonisos), Malia, Elounda and Aghios Nikolaos that you find the big modern package hotels with their swimming pools, restaurants, bars, discos and massed souvenir shops. There are some hotels, too, before you get to the old port of Rethymnon and the former capital, Chania. But go past Chania and to Kissamos Bay, take the little roads round the whole of the west part of the island and the Levkas mountains, below the mountains of the south coast, or take the little roads across the island from Heraklion, and you are in a world of old Cretan villages and farms where a passing tourist is a Man from Mars to the people – someone who has nothing whatever to do with their lives.

Drive up the hills behind that tourist belt until you run into rough tracks and you are in villages living in a different country from the people of the coast.

We always try to stay in little hotels or pensions where the Greeks stay or in family rooms rather than tourist villas. Happily some British tour operators have realized that this is where most people going to Greece want to stay and offer them on package tours. That was how we found a C-class hotel, Pela Maria, in Hersonissos, hidden among rows of souvenir shops selling imitation classical vases, Greek silver ornaments, or draped outside with Athens-made dresses, shirts and kaftans, with basket-loads of sandals on the pavement. Our fellow guests were all Greeks.

One day Manolis Tripakis, the owner, took us just five miles up narrow dirt roads to his native village. Everyone we passed stopped him to shake hands and talk. Standing among chickens and dogs in the yard of his brother's little farm, we emptied a bottle of fierce home-made raki with super rough home-made bread and sausage. Then we sat outside the only bar consuming ouzo and relays of snacks while men arrived to shake hands, children found excuses to pass and peer, old ladies in black sat opposite, knitting and

discussing us. Before we returned, we stopped at the house where he was born where Manolis's sister gave us a special cake and apricot liqueur.

It was a true flashback to the Crete of nearly forty years ago, to my days of sitting astride oil-flasks among sheep and goats on supply caiques, passing round the wine bottle. When we got back to his hotel, we sat down with him and his business friends from Heraklion and ate a five course, four-hour meal, with a magnificent fish – a luxury anywhere in Greece – and a lot of wine.

On Crete you really do need to hire a car. For Crete is 3200 square miles in size, very mountainous, so that walking takes a very long time, and the buses simply do not go to the little farming villages in the interior and mountains. The most interesting roads are simply too dangerous for scooters, so hiring one limits you mostly to bus routes.

There are really four Cretes – the old Crete of farms and villages, where the mule still reigns, the industrial and trading Crete of Heraklion and the ports of Chania and Rethymnon, the new Crete of the big tourist hotels on huge sand beaches and of discos, and the scholar's Crete of historic archaeological sites which first drew our ancestors to the island as tourists.

I have never got to love Heraklion. The frenzied traffic reminds me of Toulouse or Naples, and it is the only place in Greece outside Athens where drivers get ulcers if they are held up for a couple of seconds. Of course, it is a busy commercial town, making money, and not a place for old Greek island dreamers like me. Even the restored sixteenth-century Venetian castle, called by the Turkish name of Koules, is surrounded by ugly buildings and the old

Venetian harbour is swamped by commerce. The impressive Venetian city walls remain remarkably intact considering the wars, fighting and expansion that the city has suffered. There is a splendid market in Odhos 1866 open Monday to Saturday mornings.

You must do what everybody else does and go to Plateia Venizelos to see the impressive Morosini fountain, named after Francesco Morosini, hero of a twenty-two-year Turkish siege, and to eat at one of the tavernas. Mind you, so many people are walking past that you can hardly see the bowls of the fountain. It was built in 1620 and is superb – like a corner of Renaissance Rome. The tavernas are a little pricey, but this is the Cretan equivalent of sitting on Champs Elysées or walking round Piccadilly Circus.

At night, it is fun to eat in the Dhedhalou, a street which is really a wide pedestrian passageway, with restaurant tables lining one side. Once again, there are a lot of people passing.

Two of the original gates of the fifteenth-century city walls still exist and near one of them, Kainouria, is the grave of a great Cretan author, Nikos Kazantzakis, who died in 1957. The Greeks knew him especially for a book called *Freedom and Death*. We know him for another story – *Zorba the Greek*. Surely only a Cretan could have written the book, or the quotation on his grave 'I believe in nothing, I hope for nothing, so I am free.' In the historical museum is a re-creation of his study. But the best display is the collection of hand-woven cloth. Weaving was a folk-art on Crete, and every girl would learn to weave and create her own patterns, keeping them secret until her wedding day, when they would be displayed. In country districts girls still do that.

Try to see the fifteenth-century Aghia Ekatirini (St Katherine's) church, now a museum of religious art and especially icons. Six were painted by Mikalis Damaskinos. He was a student here when it was a monastery school, and a contemporary of Domenico Theotokopoulos, the artist later known as El Greco, who went to study in Venice then paint in Spain where he died in 1614.

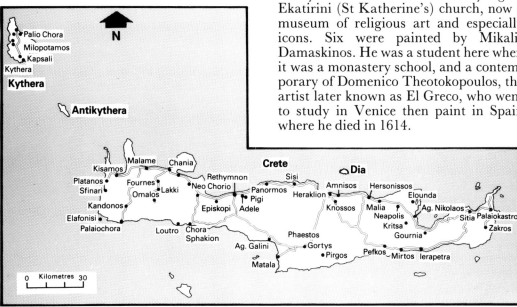

Go to the Archaeological Museum, but preferably after you have seen Knossos, then you will understand the exhibits better.

Eastward out of Heraklion the road starts through an untidy mess as it skirts the airport and army camp and the new highway inland is not much better. Offshore at Amnisos is the isle of Dia, reserve for the wild kri-kri goat with the massive curved horns – a sort of wild ibex. Dia was named after yet another of Zeus's mistresses, deported to the island by his wife Hera.

Hersonissos, first of the popular package tour resorts, at least has no 'skyscraper' modern hotels or apartment blocks, and the fish restaurants on its quayside are very good. It is built on the site of an ancient city. Malia is a strange village. A real farming centre, it is threatening to become a lively tourist resort, with hotels on the sands and the road to them lined with hotels, pensions, rooms, tavernas, bars, supermarkets and a disco; but farming continues all round and the odd sheep wanders onto the huge sand beach.

The road turns inland, but a lane left takes you to one of my favourite places on Crete, the little fishing village of Sisi, with a charming fishing boat quay. The quayside taverna is rather up-market but serves good food. Three pleasant package tour hotels have been built, some pensions and a large supermarket. Another side road before Silinari takes you to Milatos Beach which we used to call Analipsis. Now it has rooms, some restaurants and shops and several tavernas, one of which, Meraklis, is still used by the fishermen, but at the end of the village is a group of bungalow apartments with a swimming pool in an attractive setting. It won't be-come a resort until buses come here. The old village is higher up.

Make a short diversion to Neapolis, a nice Cretan country town, with interesting little shops serving the whole farming area and a big square with trees and church. Do try the local drink, *soumada*. Made from almonds, a big local crop, it is drunk iced or hot according to weather by women and children, with raki in all weathers by the men – almond brandy! Now you have a difficult choice of roads. The modern highway takes a spectacular valley route through the pretty village of Limnes direct to Aghios Nikolaos. Or you can take a winding equally spectacular lesser road to the left to Elounda. And, Oh, what a change was there, my country-men . . . or perhaps because of my countrymen.

Elounda was the site of an ancient Minoan town Olous which sank beneath the sea, and you can sometimes see the ruins beneath the water. I saw them once from a fishing caique. Elounda was until not long ago a fishing village. Fishermen's cottages are still there with their communal well and so are the fishing boats in the

little harbour, but most spend the summer taking visitors to Spinalonga island and only fish off-season. It was inevitable that it would build up a little after Aghios Nikolaos was swamped with tourists and soon there were a few modern bars, restaurants, shops and very small hotels. One was Poulis, a good, cheap taverna on the front with a simple modern pension Aristea.

Then the British made here that brilliant TV series *Who Pays the Ferryman*, starring Jack Hedley, which became popular all over the world. This drew a lot of attention to Elounda. Despite its lack of sand and its fine-gravel beach being some way from the village, it has grown into a quite-smart resort, with a number of luxury and A-class hotels, as well as C to E class and pensions, some good restaurants, discos and, the real symbol of civilization, a branch of the National Bank of Greece. No changing money in the store these days.

It is in a lovely setting, with some fine scenery around and is a very pleasant place for a holiday. Spinalonga island just off the harbour is a beautiful little spot with a Venetian fortress from 1579. It is a popular place for holidaymakers to get away from the bustle of Aghios Nikolaos, but big enough to swallow quite a lot of people. When I first stepped onto it in the 1960s, it was so deserted that I felt like Crusoe. In the Elounda fisherman's taverna they told me why. It had been a leper colony from 1904 to 1957, known as the 'isle of the living dead'. The few visitors who came this way were scared of catching the dreaded disease. The Venetian fort was so skilfully built that the Turks, who took Crete in 1669, could not take it until 1714.

The road rises past old houses, olive groves and the odd hotel or bar to Hera, up the mountainside, with superb views of Spinalonga; then it zig-zags down to Aghios Nikolaos.

I can understand people who knew Aghios Nikolaos when it was just a beautiful lively little Cretan port bemoaning the flood of tourists, and reading my own notes of 1962 makes me sadly nostalgic. But even then I was surprised that there were only about three small tourist hotels in such a delightful, likely spot, plus a beach-bungalow complex. It is still superb, despite the people, and within a length of quay from the tavernas packed with tourists, the bars, and the little crowded streets, the life of a Cretan port continues, with all manner of ships and fishing boats coming and going. A lot of its charm comes from its little freshwater lake Voulismeni, a stone's throw from the sea and joined to it by a little man-made canal. Legends have grown up about the lake. It was once called 'the bath of Artemis'. And it was supposed to be bottomless. But now it has been plumbed at a depth of about 200 feet. It was also believed to be connected with Santorini by a secret passage. It is almost certainly the emergence of an underground river. But it is a magnet for tavernas and open-air cafés built round it, and it is a most pleasant place to sit in the evening eating or drinking. There are plenty of beaches nearby.

The narrow streets are crammed with tourist shops, fast food snack bars, people, and cars. The one-way street system is inevitable. The big package hotels are mostly right away from the harbour, on the Elounda road round the north side of the harbour, or way up the hill on the way in. Even in winter, it is still a popular resort.

Kritsa, the mountain village inland from Nikolaos, is most attractive but much visited by tourists on excursions. It has a thirteenth to fifteenth century very-Byzantine church with superb murals in excellent condition, shops selling local handicrafts (weaving) and honey, and at Goulas, two miles away, excavations of the Archaic (seventh-century BC) city of Lata. Clambering around the ruins is hard work, but the view from here is delightful.

The coast is charming from Nikolaos to Sitia – sheer rocky cliffs with sandy and pebbly coves and lovely views, so it is small wonder that a number of villas have been built. If you hire one, you need a car.

The bus service is very infrequent. The modern highway reverts to an old road, and in places fields with goats and donkeys reach the shore. You pass Kalo Horio on a hill to the right, and below it on the coast at Istron clamped on a vertical cliff the truly-luxury Istron Bay Hotel, renowned for watersports and with its own caique. Then comes a little winding road right up to Gournia (Gurnia), one of the most dramatic of ancient sites.

In 1901 a farmer working in his fields found an old seal-stone which led to Sir Athur Evans, who excavated Knossos, pin-pointing an ancient Minoan town. A young American, Harriet Boyd, excavated and found the foundation walls of an entire town. Founded around 1600 BC, its townsfolk were fishermen, farmers and craftsmen, a totally different world from the Palace of Knossos. In the workshops were historic treasures – carpentry tools, potters' wheels, oil presses and cleansing tubs, wine press, copper smithy with tools. The paved staircase is akin to the donkey-step alleys of more modern villages. Try to see it if you can.

The road takes to the mountains to Sitia, a pleasant port in a bay, with tavernas round the quayside serving splendid fish, white houses on terraces joined by broad steps, and an excellent beach, with a sunken ship as décor. It is a working port for fishing and cargo boats, and some industry around the quay, but it is famous for sultanas and wine. The mid-August wine festival is said to compare with the Limassol wine festival in Cyprus for alcoholic consumption, and that is some comparison, I can tell you! For an independent traveller wanting a spot to stay where Cretans much outnumber tourists, Sitia is a good idea. It has ferries connecting with nearly all the Dodecanese islands and Piraeus, and flights to and from Rhodes, Kasos and Karpathos.

A road eastwards is marked as a highway on most maps but was still a rough old road in 1986, with signs of roadworks. It leads to Palaiokastro and beyond, on a rough driveable track through olive groves, to the bay with Minoan remains standing guard over fine sands which are often deserted, though there are tavernas. A left fork before Palaiokastro takes you to the fortified Toplou monastery, with a magnificent icon painted in 1700 by Jon Kornaros.

The main road from Sitia varies in standard. It hits the south coast near Markiyialos, with sandy beach, and continues to Koutsouras among plastic greenhouses and restored old houses rented to visitors. It skirts the coast to Ierapetra, most southerly town in Europe and only 230 miles from Egypt. It is untidy, industrial, but has two grey beaches and quite a lot of hotels and is a popular resort with Greeks. Napoleon stayed in a house near the fort on his way to Egypt. Thanks to Nelson, he had no time on his way back – without his army.

Mirtos to the west is a small fishing village with a few tavernas which seems to distance itself from outsiders, possibly from experience. The Germans destroyed the village and shot or sent to concentration camps all males as a reprisal for resistance activity. Arvi seems more welcoming. Kerkotampos is a seaside farming village with livestock and two simple tavernas, but Tsoutsouros is blossoming into quite a busy little holiday place, mainly for Greeks. There is a good choice of tavernas but it is 'ripe for development' and that is what is happening, although this coastal road is still a track. The main road runs inland behind the coastal mountains to Pefkos and Pirgos, hitting the coast again at Aghia Galini.

Aghia Galini means 'holy serenity' and in 1962 it was wholly serene, a little port with some good tavernas on the quayside which was proud of its recent history as the place where they helped the British to smuggle in arms for the Cretan resistance fighters and agents to harry the Nazis. My 1962 notes say: 'wonderful cheap fish in tavernas from local boats, narrow streets near-deserted except for men on mules, two primitive hotels (beds fifteen drachmas).'

It has certainly been 'discovered'. Over-discovered. Tour buses, cars, scooters pour people into the little place throughout summer, you cannot walk down the little main street for tables and chairs, and the leisurely harbour tavernas are hurriedly pushing out meals to coach tourists who have a deadline.

Dozens of new hotels, pensions, apartments and houses offering rooms have appeared, but it does calm down in the evening on the harbour. The discos are on the beach, reached by a clifftop walk, lit at night. There are buses to Heraklion and a much shorter journey to Rethymnon. The beaches, which have tavernas and bars, are unexciting, but water taxis and caiques will take you along the coast to beach hamlets reached otherwise by sure-footed mules. It can be very windy and squally along this coast especially when the north-easter – the Grego or Greek wind – blows. St Paul, intending to winter here, was driven to Malta. All the same, Aghia Galini is quite warm in winter.

On the road westward towards Aghia Galini you pass Phaestos, the Minoan site excavated from 1900. It delights archaeologists because it has none of the reconstruction which Evans made at

Knossos. To me, Evans's reconstruction gives me a far better idea of Minoan life. Gortys, the excavated Roman city, is further east on this road.

Matala, the old port of Phaestos, has those renowned honeycomb caves in the cliff above its beach which you recognize instantly from calendars or location shots of fashion models.

Chora Sphakion farther west is reached by road from Rethymnon or Chania or by boat from Paleochora. The British, Australian and New Zealand troops who escaped from Crete after the disastrous 1940 battle left from here. Now it is the bus station for those who have made the walk through the gorgeous Samaria Gorge, but that is a lot to do in a day and still catch the last bus. Some have cars waiting, others excursion coaches. Others stay in Chora Sphakion (try Pension Sofia by the supermarket) or in the little village port of Aghios Roumeli which can be reached only on foot, by mule or by ferry. The ferries have 'Greek Island' timetables, very variable. Delightful little Loutro, with rooms and a few tavernas, is particularly dodgy for ferries. You may get stuck for a day or two.

Paleochora, the west terminus of these coastal ferries, and reached by bus from Chania, has much to make it a fine hideaway from crowds – one of the best tree-lined sand beaches on Crete, a fishing fleet, ferry boats to interesting places, pensions and tavernas. But that lovely beach has become a pad for drop-outs as well as the pleasant adventurous back-packers and most fishermen seem to have found it easier and more lucrative to provide food, drink and rooms for tired Samaria Gorge walkers in summer. The weaving road to the north passes along hills and valleys past Kandonos, rebuilt after the Nazis

destroyed it as an 'example'. It has a large winery. Then the road winds through groves of olives, oranges, lemons and vines to join the north coast road to Chania at Tavronitis. Nearby is Maleme, another winery, with the little military airfield which was the scene of the fiercest fighting against Nazi paratroops in 1940. The New Zealanders, short of ammunition, took the airfield twice at bayonet point, only to be forced to retreat as there was no back-up. They did not know that the Command, realizing that they had not the ships or air support to hold the isle, had decided to evacuate.

The Gorge of Samaria is still awesome but no longer frightening as in the days when you could walk for an hour or two between rocky walls without meeting another person. Now at least 1000 people walk through it each day in summer, so you are unlikely to get lost or kidnapped. When Lawrence Durrell wrote of it in his *Greek Islands* he seemed to assume that you would take a pack mule, and spoke of saddle bags being scraped by cliffs only ten feet apart. Until the 1950s it was a notorious haunt of bandits, resistance fighters or any other refugees from persecution by Turks or dictators. It is still a hideout of the kri-kri Cretan wild goat, but I have never met a visitor to Greece who has seen one there.

The górge runs for only eleven miles down to the sea but falls 5500 feet and it twists and weaves and passes between *portes*, doors of narrow rock path, and then opens up to 130 feet wide in places. Much of it follows a dried river bed and the river can overflow in winter and make it very dangerous, so now it is open only 1 April to 31 October. You must walk round and over boulders and the walk takes a good six hours. Allow seven. To reach it you take the Omalos road south-west from Chania through Fournes, rich in orange groves, and Lakki until you reach a car park and the Xenia Pavilion, with just seven beds in three rooms.

The gorge side is sheer and fenced, but you go down wooden steps (*xyloskalo*) now for almost a mile. You must wear real shoes, not sandals, and it is wise to take food and a drink. Halfway along is the deserted village of Samaria with a church of 1397. After another church is the narrowest part, called *sideroportes* (iron gates). At the old village of Aghio Roumeli, deserted until recently, are a café and some restored old houses, and you can hire a mule to take you to the port of Aghio Roumeli for a ferry to Chora Sphakion and a bus. To walk back along the gorge would take about 10 hours of hard uphill work.

It is fairly easy these days to explore the west end of Crete, once very difficult. The main road west from Chania along the coast passes Kisamos (Kastelli) and turns left to Platanos. The old rough road to Sfinari now has a better surface. The first motor car did not come to this fishing village until the mid-sixties – after I first went there! It has rooms, tavernas, fishing boats and if you can pretend rocks are a beach it is a super little place to sit around a while. A mile out of the village the road becomes a track and you are climbing through zig-zag bends on a rough surface with superb views, so let someone else drive! You can hit the coast again at the nunnery of Chrysoskalitissa (Our Lady of the Golden Stair). They say that one of the 100 steps has a golden tread which can be seen only by those who have never committed a sin, but it is no good asking me which. There are beach bars nearby. I have never gone as far as Elafonisi but it

seems that from the beach you can wade across to the island where there are several beaches. Please don't blame me if you suddenly find yourself swimming.

Kisamos (Kastelli) in the north is growing each year. It is still a pleasant agricultural and fishing town, but now with tourist tavernas, restaurants, hotels and some souvenir shops. There are nice beaches nearby.

Chania, an old capital, is still charming to me, though often uncomfortably overcrowded and noisy in summer. The old Venetian harbour surrounded by tavernas and the narrow streets of the old city, which was built by the Venetians and taken over by the Turks, lure me – and, alas, most other visitors. It is rich in fine old houses within the city walls and quaint workshops and shops just outside, and around the public gardens and zoo are elegant nineteenth-century houses. The superb market nearby is in the shape of a cross, as in Marseilles. But the centre for visitors and locals in the evening is Plateia Syntravani, the square leading to the outer harbour, where the world seems to wander past or sit in the pavement bars, cafés and tavernas. Next to the tourist

office, which is in a lovely domed Turkish mosque, is the lively Plaza Hotel on the harbourside. The rooms are basically simple but you don't go to bed early. You sit in the lively restaurant downstairs, eating, drinking, enjoying the lights round the harbour, the people, the whole lively scene. You could not sleep up there, anyway, until the early hours. There are bars round the back thumping out music. But it's stimulating.

The ferries from Heraklion land in Souda Bay, three miles east, where the British and Commonwealth troops came in 1940. It is now a naval base and not very pretty! An airfield at Sternia eight miles east has planes to Athens.

To Rethymnon from Chania it is worth taking the old road through Armeni, Neo Chorio, and Vrises, through charming villages, a valley of olives, vineyards, and sheep farms. Once it was an overcrowded road with village life threatened by traffic. Now it is a quiet route avoiding the rushing traffic of the good new road on the coast. But you will meet laden donkeys. Georgioupoli used to be one of those Greek seaside villages where everyone sits around the square doing nothing. Now a British package tour company has found it. So many more people sit around or lie on the beach doing nothing. From here the route goes well inland and zig-zags through the hills around the little industrial town of Episkopi then sweeps back to the coast just before Rethymnon.

I love Rethymnon. It seems content to live in another age and let the modern world go by. Not that it is sleepy. It has plenty of visitors and the old-style harbourside tavernas are packed and lively in summer. But it has been left behind simply because the harbour which the Venetians built keeps silting up and there

are no ferries, cruise ships or other interruptions, despite a long 'new' harbour wall. The small and very attractive Venetian harbour is full of caiques and they bring in splendid fish for those tavernas where I can sit for hours in the evening. Cheaper tavernas surround Arimondi Fountain.

The walls of the Venetian fort are very well restored but there is little behind them. The domed mosque is best preserved. Local people traditionally hate the fortress. The Venetians built it with Cretan forced labour then handed it intact to the Turks.

Two minarets add a Turkish touch to the skyline and from the top of the minaret of Nerandzes mosque you have a fine view over town and harbour. The mosque is used for music recitals. The old quarter of the town is a delight. Though you see some stone Venetian houses, most are Turkish with overhanging wooden top storeys with laced wooden balconies which almost meet across the lanes.

A huge sand beach with plenty of restaurants stretches from the Venetian harbour for more than a mile, with palm trees on the esplanade. There are some big hotels on the road to Heraklion, including Rethymnon Beach, popular with Americans. The new road is more scenic if not more interesting than the old, because it follows the sea side of the mountains. If possible, make a diversion inland through Adele, Pigi and Loutra villages climbing hills to the monastery of Arkadhi, a fine old building still housing monks, who make and sell a potent raki. Entrance is free and to Cretans a visit is a pilgrimage, for the monastery symbolizes Cretan resistance to the Turks. In 1866, 943 Resistance fighters and local people were besieged there by a big Turkish force, and

rather than surrender alive to the notorious savagery of the Turks blew themselves up, taking about 2000 Turks with them. This caused a wave of pro-Cretan feeling throughout Europe and Victor Hugo and Swinburne were among writers who took up the cause of Cretan freedom.

The road to Heraklion just by-passes villages. One worth a diversion is Panormos, where they still make caiques. Fodele, just inland near Heraklion, was the birthplace of El Greco.

The one place which very few visitors to Crete would miss is Knossos, the ancient Minoan city two miles from Heraklion. As well as its historic importance and its magnificence, it is the one ancient site which gives the ordinary visitor the truest picture of the life and architecture of the ancients. An Englishman, Sir Arthur Evans, started to excavate it in 1899 and he expected to find some remains of a Mycenaean city. Instead he found a whole far-older civilization – a Minoan city of around 2000 BC which was almost certainly the capital of Minoan civilization and the meeting place of the Greek myths and human life. With the German, Schliemann's discoveries of Troy and Mycenae, it made people realize that Homer was not writing mere mythology but travel and history.

Evans's reconstruction of parts of the palaces, based on the frescoes found on the site, has upset purists among archaeologists ever since, but to ordinary mortals Knossos comes to life like few other sites in the world.

I am not qualified to describe it all to you nor would I have the space. You need a guide book, which you can buy on the spot. A good one, by an archaeologist Anna Michailidou, has been translated into English (*Knossos – A Complete Guide to the Palace of Minos* published by Prentice-Hall). Another excellent guide you can find on the spot is *The Archaeology of Crete* by John Pendlebury, a British archaeologist who used to live alongside the site in Evans's old home, Villa Ariadne. During the German occupation of Crete, Pendlebury fought with the Resistance.

Most visitors to Knossos are interested especially in the labyrinth where they kept the half-man, half-bull Minotaur, born to the wife of King Minos. And in all the stories attached to this sorry tale of lust and passion.

Minos and his wife Pasiphae lived in Knossos palace, and she had already borne him four sons and four daughters when the god Poseidon made her fall for a white bull. The queen's passion for the bull was so great that the engineer Daedalus fashioned a model of a cow in which he concealed her so that she could enjoy her fancy. When the Minotaur was born, Daedalus built the maze to keep it out of sight.

Minos made Athens send seven boys and seven girls each year to satisfy the Minotaur's appetite for humans. Theseus, son of the King of Athens,

volunteered to join the third death squad. Minos's daughter Ariadne fell for Theseus, persuaded Daedalus to make an unbreakable thread which was tied to the entrance to the labyrinth so that Theseus, after killing the Minotaur, found his way out.

Minos was very angry. Daedalus made wings so that he and his son Icarus could flee but Icarus flew too high and the sun melted the wax so that he fell into the sea, which was named after him.

Theseus fled with Ariadne but abandoned her asleep on the beach in Naxos. But the god of wine, Dionysus, turned up and seduced her and she soon forgot her hero.

The first Minoan palace built around 2000 BC was destroyed by the great earthquake around 1700 BC, the reconstructed palace by an earthquake around 1600 BC and the rebuilt palace by the great earthquake in Santorini in 1400 BC which also sent tidal waves which destroyed most of Crete's coastline buildings.

Discoveries are still being made. The Royal Road to a minor palace is particularly interesting.

I have been to Knossos several times and still find it very fascinating indeed. Don't miss it, even if you don't think much of old stones.

There are two wonderful things about Crete – its variety, so that no one could really be bored, and the Cretans themselves, with their carefree courage, dignity and genuine hospitality to people of goodwill.

CRETE (KRITA)

The most individualistic of Greek islands, most varied in interest and perhaps the most rewarding. Don't risk a scooter except on paved roads, and then not in the mountains.

Air ...... Charter flights from many European countries. Athens: Heraklion six or seven flights daily (45 mins); Chania four to five daily (45 mins). Also: Heraklion to Mykonos daily (1 hr 10 mins); Heraklion–Santorini four times weekly (40 mins); Heraklion–Paros thrice weekly (45 mins); Heraklion–Rhodes daily (40 mins). Sitia to Rhodes thrice weekly, Karpathos twice weekly, Kasos weekly.

Ferries ...... Heraklion: Piraeus twice daily, overnight (9 hrs); to Santorini six weekly; Ios, Paros, Mykonos all twice weekly. Chania: Piraeus daily (9 hrs). Aghios Nikolaos: very useful connections at various times of the week with Rhodes, Kasos, Karpathos, Chalki, Symi, Chios, Lesbos, Limnos; also mainland at Piraeus and Kavala by circuitous island route.

Kythera, Elafonissos and Antikythera

Kythera (Kithira) and Antikythera (Andikithira) are on the ferry route from the south Peloponnese and to Crete, although they are classed as Ionian isles. So many of the people emigrated to Australia that the population has been halved, there are 100 000 Aussies of Kytheran origin, and other Greeks call it Kangaroo Island. Here is a place to get away from your fellow tourists, apart from a few rich visiting Greeks with summer villas. But you will meet Aussies 'coming home'. And some return here on retirement, so a form of English is spoken.

The Chora is an attractive white town with a tall Venetian castle and delightful views of two bays and the port. The island's one hotel is here.

Its port Kapsali – a village in a horseshoe bay – is the nearest thing to a 'resort'. There are four tavernas on the waterfront and some attractive white villas above the sandy beach, backed by green pines and silvery olives. You can book the villas through a small British company.

The splendid caves of Milopotamos contain some of the most awesome stalagmites and stalactites in Greece. But you must now ask the police to have them opened for you. Vandals have been at them.

Kythera is still very Greek, though more Peloponnese than island, but its bus service is very 'Greek Island' and infrequent, and roads are rough.

It is only twelve miles by eight miles, though hills abound. But it has a certain beauty. After all, it was good enough for Helen of Troy's honeymoon. And despite what Cypriots say, the Greeks believe that Aphrodite, goddess of love, rose from the sea here in rather nasty circumstances. To gain control of the world from his father Cronus, that nice god Zeus castrated him and threw his bloody members into the sea, which gave birth to Aphrodite. Kytherans say that she only went to Cyprus later.

History, ghost stories and legends of the island centre on the ruins of Palio Chora, a Byzantine fortified town high on rocks and hidden from the sea.

Elafonissos is a little isle north of Kythera and very close to the mainland near Neapolis. It has two beaches and a port with tavernas.

Antikythera, between Kythera and Crete, is a rocky islet with 150 people, many more goats, few trees and two small villages. A *real* Greek island hideout for solitude and tranquillity.

KYTHERA
Air ...... Athens twice daily (1 hr 5 mins).

Ferries ...... Piraeus twice weekly; Crete one or two weekly; Monemvassia and Neapolis on mainland (frequency varies seasonally); hydrofoils in summer weekly Piraeus, Nauplion. Antikythera weekly.

ANTIKYTHERA
Ferries ...... Kythera, Crete one or two weekly.

DODECANESE 1

Rhodes (Rodos) and Chalki

Rhodes is a singular island, so set apart from other Greek isles that to some of my Greek friends it is 'foreign'. It was not freed from the Turks until 1912, and then the Italians took over until 1943, the Germans until 1945. It has had little time to regain its true Greek character.

Previously, from 1303 until 1522, it was held by the Knights of St John of Jerusalem, that exclusive order to which only younger sons of the flower of Europe's aristocracy could belong, and although the Order was international the majority were French and Spanish. Theirs was really a foreign occupation. And even in ancient times Rhodes was so powerful and independent that it was at war with Athens and much of Greece.

The Italians gave Rhodes material prosperity with tyrannical rule. Mussolini treated the whole Dodecanese as an Italian colony, with all hints of freedom ruthlessly put down. Rhodes was a holiday resort for the upper crust of the Fascist party and Roman society. They turned the Palace of the Grand Masters of the Order of St John into a holiday home for Mussolini and King Victor-Emmanuel,

bringing in lovely mosaics and Hellenistic sculptures from Kos, a lift, central heating and modern plumbing. They also built 'Mussolini Gothic' heavy public buildings, aptly described as 'ungainly piles', though the Italianate Evangelismos church is beautiful – modelled on the Knights' Church of St John destroyed by an earthquake.

In 1937 it was forbidden to speak any language but Italian in public places. But at least cooking on Rhodes is good because the Italians superimposed their high standards on what the Turks left.

Because of all this, tourism came late to Rhodes, but when it joined Greece in 1947 it caught up really fast. Some villages of the interior became almost deserted as the men moved into Rhodes city to build hotels, restaurants and bars, and old Rhodes was soon surrounded by high-rise hotels which stretch for a mile or two along each side of the city promontory. British and German package-tourists abound, but I think they are outnumbered by Scandinavians, especially in winter. You will find smorgasbord in restaurants and a separate post-box for

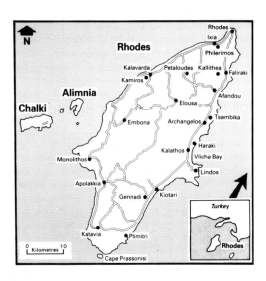

Swedish mail in the post office. There is little respite in winter, for Rhodes is warm enough.

It was all inevitable, for Rhodes has the climate, the superb beaches, wonderful old sites to see, fine harbours for cargo and cruise ships, ferries and yachts, a good international airfield, above average Greek cooking, and Rhodes town is a free port. But, if the building has been over-done a little upwards and sideways, it is fairly elegant and the old areas of the city, so well preserved, give it great charm, especially for eating and drinking at night. There are hundreds of bars and discos, of course, and a casino, and there is even a touch of a modern Cannes about the town, with people tending to dress up a bit for dinner.

The old city walls are two and a half miles long and well preserved. Built by the Knights of St John on Byzantine foundations, they average forty feet thick, are curved to deflect missiles and used to have a large moat on the landward side. The knights were divided into 'inns' for each 'tongue' or nationality, and each was given part of the wall to defend. By raiding shipping, the Knights made a thorough nuisance of themselves to the Ottoman Empire, which regarded them as pirates just as they regarded the Turks. The great Sultan Suleiman the Magnificent, who so nearly swept through Europe, attacked them in 1522 and finally forced them to surrender after a six month siege.

For their valour, he allowed them to leave unharmed. He probably regretted this chivalry later. From Malta, they played havoc with his shipping and his long siege was a costly failure.

The old town is divided between the Castle of the Knights and the alleyways and arches of the old Turkish quarter by the main street Socratous. Though many of the streets on the 'Knights' side' are lined with tourist shops selling brass and fur coats (not much use on Rhodes but invaluable no doubt in Finland, Sweden and Norway), Ippoton Street, known as the Street of the Knights, is free of souvenir shops. Here or in alleys nearby are many of the inns where the Knights lived, including the inns of France, Italy, Provence and Spain. At the end is the Palace of the Grand Masters and there are more inns at the other end in Argyrokas-tro square, with the English inn nearby. Built in 1483, it has been rebuilt twice by the English after earthquakes and bomb-ings and despite the English being thrown out of the Order after the Pope excom-municated Henry VIII.

The hospital of the Knights, rebuilt by the Italians, houses the Archaeological Museum which among many treasures includes the lovely Aphrodite of Rhodes.

Even in recent times, the Greeks re-garded the Turkish streets as something of a 'no-go' area, especially during the troubles in Cyprus. Barbara and I were warned one night not to risk going there or we might get our throats slit. That to Barbara was a direct challenge. The Turks were so pleased that visitors had come that they plied us with wine and food all the evening, and Barbara finished up dancing with the men in turn on the large open-air table of a taverna. We went away laden with bottles of wine.

The slender minaret of the lovely Mosque of Suleiman built in 1523 is the landmark of Socratous Street, which is so full of tourist shops it is almost an Eastern bazaar.

Throughout July and August buses pick up revellers to attend a wine festival, where for a few drachmas you can drink all the Rhodian wine you can lap up, and Rhodes has a fair variety of wines, from retsina to the red Chevalier de Rhodes, the good dry whites of Embona in the north and Lindos and very good sweet Muscats akin to Samos. The wine bibbing takes place in Rodini Park where peacocks strut. Here in 303 BC was built the School of Rhetoric attended later by Cicero, Julius Caesar, Mark Antony and Cassius, who repaid Rhodians by sacking the island. The rhetoric at the wine festival can be interesting, too.

The ancient Colossus of Rhodes stood astride the entrance to Mandraki harbour. It was a statue of the sun god Helios, in bronze, took the Lindos sculptor twelve years to complete and was somewhere between 90 and 120 feet tall. It was one of the Seven Wonders of the World, it cost 20 000 pounds of silver and was not worth it, for it crashed to the ground in an earthquake only sixty-five years later. According to local history, it lay on the ground for nearly 900 years, then in 653 AD the Saracens, who had captured

Rhodes, sold it as scrap metal. It took 900 camels to transport it to the ship. Now on the stone pillars on which it was said to have stood there are two impressive bronze deer.

The Colossus was made either by melting down or selling a huge siege engine left behind by the great general Dimitrios, who had besieged Rhodes with a Syrian army and the Phoenician fleet. After the death of Alexander the Great, Rhodes refused to fight with Dimitrios's father, Antigonas, against Ptolemy of Egypt because the Rhodians had lucrative trade with Egypt. So Dimitrios besieged them with various ingenious machines including the nine storey Heliopolis siege tower which carried catapults, grappling irons and a drawbridge to release troops over a wall. The Rhodians dug a ditch in its path and it fell over. After a year, the two sides made a deal.

Though there are tourist excursions to the major sights of Rhodes, you need a car to explore the interior, which is a world apart from the tourist areas. Here people go about their business of farming as if the hotels of Rhodes town are on another planet. Most of it is mountainous and

wooded, and it is good country for really hardy walkers. In the south roads are often mere tracks and you can drive for two hours or more and see nothing but a couple of goats, so take some food just in case you have a breakdown, and, in the mountains, take something warm for the night. Most of these mountain roads are dangerous for scooters, even if you do see some intrepid scooterists pop-popping along them. And the mountains are far too rugged for them. The coast roads are fairly good except in the south-west, but the traffic can be formidable.

The east coast is the best for beach loungers because the west is windy. There are superb often-deserted beaches south of Lindos. They are sometimes windy but most have dunes for cover and a few have tavernas open from spring to autumn, and noted for seafood. Those at Kiotari, a fishing and holiday village, are famous for fish. There are rooms at Gennadi and Plimiri, which has a sand beach and a restaurant. By walking for a while, it is still possible to have at least a half mile of beach to yourself, even in summer. The road swings inland at Plimiri to Katavia, nearer the west coast. Just before, a track, marked as a road on most maps, and driveable with care, leads to Prassonisi cape, the island's southern tip – a desolate spot. It is really an island connected to Rhodes by a sandbank about 1000 yards long. According to the way the wind blows, the sea can be really rough on one side, calm on the other.

I have never met anyone who has spent a week or more in Rhodes who has not been to Lindos. If you can stay overnight, it looks superb in the evening light, and even better from the sea with the sun behind it. You see the formidable walls of the Knights' castle looming menacingly over the little white town of flat-roofed houses, built halfway up the 400-foot hill which ends in a sand beach and the harbour where fishing caiques and yachts anchor. The Acropolis, dedicated to Athena, stands on the highest point of the rocky hill, surrounded by the walls of the Knights' fortress. There is enough left of it to see its form. The original temple was probably built around the ninth century BC by the warlike Dorians, but was destroyed by fire and this one dates from the fourth century BC. The original statue of the goddess was famed throughout the world but looted by a Byzantine Emperor Theodosios II, who took it to Constantinople. Many of the other statues were stolen by Cassius, one of the murderers of Julius Caesar, when he attacked Rhodes for siding with Mark Antony. The view from here over the village to the sea is beautiful. To the south is a charming second harbour almost enclosed by rocks, with a small sand beach. Here it is said St Paul landed to convert the people.

Lindos is still a magic place although its beauty and its beach have made it a resort offered by package tour companies, and the forest fires of 1987 have harmed its setting. Its houses have been restored instead of new ones being built and no one may build an hotel there. But there are 2000 beds let to visitors in houses. The 'Houses of the Captains', from the sixteenth to eighteenth centuries, were deserted when I first saw them, but have been beautifully restored with the help of the Archaeological Service. They are charming. Steps lead often to balconies with rooms resting on pillars, a wonderful place to eat or rest on a hot day.

It is a long, steep climb from the village to the fortress, and most people go by donkey. But not me. I was once told: 'We have not a beast big enough to take a man of your strength. Yul Brynner could have carried you but he is having his dinner.' Donkeys are so much part of the family that they are named after family members, friends, mothers-in-law, favourite film stars or footballers. Onc in those days was called after footballer Bobbie Charlton. I should not have liked to be kicked by him.

There are long beaches just up the coast at Vlicha and Kalathos, and at Haraki is a good view of Lindos and good fish tavernas. Just north of it a track leads to a lovely little sandy cove, often nearly empty. On a cliff above is Faraclos Castle, the last stronghold to fall to the Turks. The Knights took it from pirates who had built it and used it as a sort of Colditz for prisoners of war and Knights who had broken the rules of the Order.

You can reach Archangelos by a surfaced inland road through Malona and Massari in the fertile Naithon valley, rich in orange and mandarin trees, grapes, walnuts and olives. For many hundreds of years Archangelos has been known for carpet weaving, pottery (some lovely traditional plates made here since Byzantine days) and goat-skin boots, which the cobbler will make to order if you are around for a few days. Many local women wear the traditional local costume. There are 4000 people and 2000 donkeys, and between them they produce 800 000 oranges a year.

There is another superb sand beach at Tsambika and views over several beaches from the rocky steep hill on which the monastery stands. When the monks were there, women would walk uphill barefooted and pray in the church for a baby. Since the monks left, there are far fewer children called Tsambika or Tsambiko.

Much of the film *The Guns of Navarone* was filmed on the Tsambika promontory.

Afandou is so hidden among hills that it is called the Invisible Village. This is the heart of fruit country, producing apricots, oranges, lemons, pomegranates which ripen in October, mulberries and olive oil. They get a kilo of oil from five kilos of olives. Afandou has a golf course, but our memory is of the smell of baking bread from the outside ovens which many women still use and the lovely smell of fish cooking in the beachside tavernas.

There are two miles of golden beach at Faliraki and plenty of package tour hotels, only seven miles from Rhodes town, but it is not crowded by many standards. The fading Italian spa of Kallithea no longer offers drinks of curative water or baths in its odd Italian-Moorish building. Perhaps the wine festival has taken over the recuperative business.

The *meltemi* north-west wind which blows in late summer can whip up the winds on the west coast, but it is not quite so hot as the east in July and August, which is a relief. Ixia has some good package-tour hotels and all that goes with them, but is plentifully endowed with trees, even on the beach. Shortly after, a road leads to Mount Philerimos and the remains of the ancient city of Ialysos, renowned in the ancient world for the prowess of its sportsmen, including a boxer Diagoros who won the Olympic boxing event three times. Two amateur archaeologists, Biliotti and Salzmann, found the site in 1876 but many of its treasures are now in the British Museum and the Louvre. The acropolis is most interesting.

From Soroni a paved road leads to Petaloudes, the Valley of the Butterflies, where in June, July and early August you only have to clap your hands and millions of butterflies will take off. Some are a gorgeous red colour. For the technically minded they belong to the species *Callimorpha Quadripuntaria* and are attracted by resin in the storax trees. Retsina addicts! Alas, excursion coaches bring so many people that the clapping could easily break into a round of applause. The valley is very beautiful, with rustic bridges crossing the little river and ravines. I have enjoyed it most in May before the crowds arrive.

Ancient Kamiros was one of the most unusual finds of ancient Greece. It is also one of the most beautiful. Stand above it looking over the ruins of the old walls and pillars towards the sea with the waters of the bay changing from shallow blue to deep blue and aquamarine and the mountains of Asia Minor beyond, mauve against a bright blue sky, and you wonder why anyone left this lovely place.

And that is what they did – just *leave* it. Nobody knows exactly why. Kamiros was

a farming community, producing figs, oil and wine which were exported, so pottery was an industry, too. It reached its zenith in the sixth century BC, but after Rhodes city was founded in 408 BC the people drifted away. A small town remained until the fourth century AD, when it was deserted. Pirate raids may have driven out the people, or pirates preying on their ships, making exports impossible. Earth, sand, then woods and fields covered the site. Not until 1859 did some farmers turn over graves by chance and the archaeologists, Biliotti and Salzmann, dug up the necropolis with rich finds of pottery. Most of these treasures too went to the British Museum and Paris Louvre. Stones and layout give you a superb idea of a city of those days. You can even walk the streets. There are remains of the temple of Athena dating from the sixth century BC, a market place, other temples, a row of houses, shops and public baths, in the Roman style, with water from a cistern, and a water tank and plumbing to supply at least 400 people. It seems that the houses had no windows onto the street – only to the rear. Alas, many of the treasures of Kamiros are in London, Paris and the US, though some are in Rhodes museum.

From Kalavarda, north east of Ancient Kamiros, a paved road runs south along the lower slopes of Mount Profitis Ilias through beautifully green country. Later a right fork leads to Embona, which produces some of the best wine on Rhodes. Tourists have found it, and Barbara, who adores Greek honey mixed with yoghourt, tried in 1987 to buy the famous local honey but other tourists had cleaned it out. Blessedly they had not drunk all the wine. It is a delightful village and a delightful route to it. Take the left fork earlier to Apollona and you can sit outside one of the three mountain-top hotels drinking Embona wine and admiring a magnificent view, including a charming Byzantine chapel.

The road continues across the island to join the east coast at Kolympia, near Tsambika. It is not a paved road, but is quite a highway compared with interior roads on many islands. Past the hotels at Fountoukli is the delicious little Byzantine church of St Nicholas, with interesting wall paintings. It is among trees with a spring from which you can drink, and on a hot day you will be tempted to lie in the shade and snooze. Beyond lies Elousa, an attractive village built round a square with the impressive Italian Governor's summer residence.

Back on the west coast, you reach modern Kamiros Skala, a fishing village from which a caique once took me to the isle of Chalki (Halki). Now there is a daily launch service. The tavernas still serve good fish. You can also get a boat to the offshore island of Alimnia, where there is a ruined Byzantine castle.

Monolithos, further down the coast, is built on terraces with more superb views. A narrow difficult path leads down to remains of a castle built by the Knights atop a cliff. Inside the walls is a fifteenth-century chapel, well renovated, and with frescoes. The view is beautiful but truly awesome.

Apolakkia is a delightful village and produces delicious water melons. You wonder at first why there are no tourist hotels down here. The trouble is the wind, persistent even by the standards of this windy west coast. Low sand dunes give you protection but the sea gets too rough for bathing.

The southernmost village Kattavia is known for fish good even by Rhodian standards. If you cannot find rooms here, take the track from half way to Apolakkia to Skiadi monastery which has sea views and a hostel sleeping thirty. The caretaker divides you up for sleeping – men in one room, women in another. You get coffee in the morning and no bill, but you are expected to contribute towards the monastery's upkeep.

The coastal road round Rhodes is about 200 miles but it would be both hard work and quite ridiculous to drive it in a day. There is so much to see, so many views to admire and taverna dishes to taste. Bus routes are good, but miss whole areas of the interior and south. The east coast temperature hits eighty-five to ninety-five degrees Fahrenheit in mid-summer, and the west coast, though cooler, is windy. It is an all-year island for visiting and you can bathe in November, but the nicest times for me are spring, when the island is green and ablaze with wild flowers, and late September to October when it is pleasantly hot, not crowded and the winds have usually dropped.

There are many guides to old Rhodes city, Lindos, Kamiros and other ancient sites, but the one I like for interested but inexpert people like me is the English version of the Ekdotike Athenon book *Rhodes* by an archaeologist A. B. Tataki, which you can certainly buy there and possibly in Britain and America.

'Nothing happens on *Chalki*,' I was told before I went there. 'Good,' I said. But, of course, they were wrong. The men of Chalki were busy fishing, the tavernas cooking the fish and serving it much cheaper than on Rhodes. True, many fine old Venetian houses were sightless, empty and decaying and the one road built in the rich days of sponge diving to the almost

abandoned Chora was breaking up. The population was down to 400 people because more than half had emigrated to Australia, America or Athens. Nearly all of them lived in the port, Emborio (or Skala), but even there the once-elegant neo-classical mansions were derelict. Rabbits ran around town.

This may all sound depressing. It wasn't. Chalki (sometimes written Halki) was extremely peaceful, with no cars, Greek music rather than international pop in the tavernas, empty beaches, sand and shingle, to which you had to walk or persuade a fisherman to take you, and the inevitable Dodecanesian ruined castle of the Knights of St John. It had the magical air of a sleeping island awaiting its awakener.

The daily caique from Kamiros Skala on Rhodes brought everyone to the quayside and I sat up with the rest of the males, drinking in a taverna until after midnight, to await the big moment of the week – the hooting into harbour of the ferry on its round trip from Piraeus and on to Kassos and Karpathos. It was far easier to arrive from Piraeus than to get back there. The best way to return was to cross to Rhodes.

The highlight of my trip was going fishing and being left for half a day by the fisherman to explore the uninhabited isle of Alimnia, with a ruined Byzantine castle and a good beach.

Some of the glorious old houses on Chalki have been renovated. A number have become pensions or houses with rooms to let, so it is easier to stay. Fish is still cheaper than on Rhodes. And you can still find peace when you want it.

Chalki will never be 'spoiled'. It has not enough water and it is not beautiful enough. But it is a very pleasant place to idle away a few days. When the winds blow, boats are sometimes cancelled, so don't risk it if time presses hard.

The Greek government has come to the rescue of the little isle of *Megisti*, known more often as *Kastellorizo*, which was becoming almost abandoned. I am sure that they would not have liked that to happen for, although it is reached from Rhodes by boat once or twice a week, that is seventy-two miles away and the Turkish town of Kas is only half a mile. Turkey owned it as recently as 1913. Its population dropped to 200, but the Greek Tourist Board has set about putting that right with a real will. When Barbara was last on Rhodes in 1987, they were tempting visitors to Megisti with free boat tickets.

In the nineteenth century, during its heyday as a seafaring isle, Megisti had 15 000 people, and many owned land over in Turkey. Under the Italians it remained important right up to the Second World War, finally as a base for refuelling and victualling seaplanes. Like Symi it was rich. When Italy joined Hitler in the Second World War, the people were taken to the Middle East, and had to leave their possessions behind. The occupying troops looted their houses and burnt a lot down to cover their crime. Then the ship carrying the people back at the end of the war sank and many were drowned. Those that returned found that they had lost almost everything. No wonder so many emigrated.

Now there are more immigrants from the island in both Australia and America than on the island. But many come home for holiday visits and now that it is possible for Greeks to get help with renovating the old mansions, some are returning to retire. There is a hotel-pension and simple tavernas. But you are still likely to see houses inhabited by chickens and cats, and turkeys strutting the streets.

Strangest of all, islanders go shopping in Turkey.

Megisti, the official name, means major or biggest, which may sound strange for an isle only four miles by two miles, but it is the biggest of its group of twelve. Only two of these are inhabited – by lighthouse keepers! You can swim to some of these islets, get boats to others, including a good swimming beach on Aghios Georgios. Megisti has no beaches but you can swim from rocks in gloriously clear and clean water.

The Blue Grotto is Megisti's pride. It is as big as the Blue Grotto of Capri and even higher – sixty-five to eighty feet. It is a three hour round trip by boat and the afternoon is the best time to see the light reflected off the water onto the stalactites. You might even see a seal – but not a blue one.

RHODES

With Crete, Rhodes has the best national and international communications of any Greek isle. An all-year holiday island.

Air ...... Many international charter flights from Western Europe, all the year, New York and the Middle East. Athens (55 mins) three to five daily; Karpathos, Kos and Crete (Sitia) one or two daily; Santorini, Kassos, Mykonos two or three weekly.

Hydrofoils ...... Daily to Patmos, Samos, Kos; twice weekly to Tinos.

Ferries ...... Almost daily to Piraeus (16–24 hrs according to boat and routes); also to Kos, Patmos, Leros, Symi (many excursions to Kos and Symi, too). Twice weekly to Kassos, Karpathos, Crete (Sitia, Aghios Nikolaos), Tilos, Nissiros; weekly to Lipsi, Kastellorizo, Astepalea, Samos, Chios, Limnos, Ikaria, Amorgos, Paros. Several boats weekly from Kamiros Skala to Halki.

Weekly boats to Cyprus and Israel.

Karpathos

Karpathos was until very recently the forgotten island of the Dodecanese. Writers and travellers hardly bothered to mention it, few outsiders visited it except emigrants on nostalgic voyages of return from the US. It is a long island and the fertile south and the mountainous, poorer north were in two separate worlds, connected only by boat or mule. Not until 1979 was a road built between them. And when Barbara was there in 1987 unheard-of winter snow had washed a lot of the road away, so that the local taxi driver took three hours to drive from the port of Pigadia to the glorious mountain village of Olympos in the north. Previously he had done it in two and a quarter hours. There is still no bus on that unpaved road. There is a minibus occasionally from the northern port of Diafani – but not many rooms in Diafani for visitors.

It was Easter and Barbara was very glad she went. Like many places once nearly isolated, Olympos has many festivals and celebrations, but none quite so important as Easter. Everyone, from the tiny children to the oldest folk, was in colourful traditional dress – not for the cameras of tourists or for self-conscious local colour but because it would be quite wrong to wear anything else. Older women wear the costume every day.

Many of the younger women wore strings of gold coins round their necks. These had been brought back from abroad, anywhere from Egypt to the United States, by their grandfathers or great-grandfathers who had worked abroad until they could make enough money to return and marry a local girl.

When a girl marries she puts away her gold necklace to keep for her eldest daughter. Basically, family inheritance goes to the eldest daughter, not the eldest son, which is why so many men emigrate to make their fortunes, even if they return later.

Olympos is clamped to a stark moun-

tain ridge, its white, blue, and beige houses terraced upwards, joined by steep alleys and donkey steps, and no car can get past the first taverna. Down the edge runs a line of windmills, one still used for grinding corn, and the houses seem to be stacked on each other. Some still have decorative painted balconies, even with the Byzantine eagle on them. From the village, the mountain descends to the sea on one side, and on cultivated terraces to a fertile valley on the other. Despite bare rocks of the mountains around, the scene is beautiful, dramatic and exciting. That is true of the island – dramatic and exciting, yet restful and tranquil.

By mid-morning that Easter Sunday, there was not yet a woman in sight. They were at home preparing vegetables, roasting the traditional Easter lamb. The Easter procession had been at midnight before. The tavernas were full of men. Barbara did the rounds. There was a delicious smell of cooking from all of them, Greek music, noisy conversation and a

festive air. The Easter Sunday lamb lunch is a traditional family affair all over Greece. The men drifted off noisily before one o'clock, and Barbara joined the taxi driver in his favourite taverna and they ate with the family. Then the whole village went to church. Barbara stood at the church door because, after kissing an icon, the women were banished to a balcony. But people wandered about talking to each other during the service and others came and went.

Many of the men returned home via the tavernas or returned later in the evening. The one disappointment was that she did not hear the island's traditional music – not the usual slow, dirge-like tunes which seemed to have been left behind by the Turks but fast and furious rhythm played on a three-stringed lyre, guitar and goatskin bagpipe called tsabouna. It seems that the best time to hear that is at a wedding, which may go on for several days.

On Saturdays the women do their weekly bread baking in outside ovens and the smell is delicious. Olympos is the place to buy traditional goatskin sandals and particularly the boots (*tastivania*) which are worn with the costume and which are sent by the two cobblers here who make them to Karpathians all over the world. The boots will cost about 20 000 drachmas, but last a lifetime. They are in light or dark brown goat leather with red, blue or black embroidered toes and heels.

Some believe that the people of Olympos are descended from Dorian Greeks of 3000 years ago. They speak a very old dialect.

A taxi day trip from Pigadia port to Olympos cost 7000 drachmas in 1987, so try to find others to share with you. In summer, boats run from Pigadia to the port of Diafani, where you can get a mini-bus or take a much shorter taxi ride to Olympos. But *do* see Olympos.

Karpathos is a fairly rich island. Citrus plantations and vegetable gardens of the fertile south give it money-making exports and it is said to have the highest income of any Greek island from emigrants working abroad. Furthermore many of these make their little pile in America and return home where it buys them a better life than they dreamed of before they went. The island does not really need tourism, but the people are friendly and hospitable to visitors, treating them as guests, and meals are fairly cheap because little needs to be imported.

Incidentally, the emigrants in the US keep up a community relationship and Karpathian culture, publishing their own magazine, and even choosing an annual 'Miss Karpathos'. The men almost all marry Karpathian girls – even if they go home on holiday to find one. They have a Pan Karpathian Society of America. Pres-ident for two years was Telly Savalas.

The port of Pigadia curves round one side of a bay where the mountains meet the sea, with a long curve of sandy beach beyond. It is a busy, thriving little port with quite a lot of small hotels, pensions and rooms to let. Quite a lot of English is spoken. There is a good choice of tavernas, too. The town is expanding, so there should be more rooms soon.

There just are not enough roads or rooms to make this a tourist isle. In 1987 you flew from Rhodes, thirty miles away, or Crete, in a fifteen-seater Skyvan and the landing and ground procedures were rather like a pre-war local airfield. After Barbara landed, she got in a bus to see another plane landing straight at it, so she

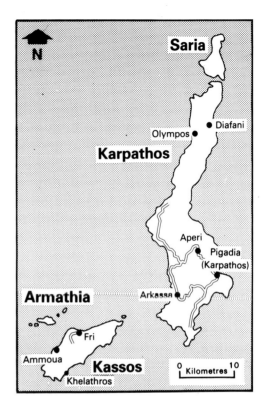

got out fast. The driver rushed over and moved it just in time.

A reasonable road leads to the nearest thing to a beach resort – Ammopi, with a string of small beaches, tavernas and rooms. Another road crosses the island to Finiki, often called Arkassa, a large fishing village with rooms and an out-standing fish taverna. Just south are the relics of ancient Arkassa, which stood on a clifftop. There are good mosaics from some Byzantine churches, but most were taken to Rhodes by the Italians. A beach lies beyond. A rough road leads up this west coast to Lefkos, a lovely spot with a white sand beach, pines for shade, a small hotel, some rooms and tavernas;

nearby are archaeological sites and a small mediaeval fort.

A warning about scooters on Karpathos – not only are most roads dangerously rough but mountains are steep and you cannot get petrol in villages. Many visitors have been stranded.

The road to Olympos is quite good as far as Aperi, overlooking Vrontis Bay. It was once the capital and has a cathedral with an icon of the Virgin credited with several miracles, including saving the life of a boy who fell over the cliff. He became a successful lawyer in the US and paid for most of Aperi's new buildings. Quite a good road crosses the mountain from here to Piles.

The road onward north to Olympos begins to deteriorate but has some splendid sea and mountain views round hairy corners. The scenery around Apella is truly dramatic – rugged rock formations, deep, steep-sided gorges, huge boulders which at some time crashed down from the mountain. Karpathos was the legendary scene of the Titans' battle. Here these wild giants of Greek mythology tore out bits of mountain and hurled them at each other. On the pebble beach below are remains of a Byzantine church with frescoes, but you can reach it only by boat and you may have to swim ashore. A more rewarding place for a caique trip is just north – the attractive fishing village of Aghios Nicholaos, hardly known to any tourists. There are a few rooms here, and one taverna is owned by a fisherman whose wife cooks the catch. A delightful hideout.

All ferries to Karpathos stop at both Pigadia and the tiny northern port of Diafani, built by the people of Olympos in 1897. It is a pleasant little place, with a track road to Olympos, a good sandy beach with a background of pine woods, a few rooms and tavernas. But that is the only road, so it attracts mostly rugged hill walkers. There are boats to and from Pigadia, and on Sundays a boat to the little isle of Saria – once a kingdom with a basilica, now deserted apart from shepherds in summer. A hard walk takes you to Ta Palatia (the Palaces), small stone domed houses on terraces. These formed a genuine pirate base.

To avoid the north wind – the *meltemi* – go in April, May or October. It blows so hard near Olympos that trees are bent over.

Boats go also to the tiny isle of *Kassos* (Cassos), three miles away at the nearest point. Its shores are of volcanic rock and it has a gaunt look. Though it may look uninviting, it is a great place for parties. Anything is an excuse for a party, from a saint's day to someone's birthday. Many are held in the churchyard at Fri, the fishing port, with dancing, ouzo and retsina, and a running supply of those tasty snacks called metzes. An American friend swears that he went to four parties in one week.

The people are certainly some of the friendliest in Greece and seem genuinely pleased that you have chosen to stop off in their island. They have made flourishing sheltered gardens, often with lemon and orange trees, and wild flowers abound, with white crocuses near the shore and anemones in flower in December.

Few tourists visit Kassos and the young leave the island to make a better living, so there are many empty, crumbling houses in the streets of the five villages, and uncultivated terraces going wild. Fri is a charming fishing port, with a mountain overhanging it. It has a handful of tavernas, two little hotels, pensions and rooms. From here boats go fishing, the main occupation of the island. The other small port across the bay, Emborio, has tavernas and cafés. One little road runs inland from Fri to Arvaniohorio, a pleasant hillside village. The island bus runs to it, past another hillside village, Aghia Marina, and also along a rougher road to Poli, an old capital down to 100 inhabitants. There is an airstrip near Fri, with little planes to Rhodes, Karpathos and less frequently to Crete. Beyond it at Ammoua is the nearest thing to a beach and a beautiful cave with stalactites. If you must have a beach, get a Fri fisher-man to drop you on the inhabited isle of Artmathia. There are excursions in summer.

Kassos is truly a walker's isle, with fine coast walks and a silent walk of solitude to the middle of the island and southward past olive groves and fields where the sudden sound of goat bells can startle you. The track descends gradually to the coast at a beautiful cove at Khelathros harbour, with a small sandy beach. You might see someone working in the valley behind, but no one lives here any more. The only sound is of many kinds of seabirds which wheel over the cliffs.

KARPATHOS (CARPATHOS)
Ships call at Pigadia and Diafani. Airport is in south.

Air ...... Twice daily Rhodes (55 mins); Crete (Sitia – several weekly); Kassos (weekends).

Ferries ...... Thrice weekly Piraeus (23 hrs); twice weekly Rhodes, Kassos, Crete, Halki.

KASSOS (CASSOS)
One of the most remote Greek islands. Take good walking shoes.

Air ...... Thrice or more weekly Rhodes; weekends Karpathos, Crete (Sitia).

Ferries ...... Four weekly Piraeus (20 hrs); twice weekly Karpathos, Rhodes; weekly Crete (Sitia).

Weekend caique from Finiki, Karpathos.

DODECANESE 2

Kos (Cos)

If the Knights of St John from Rhodes had lasted as long as the solid mediaeval fort they built to protect Kos harbour, they would surely be staring in disbelief today.

In place of the galleys from which they landed their loot and prisoners following Christian raids on Moslem fleets and territories are yachts from around the world, a never-ending stream of trip boats, noisy but useful hydrofoils, topless girls sunbathing on the beach opposite and, overhead, hang gliders galore suspended aloft as if by magic.

I confess that I did a bit of staring when I returned to Kos after ten years. In a mere decade there had been a revolution, brought about by the arrival of charter jets since the airfield was extended.

Yet Kos is still a farmers' and fishermen's island. Only Kos town and the other old port of Kardamena have changed from pure Greek dancing to disco.

The lazy waterfront, backed by decaying Italian mansions and long overgrown gardens, has become in summer a bustling, crowded place, bristling with clothes, leather and liquor shops, and dozens of travel agents offering excursions to the other eleven major isles of the Dodecanese. The tables outside the tavernas and restaurants are all taken by noon or early evening, while crossing the road is fraught with peril, such is the number of taxis and coaches taking tourists round the island, not to mention the greatest menace of all – cycling tourists, many of whom probably have not ridden for twenty years or more. Round the corner of the harbour towards the long beach are new roads with pleasant little shops, cafés, pensions and tavernas.

Romantics may sigh for the idyllic isles of our youth, but they were never idyllic to the Greeks. Hundreds of thousands emigrated to the US, Canada and from Kos particularly to Australia where they could earn a living wage and live in a house with a real bathroom and flushing toilet. Many are back taking part in tourism.

The modern taverna-hotels may not have the atmosphere of the old ones, with their bare wooden floors and primitive shower room, probably shared with the family. But you get the same friendly welcome and a fairly up-to-date shower and toilet that usually work – unless there is a mid-summer water shortage.

I think it's a mistake to book in to one of the few new 'Costa' hotels with swimming pool and night club and compulsory half-board on Kos. I have returned several times since the charters came and many of the people staying in those hotels are disgruntled. No one wants to be tied to a hotel 'international' meal on a Greek island. Much of the evening fun is to eat and mix in a taverna. You might as well be anywhere in these hotels. They have none of the Greek island atmosphere. And some of them are almost literally 'nowhere'. Not only are there no bars or tavernas nearby but it costs a bomb for a taxi or you must get up very early to catch a coach when you want to explore other isles, for nearly all boats go from Kos town harbour.

And the joy of Kos is that it is such a good centre for island exploration. There are ferries, caiques or hydrofoils to nearly all the other twelve islands of the Dodecanese and excursions in summer to all of them.

That is why we book a cheap Intasun package with a small flat or preferably a small modern bed and breakfast hotel in Kos town within a short walk of the quay. We know a good little hotel called the Bristol for bed and breakfast, and the family also own an excellent restaurant in a flower garden near the Knights' Castle where they give you reduced prices if you stay in the hotel.

Though crowded with visitors in summer, with many ferries, yachts and yacht-flotillas coming and going, and too much traffic, the harbourside has not lost all of its old touches. The fishermen still sell their catch on the harbourside and drink in the café-bars, the chairs and tables of the tavernas spread down to the sidewalk, visiting sailors still tie up their yachts in the evening alongside fishing boats and sit drinking on deck. Palm trees still grow around the Knights' Castle.

The town has been much repaired and tidied up since its decaying days just after the war, with flower gardens around the harbour and beside the beach. The noisy hydrofoils come and go from another quay round the corner, so do not kill all conversation in the harbourside tavernas. The ornate Italian town hall on the waterside near the castle is kept well painted. An earthquake in 1933 knocked down much of architectural interest but one good side effect was that it opened up new archaeological sites which are well displayed. But the Turks must have built well, for mosques and minarets still stand, and the Defterdar mosque, which ironically dominates Freedom (Eleftheria) Square and the important fruit market, is still used by the few Turkish families remaining.

I find Kos much noisier and much happier. There seems to be a party atmosphere all round the town. Perhaps that is because, like the rest of the Dodecanese, it has been granted tax concessions, spirits are cheap and liquor shops abound. It is certainly a good place to eat, with outstanding cooking, probably a legacy from the Italians, but there are also fast-food restaurants with dishes advertised by ghastly coloured pictures. Waterfront restaurants tend to be dearer, but have superb fresh fish. Wines are above Greek average.

Ancient ruins are scattered all round town and there are so many that the local people treat them very casually. The well-restored amphitheatre is sometimes used as an open-air theatre. The museum is unusually interesting, even to a non-classicist.

The Castle of the Knights was begun in the 1390s. It fell to the Turks in 1522 and they ruled until 1912 when the Italians came in as 'liberators', declaring that Kos was Greek and must remain Greek. But when Mussolini gained power the Fascists started to Italianize Kos and all other Dodecanese islands. All children were educated in Italian or not at all and the farms were given to Italian immigrants, turning Greek farmers into farm workers. The Nazis took over in 1943, then the British army came in 1945 and started to rebuild. Kos joined Greece in 1948 and it is amazing how they have kept their Greekness through so many centuries of occupation – since the Romans took over in 197 BC.

The most important site is strictly Greek. Kos was called the Isle of Healing. Hippocrates, 'Father of Modern Medicine', was born here about 460 BC and there is a huge old twisted plane tree by the castle under which he is said to have taught his pupils. Alas, it is only about 600 years old. His methods, involving scientific diagnosis by observation, treatment by baths and special diets upset the priests, who believed in magical cures.

The Asklepeion, two miles south-west of Kos, was discovered by the German Herzog in 1902. It was built in the fourth century BC after Hippocrates died and was one of the most sacred shrines to the healing god Asklepeios, worshipped by a secret sect of priests who, among other beliefs, held that baths in a beautiful setting were good for body and soul. Snakes were their cult symbol, as they were believed to hunt out healing herbs.

This temple became a sort of ancient Lourdes where people went to seek cures from just about every illness and affliction from blindness to baldness. Payment for treatment was a chicken, to be sacrificed. The site is most impressive, set on three terraces of a hill, with wide steps. It was built on the site of a sacred wood of Apollo near springs with iron content, which probably did more good than magic. The Knights stole much of the stone from here to make their castle.

Nowadays there is an international Hippocratical Foundation nearby, to encourage international co-operation in medicine. Dr Christiaan Barnard, the heart surgeon, once presided over it.

Kos has many good roads and it is one island where scooters are fairly safe, in the hands of experienced riders. Bikes are useful for shorter journeys. But do remember that donkeys still have the right of way.

The beach north from the harbour of Kos town is lined at first with open air tavernas but stretches far outside the town to Cape Scadario. We used to walk to Lampi, near the cape, to eat in an isolated primitive taverna (Faros) where you entered through the kitchen and chose your meal from fish and meat raw on the slab and copper pots on the cooker. While you waited for it to be cooked, you had a bottle of wine and *saganaki* – goat cheese dipped in milk and flour, fried quickly in olive oil and flambé in brandy. Absolutely delicious! We went back recently and

although there are new small hotels nearby little else had changed except that with much ceremony the owner brings in the *saganaki* already flaming. We ate it Greek-style with spicy sausages, then had little mullet and a really good moussaka. The bill was strictly for the Greeks, not for tourists. The new little Cosmopolitan Hotel is very welcoming.

There are good sand beaches all round Kos, and although those reached by paved roads can be fairly busy, there are others reached by mule track which are still almost empty.

Next beach down the north coast from Lampi is Tingaki, where there are a few new package hotels and tavernas very good for fish, but considering the sand is fine, the village only seven miles from Kos town, it is often surprisingly empty. Working salt pans are nearby.

The fishing village of Marmari is becoming a little 'resort' by Kos standards, but nowhere will you find the high rise, massive hotels as on Rhodes. Even the few big hotels that have been built are low-profile, well-designed buildings in gardens. There is a long, near-deserted beach southwards.

We like Mastihari. It has a nice beach with trees for shade, and is quite a busy village with fishing boats. You can get a small ferry here to the isles of Kalymnos and Pserimos. There are a couple of hotels and some tavernas. Further south, a simple side road leads to the beach and to the delightful mini-port of Mikro Limonias – a handkerchief-size haven made with boulders. When we saw it, it was hosting two fishing caiques and three rowing boats.

Southward, just inland from the east coast, is Kefalos, on a hill, with another ruined Knights' castle above it. In the Middle Ages they told of a dragon living in a cave in the castle. The most imaginative travel writer of them all, Sir John Mandeville, who wrote in the 1360s, called it the Dragon Maid. He said that it was the daughter of Ypocras (Hippocrates) turned by the goddess Diana (Artemis) into a hideous looking but harmless dragon and would stay that way until a knight kissed her on the lips and transformed her back into a girl. Several knights went there intending to be gallant but one look at her sent them shaking away. They usually died. He used the Turkish name for Kos – 'Lango'.

There is a beach half a mile from Kefalos at Kamari, which has a fishing boat quay and a taverna. Barbara persuaded a fisherman to take her out to the islet of Aghios Nikolaos, just a rock with a fisherman's chapel. Along the long sandy bay north from Kamari are several tavernas and at the end a big Club Mediterranée hotel where they have their own sailing boats and wind surfers, so that the bay, sea and tavernas are not entirely empty. Nor are the rocks, where nude sunbathing is the fashion. The sea is superbly clear and blue, and is made for swimming, scuba diving or any watersports. And in the grounds of the Club are the remains of the basilica of Aghios Stefanos, found in 1928. Past this begins Paradissos beach, called Almiros by the fishermen but a paradise to sun, sea and sand beach loungers. But there is no natural shade. If the sea appears to be bubbling a bit and warm, don't worry. It is bubbles of air from the volcanic sea bed. But you are not likely to be blown up to paradise.

Kardamena, up the coast, has given me my biggest shock on Kos. It was a fishing port with fish tavernas on its quay, ceramic workshops and a few knowledge-

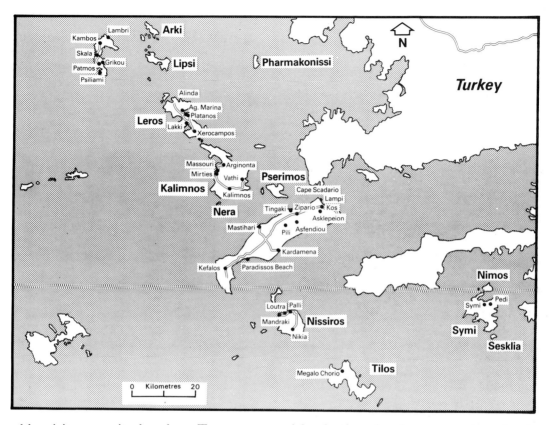

able visitors on its beaches. Ten years later, the tavernas and bars were full of tourists and the beaches fairly draped in browning bodies. Now it is a lively resort as much as a fishing port, with hotels, small new apartment blocks, tavernas crowded in summer and the bodies stretch on sands east and west, past German machine-gun bunkers. There are discos in summer. But the fishing port atmosphere is still there, so is the smell of fish. It just costs a bit more in the tavernas. There is nothing posh about these, either. And the hotels are small, though there is a big one two miles along the beach. But Kardamena is not a good base for seeing other

islands, though caiques go to the volcanic island of Nissiros. It is twenty miles from Kos town and boats to most islands go from there fairly early, so you have to take an excursion bus or, if freelancing, hire a taxi. And those motorized water scooters which skim on skis across the sea may be great fun to the kids on them but don't add to the fishing village atmosphere. I prefer noiseless windsurfers.

The road from Kos town to Kardamena takes you inland through Zipario where you can take a road to the pleasant mountain village of Asfendiou. Kos is a green and fertile island, and the villages nestle among trees, their houses freshly painted white with blue doorways and window frames, and the white churches have bright blue domes.

Asfendiou is on the slopes of Mount Dikaios and is really four hamlets up the mountain, plus a new one on the main road in the plain. A few years back, some of its houses were empty because people had moved into Kos town, but the community has been renovating them and letting them to visitors. Ask the tourist office in Kos town if any are free. One of the hamlets – Lagoudi – is very attractive and Zia, higher up, is beautiful. They are rich in flowers, the traditional houses have courtyards where they still bake bread in open ovens, and baking and flowers mingle in a delicious aroma on bake days!

The steep white alleys of Zia are delightful, the views of the island are lovely but inevitably it has become the traditional village for excursions. The round-the-island coaches call during the day, and on summer's evenings excursions arrive to see the sunset over Kos, staying the whole evening to eat, drink and try their luck at traditional Greek dancing. As this is a wine district, it is a lively evening.

The view from Pili further down the road is even more spectacular. You can often see the isles of Pserimos and Kalymnos.

May and September are very good months to go to Kos. There may not be quite so many boats to other islands, but you will have more peace at Kardamena at night, more room in the tavernas and you will be able to eat and drink at sunset in Zia in peace.

Pserimos is so small that a lot of guide books just don't mention it. It is little more than a tiny rock of six square miles with one village on a sheltered creek, an hour's boat ride from Kos. There are three tavernas, a nice little pension, Tripolitis, some nice quiet walks, and one of the best sand beaches in the Dodecanese. But day visitors arrive from Kos and Kalymnos, and they take over the tavernas at lunch time. By around five or six o'clock they have gone and you can drink and eat in peace. Be prepared to sleep on the beach if you cannot get into the pension.

Nissiros is a volcanic island and I cannot stand volcanoes – they smell so dreadful. But if volcanoes are unavoidable, then Nissiros is an attractive place – once you have braved the rough caique ride from Kos.

It's a prosperous island, none of its people have to emigrate to make a living, its lively tavernas and its three hotels with restaurants are for the locals rather than tourists, and so it stays fairly lively even in winter.

You pass the reason for its success on the way in. The little isle of Giali is made of pumice, and in quarries there the men from Nissiros are gradually breaking it up and shipping it around the world. Oddly Giali has the one golden sandy beach. The others are black sandy.

The port of Mandraki is most attractive. There's a long promenade by the sea but then a maze of alleys too narrow for traffic winds upwards, the balconies of the houses almost blotting out the light. There is a new fashion for painting houses contrasting colours and some are decorated, so the town has a bright unusual appearance. There is a fine selection of restaurants and tavernas, the better ones on the quay, the cheaper, simpler ones into the town. And there is the inevitable Knights' castle at the top. Inside it is a working monastery.

The smell near the sea is of wild flowers,

figs and almonds, once exported in tons, now often just left on the trees.

The smell of the old, faded spa of Loutra is of sulphur from its hot volcanic springs, still used for treating arthritis and rheumatism. The mineral water is piped to the hotel. The best beach is Palli, where there is an hotel and several tavernas.

But the great excursion is to Plybates, the volcano. Buses go regularly and there are plenty of taxis. In spring, the mountainside is green and rich in wild flowers, and you pass many healthy vineyards on the zig-zag route to the villages of Emborios and Nikia on the crater's rim. Then fields give way to a barren landscape of rocks and scrub. The bus stops near the heart of the volcano in a spectacularly ugly technicolour moonscape of brown, grey and a nasty yellow. You must have stout shoes and preferably sun glasses to walk further. You can feel the heat and movement of the volcano beneath your feet and you can hear the bubbling beneath you. Steam jets from little holes and there is a strong obnoxious stench of bad eggs, like an experiment in a school laboratory. The ground is spongy in places and you must tread on rocks. Some of the holes send up a low, deep groan. These are the groans of the giant Polyvotis, trying to break loose from the huge rock which the Titans tore from Kos to crush him.

Emborios and Nikia are tiny villages, both with spectacular views. Below Emborios is a cave with a natural sauna, far too hot for me.

Some almonds are picked to make a sweet non-alcoholic drink, *soumada*. But I recommend local wine to wash that foul bad-egg taste from your throat.

KOS
One of the best Greek islands for outside communications.

Air ...... Charters from several European capitals; many from London. Athens flights one to three daily; Rhodes most days; Mykonos four weekly in July and August.

Ferries ...... Six weekly Piraeus, Patmos, Leros, Kalymnos, Rhodes; two to three weekly Nissiros, Tilos, Symi; twice weekly to various smaller Dodecanese isles; irregular services to Chios, Lesbos, Limnos, Crete, Santorini, Milos. Excursions in summer – daily to Patmos, Rhodes, Kalymnos; five weekly to Pserimos; four weekly to Nissiros; three to Leros; weekly to Samos. Hydrofoils June–September to Rhodes, Patmos, Samos and Leros.

Nissiros: Ferries – Piraeus, Amorgos, Astipalea, Kalymnos, Kos, Leros, Lipsi, Paros, Patmos, Rhodes one or two weekly; excursions from Kos June–September four weekly.

Pserimos: Ferries – Kos five weekly in summer, less in winter; Kalymnos twice weekly.

Symi (Simi) and Tilos

Symi is a seducer. It is not the *most* beautiful of Greek islands; it has too much bare rock. It has no idyllic beaches of golden sand. But it has a beautiful serenity – except in the port for about three hours a day when day trippers arrive from Rhodes and Kos. Then natives who are not trying to relieve the trippers of their money walk round the bay past the boatyard to Nos beach for a swim or an ouzo in the taverna and knowledgeable visitors take a truck-ride of exploration into the interior and mountains green with pine and cypresses, or take the island's only little bus to the tiny harbour and pebbly beach at Pedi, where there is an hotel, one or two tavernas and caiques being repaired. Better, they *walk* to Pedi past fields of oregano, the herb of peace and happiness to the ancient Greeks and Romans. Better still, they take a caique to one of the many deserted beaches which you can reach only by hours of hard walking or by boat. By early evening, serenity has returned.

Symi has kept its serenity because of its shortage of water. They dare not allow any big or luxury hotels to be built, nor encourage too many people to sleep there. Not that the island dies at night. The cafés are full of fishermen drinking ouzo with the visitors, the tavernas buzz with talk and laughter until late. But they are not just there for the tourists. Local people join in, too. And there is even a disco in mid-summer at the taverna on Nos beach, where young locals go.

Strange that Symi is regarded as the dream Greek island, for it is just four miles from Turkey. You feel that you could nip across for a raki before dinner. Turkish fishermen *do* nip across – in the night to the far side of the isle of Nimos to collect goods from the Greeks to smuggle into Turkey. In the days when wooden boat building made Symi very wealthy the people owned land over in Turkey to grow grain and vegetables and particularly trees to provide wood for the boats.

Sailing into Symi harbour is unforgettable. As you sail past steep cliffs dropping sheer into the waves and round the point, the long harbour stretches before you like a sunny fjord of deep blue water to the town of white and ochre houses with red roofs climbing a hillside to green-brown hills and a vividly blue sky. Then the houses are on both sides of you, beautiful neo-classical mansions. They too are left from the days of Symi's prosperity – mostly built last century from profits of ship building and sponge diving. Palladio himself would not have been ashamed of them.

When I first saw these houses they were in sad decay – sightless, crumbling, unpainted, their elegant pointed pediments cracking, even the mosaic floors of their courtyards breaking up. Now each year more and more are restored, and each year they and the smaller houses are re-painted, so that the town always seems fresh and bright. One house on the very quayside round the first headland has been converted tastefully into a beautiful fifteen-bedroomed 'A' class hotel, the Aliki, but you will need to book ahead to get in. Others have been divided into most attractive holiday apartments.

The port is really two towns – Ghialos, round the harbour, for shipping and shopping, joined by a 'high street', Kali Strata, of 357 winding steps to Chorio, the high town. Once the people of the two towns hardly crossed into each other's territories except on important business. Another 275 steps lead to a monastery.

No cars can get through the narrow stepped streets, and the only bus has to drive along the waterside and double back on the road outside to reach the top of the town. Mules and donkeys still carry most things. Trains of mules carry the sand, gravel and cement for restoration of houses.

Even the port scene is of another age. A fishing boat comes in with lobsters and the famous prawns of Symi and the skipper carries them around the tavernas, haggling over an ouzo. Next to a converted caique taking visitors to remote beaches, a sponge boat ties up, the black sponges are washed and beaten then taken across to the shop where they sell them in basketloads, to be dried and treated. A boat from Rhodes unloads vegetables. A caique from Samos unloads wine. The rest of the fish are taken to the little market behind the beautiful customs house and the fishermen spread out their nets to dry and mend. The church bells ring – the sound of Symi.

We saw the whole town turn out one afternoon to see four men in boats chase and catch a swordfish which had strayed into the harbour – and Symi mostly sticks to the siesta.

Round the harbour just before Nos beach men work in the shipyards, repairing wooden caiques. Perhaps there's the skeleton of a new boat being built. Their skill as shipbuilders made the people of Symi prosperous and relatively independent for centuries. Homer reported that they sent boats to the Trojan Wars. When

the Knights of St John were here they let the Symians go much their own way so long as they made them solid, fast ships. The Turks were so pleased with their ships, fast sailing *skaphes* which they used for courier boats, that they allowed Symians to own land on the Turkish shores and gave them the valuable right to dive for sponges in any Turkish waters. It is said locally that they got this right by giving fine sponges to Sultan Suleiman – for his harem ladies, perhaps. The gift became a yearly tribute. Being so near Turkey, the Symians were in no position to resist Turkish invasion in 1522. The Turks called the island Sumbequi – 'place of ships'. All they asked for was ships, a yearly tax, and sponges.

Symi was producing 500 ships a year when the age of steam started the decline. But caiques were still needed, so were sponges. The real depression started when the Italians took over in 1912 and cut them off from their lands and woods in Turkey. In 1945 Symi joined Greece again. A plaque commemorates the signing in the pleasant taverna-restaurant Les Katerinettes. The population dropped

from 20 000 to 2500 as the young emigrated to Rhodes, Athens, America and
Australia. Now tourism and fishing are
bringing back prosperity.

Caiques take visitors to *Nimos*, the isle
to the north, home of sheep and
shepherds, for swimming, fishing, walking and solitude, and to fertile *Sesklia*, to
the south, where fruit and game abound.
It is owned by the monks of Panormitis
monastery, and may not have quite the
same solitude in summer, for caique owners do organize barbecue trips with roast
lamb or fish.

The Panormitis monastery is right on
the water of a horseshoe bay to the south of
the island, and boat excursions from
Rhodes call here before or after visiting
Ghialos port. The monastery is a long
white elegant prosperous-looking building, mostly eighteenth century, with a
mock Baroque bell tower built in 1905.
Inside the little church is a remarkable
carved wood icon, eighteenth-century
frescoes and gold and silver votive offerings from grateful sailors. More sailors'
offerings in the museum include beautiful
models of ships and little bottles which
passing sailors threw out to drift ashore
with money in them for the monastery.

The monastery has a restaurant, café
and food shop and rooms to rent. It is as
much a tourist complex as a religious
sanctuary. Services are often held to co-
incide with the arrival of an excursion
boat. The rooms are rather cell-like but
you don't pay for them. You are expected
to give to the church when you leave. It is
now connected to the port by a road which
runs right down the island, but there is no
bus. Excursions by road are organized.

Do get back to the port in the early
evening to sit outside a kafeneion having a
drink among the fishermen. Sunset over

the town is a beautiful sight. As the sun
goes down the rose-coloured light reflects
in the harbour water, then turns to orange
as if the sea is catching alight, but within
minutes it turns to mauve and black with
the reflection of the harbour lights playing
in the water. That is the time to have just
one more glass of wine or ouzo before
wandering off to a taverna to choose your
meal – prawns fried in olive oil, perhaps,
or even lobster.

Tilos, south-west of Symi and about the
same size (twenty-five square miles) is less
known and less visited. Fewer than 200
people live there but there are 10 000
goats. It has one very simple old hotel, a
small new hotel, Irini, mostly booked by a
British company (Laskarina), some holiday apartments let to a package-holiday
company and a few rooms in houses. Possibly it is the least changed of all Greek
islands over the last twenty years.

It has a natural harbour in the port,
Livadia, where most islanders live. Five
miles up the road is the capital, Megalo

Chorio, on the site of an ancient city. The Venetians built a castle incorporating a classical gateway and stone from the ancient acropolis. At Nausica nearby is a nice beach with a taverna, and there are paths to other sandy coves, or you can hire a boat.

The village of Mikro Chorio is deserted. So very often is the good sandy beach of Eristos. Livadia has two simple tavernas and a shop which opens on demand. Apart from goats' cheese and milk, all fresh food comes by boat from Rhodes – even bread.

SYMI
Prebook rooms in high summer.

Ferries ...... Rhodes daily in summer, less in winter; one or two weekly Piraeus, Astipalea, Amorgos, Kalymnos, Kos, Leros, Nissiros, Paros, Patmos, Samos, Tilos.

TILOS
Nothing direct from Piraeus; waters can be rough, boats often cancelled in winter. Boat weekly via all small Dodecanese isles; excursions twice weekly Rhodes May–Sept; occasional hydrofoils Rhodes in summer.

Kalymnos, Leros and Lipsi

Pothia, the port of the mountainous isle of Kalymnos, is a frantic place. The rushing, the noise, the shouting, the crowds on the waterfront, make you think that everyone is preparing to leave in a hurry. Some are. Mainly because of its history of sponge diving and the sponges of all shapes, sizes and qualities hanging on strings from shops and stalls and piled in baskets, Kalymnos gets more than its share of day trippers from Rhodes and Kos and visitors from cruising boats. But the mystery to me is that the noise and bustle goes on about eighteen hours a day from Easter until at least October. A man from Kos said to me: 'Kalymniots seem to live every day as if it's their last.' And perhaps the volcanic rock under whose shadow they

live and the dangers their young men face when sponge diving makes them feel that way.

I find it all great fun, so long as I can escape occasionally across the island for a little peace. Sitting outside a harbourside taverna watching the crowds pass, the traffic getting in a muddle, people all round eating and drinking, is very stimulating.

As you approach the island, its barren grey and purple hills look forbidding. You cannot see the fertile valleys between, rich in figs, mandarins, lemons and vines. Then you see the amphitheatre-like harbour packed with ships and the port all round the bay, with its buildings painted in blue, green, yellow and brown rising up to barren slopes, and you know that Kalymnos must be a warm, bright sort of place. There are tavernas and hotels right round to the small beach and yacht club, and in the roads behind the shops of the truly Greek type intended for locals rather than tourists. There are some fine old mansions, too.

Like Symi, the isle is thick with churches and monasteries. Greek sailors are often deeply religious, especially those with risky jobs like sponge divers. Aghios Ekaterini church on the harbourside has beautiful gold, blue and brown decorations and a virtual art gallery of icons by famous local artists. Two sculptors, Michail Kokkinos and his daughter Irene, have adorned Pothia with statues. Look particularly for Poseidon by the Olympic Hotel, Winged Victory in Liberty Square, and the towering statue of Liberty with a relief showing the history of sponge diving (by Michael Tilianos).

A huge cement cross standing above the town is lit at night.

One place most tourists visit is the sponge factory. When the sponges come out of the water they are black and have to be washed and dried. Then they are treated with acid which turns them the pleasant golden-yellow.

There is a school for sponge divers. The boats leave after Easter following a week of celebration – eating, free drinks, music, dancing in local costume. The last night is called the Night of Lovers. Then church bells peal to call the men to the boats, the whole town lines the quay to wave handkerchiefs and the boats circle three times before heading for sea. They return with their sponges in October, while families pray that they will all come back. Then another round of celebrations begins.

In old days sponge divers strapped heavy stones to their chests to take them to the sea bed, speared the sponges with a trident and were raised by a lifeline when they gave the signal.

Now they wear oxygen tanks and dive to 300 feet, attacking the sponges with axes. And they go for only four months instead of eight because they can only dive now in Greek and Italian waters and the competition from cheap sponges from Florida is spoiling the business. A lot of Kalymniot divers were lured to Tarpon Springs, Florida, but they co-operated with their relatives back in Kalymnos to fix production and prices. Then in the early 1980s the Cubans began to dive in the rich sponge fields off Florida Keys and undercut the Greeks in price, mostly because of fuel bills. The Cubans even came to Kalymnos to sell sponges to the shopkeepers to sell to the tourists!

So many young men being away for so long has made men and particularly women of Kalymnos very independent. The Italian Fascists discovered that. When the Italians closed Greek schools the islanders painted their houses in Greek colours, blue and white, and even the streets and the churches. As so many men were at sea, the women held a mass protest meeting and march which finished in a violent clash with Fascist soldiers by the custom house. But the women had always fought for their emancipation, making up poems and rallying songs about their complaints of overwork and hard life.

From Pothia caiques will take you to the little isle of Nera, with a monastery and a small taverna, or to Kephalos caves, discovered in 1961, found to have been a sanctuary of Zeus. There are many coloured stalagmites and stalactites, but the cave has not been fully explored. Nor has the Cave of the Seven Virgins at Flakas, even believed to have a bottomless pool. Seven young girls hid here from Turkish pirates and must have got lost, for they were never seen again.

The bus service is not good but there are plenty of taxis which you share. A few buses do run to Vathi, a delightful fishing hamlet with a tiny harbour and two tavernas at the mouth of a long fjord. The fertile valley behind has three villages growing lemons, oranges, mandarins and roses. It smells delicious. I prefer to take a boat here and return by road, for the arrival through the fjord is quite spectacular. Little boats bring the fruit from the harbour to bigger boats outside for export.

As you cross the island from Pothia the contrast becomes startling. You come first to the old capital, Chorio, which grew up around the mediaeval castle. The village inside its walls was a place of refuge from pirates from the eleventh to the eighteenth centuries. Although it is in ruins now, its nine chapels are kept faithfully whitewashed.

In the more fertile stretches along this road are attractive villas, built by sponge-boat skippers who managed to survive past forty years of age or by 'Australians' returned to their island. The names are a clue to where they lived Down Under.

The road reaches the coast at three sandy beaches, shaded by trees – Panormos, Myrties and Moussouri, all favourites with longer-stay holiday-makers. So there are a few hotels, holiday villas and rooms to let. Panormos is an old resort with big old hotels and good restaurants. Myrties is a sweet little port with red-roofed houses among trees and a domed church beside the beach. Flowering shrubs line the beach path and taverna tables are shaded by arbours.

Try to stay here at least one night, if only to see the sun setting in an orange blaze behind the isle of Telendos. Telendos is a bare mountain with beaches round it. It was joined to Kalymnos until an earthquake sank the town in between. Boats from Myrties take just ten minutes to reach it. A few fishermen live there and it has two simple tavernas, a ruined castle but little shade.

At Moussouri more of those fine villas have been built. Northwards the paved road and bus route stops at Arginonta, a seaside village where they raise cattle, but taxis can take you along the track road to Emporios, which has a beach, two good tavernas and no rooms, but in summer you could sleep under the tamarisk trees. Whether you get away with it depends how near the police are and how they are feeling.

Though you can fly from Athens, get almost daily ferries from Kos and Rhodes or take a hydrofoil from Kos to the strange little isle of *Leros*, the nicest way is to take the little boat from Myrties on Kalymnos to the little port of Xerokampos. It is very Greek, with some tavernas, rooms and a small harbour for caiques – quite different from the main port of Lakki, which looks decaying Italian, which it is.

Lakki is in a large, almost enclosed bay, one of the best natural harbours in the Greek Isles. In 1916 the British Royal Navy built a naval base there. When the Italians took over in 1923, Mussolini strengthened it considerably. So the town looks like a rather seedy and decaying set from an old Italian film, with well-paved, wide streets, big 1930s Mussolini gothic and art deco buildings and lots of statues, imported palm trees, and little gardens. Most buildings stand forlorn and empty, and so do the streets except when a ferry comes in, often around midnight, which adds to the ghostly, deserted effect. The once-Grand hotel is part of the scene.

There is a huge grim military camp at Partheni, and during the military dictatorship of the Colonels (1967–74) it was a prison for democratic leaders. To add to the feeling of past tragedies, there is a British cemetery from 1943 when a small British force freed the island but did not have enough men there to hold it against German attacks. While the British were there Dodecanesians in New York prematurely announced the union of their isles with Greece. The British came back in 1945 with a crack Greek regiment and cleared the Germans out.

It is a fairly green and attractive island, with tree-shaded beaches and many inlets. The best beach is at Koylouki, a mile from Lakki. The capital Platanos has its own little port at Aghia Marina with brightly painted boats beside the quay and real old-style tavernas, and just round the bay at Alinda on a sand beach is a small resort with small hotels, restaurants, tavernas and rooms. Most holidaymakers are Greeks from all over the country. That was a mystery I could not solve at first. Why should Greeks come so far to this one little Italianate island in the Dodecanese? What did it have that I had not noticed? Then I was told. The Italians made it not only a naval base but a hospital island for the mentally sick. There are three hospitals for mental patients, and relatives combine a visit with a holiday. And that accounts for the number of Greeks on beaches and in discos. About 1800 of Leros's 8000 people work for these hospitals.

You can take a boat to the islet of Pharmako, twelve miles from Lakki. Julius Caesar was once held here as a prisoner by pirates. When his ransom arrived, he was freed, but he went back, captured the pirates and crucified them.

As you sail towards *Lipsi* (Lipsos), the tiny isle of six square miles between Leros and Patmos, it arises from the sea like a mirage. The village is crowned by a church with three turquoise domes and similarly domed chapels seem perched around the coast. The village is uncommonly colourful, the cube-shaped houses painted in vivid colours, the shops in red and yellow.

Its population is under 600 but it is a busy little farming island, buzzing with the sound of farm machinery in season. When I first went there the farming was

done by hand and the only sounds were of the fishing caiques coming and going and the local musicians who played in the taverna at night. Now there are a few mid-summer excursions from other isles, of visitors determined to brown themselves as evenly as possible all over on the little beaches nestling along the jagged coastline.

Nearly all the population live in the village of Lipsi around the waterfront. It has a D-class hotel fittingly called Calypso, a small pension and some village rooms. The tavernas are good and fairly cheap, and the fish deliciously fresh. Try Lipsos Taverna, by the harbour.

The one taxi will take you to the best beach to the south, Plati Yialo, with one taverna, but you can walk it in half an hour. There are no real roads and it is a walker's isle. Near the village is a valley of vines where a quaffable wine is made.

A ferry from nearby isles calls once or twice a week. The same ferry usually goes to *Arki*, north of Lipsi, where about fifty fishing families live. There is no electricity, food is basic, and rooms very limited, so take a sleeping bag. Just outside its harbour is *Marathi*, an islet with a sandy beach and a taverna open in mid-summer. You must hire a boat from Arki.

The ferry goes on from Arki to a remoter fishing island, *Agathonisi*, with two villages.

KALYMNOS
Ferries ...... Piraeus, Kos, Leros, Rhodes four to six weekly; Patmos, Pserimos thrice weekly.

LEROS
Air ...... Athens daily; Kos thrice weekly.

Ferries ...... Piraeus four to six weekly; Samos one or two weekly; Kalymnos, Kos, Patmos, Rhodes weekly via all Dodecanese isles; caiques Lipsi high summer.

LIPSI
Daily caiques in high season Patmos, Leros; irregular weekly boat connecting Lipsi with all Dodecanese isles.

ARKI, AGATHONISI
Connected to Lipsi by irregular boat connecting all Dodecanese isles.

Patmos

For a beautiful, holy island, Patmos is sadly commercialized. But only in its port, Skala. Cruise boats and excursion boats and hydrofoils in high summer unload thousands a day from Kos and Rhodes. They have come to see the gaunt, forbidding, but impressive, white-painted monastery high on the hill which, since St Christodoulos founded it in 1088, has contrived through courage, cunning and perhaps the help of a Higher Hand to survive the rampaging pirates who looted and pillaged these isles for centuries, raids by Arabs, Turks, Normans and Crusaders, Venetian conquest, Italian Fascist rule and two years of the Nazis, earthquakes and famines.

It is still one of the richest religious houses in the world, with such priceless items as an eleventh-century icon of St Nikolaos in a silver frame and a bishop's crozier of gold and enamel studded with sixty-two diamonds. Frescoes from the thirteenth century decorate the chapels. The most prized possession is the library, with many thousands of old rare books, manuscripts and codices, but you must have the abbot's permission to see it. This is not surprising. Over centuries scholars have 'borrowed' many rare and priceless items, which are now in national libraries of France, Germany and England.

It is the monastery of St John the Theologian. For it was on this island that the apostle John, exiled here in 95 AD, heard the voice of God through cracks in the ceiling of a cave and dictated to his disciple Prochorus the doom-laden prophetic poem the Apocalypse, which we call Revelations. In its St James Bible English translation it is a magnificent, awe-inspiring poem. Lawrence Durrell says that it is 'worthy of an early Dylan Thomas' and if you do not think that is sacrilegious, you will probably find it true.

The cave where John heard the voice, a fifteen-minute walk down the hill, then down a flowered stairway, is now a little chapel of the Monastery of the Apocalypse. You can see the massive roof split in three by the voice of God and the shelf of rock used by Prochorus as a desk. He must surely have written a form of shorthand. Alas, the cave is not always open. You must find a monk.

The St John Monastery was really a town fortified against pirates, and in narrow streets are fine merchants' houses hiding patios and gardens. They are from the seventeenth century, when Patmos had a powerful merchant fleet. They are

only used in the summer and I am told that the whole Chora can look sinisterly bleak in winter. But in summer there are stalls and shops selling souvenirs to the pilgrims, ice creams and snacks.

Buses and taxis go up now, but through piety or because of the superb views over Skala, the fjord-like entrance to the port, and isles of Ikaria and Samos, many walk up the old donkey track, a hard hour's walk in heat.

Because of pirates, Skala was little more than a quay until around 1820. Now it is a pleasant town with a big quay and little square which has not lost its Greekness despite the crowds, the souvenir, clothes and jewellery shops, bars, and new small hotels and apartments. Life is much calmer in the evenings. Even nightlife is discreet and sophisticated, in music bars and two small discos. And life on the rest of the island is calm and quiet.

There are only fourteen miles of roads and some good walks within sight of the sea. But the best way to see the island is by boat. The fishermen put up a board on the quay at Skala telling you where they are going next day. At Grikou, where about fifty people live round a horseshoe bay, a mini resort has grown up with a restaurant, taverna, beach surfing and a B-class Xenia hotel. The best-known beach is in the north at Lambri, covered in many-coloured patterned pebbles.

Northward, the bus stops at Kambos, with a long beach with bars and tavernas, windsurfing and waterskiing and an enchanted upper village. Psiliamo has fine sand – go by boat.

Incidentally Patmian House restaurant up in Chora is said to produce some of the best food in the Greek isles, and the owner lets out some apartments in Grikou Bay.

PATMOS
Many excursions from Kos and Rhodes in summer.

Ferries ...... Piraeus, Rhodes, Kos, Kalymnos, Leros six days weekly; Samos thrice weekly; Ikaria one or two weekly May–September. Weekly Dodecanese island boat; daily caique Lipsi in summer. Hydrofoils summer Kos, Rhodes thrice weekly; Leros twice weekly.

Astipalea

This fertile, deep-sided isle shaped like a moth is the most westerly of the Dodecanese, and would seem to be closer connected with the Cyclades. You can see the Cycladian isles of Amorgos and Thira on a clear day, and its looks are of the Cyclades, in the cube style of its houses and the steep white steps joining buildings on cliffsides.

The Italians ruled from 1912–43, the

Italian influence is there, but so is the Turkish, in the houses with ornate wooden balconies.

The port of Astipalea is on the western 'wing' of the island, its houses tumbling down from a hilltop Venetian fortress to the quay where are most of the island's tavernas and the three hotels and rooms. There are more tavernas by the beach at Livadia at the end of a fertile green valley. You can camp or rent a room. There is sometimes a lot of seaweed on the beach.

You can take a taxi over the narrow strip of land which joins the two wings of the island to a fertile plain of citrus and vegetable gardens called Maltesania, because it was once the lair of Maltese pirates, and onto the beach at Analipsi where there is little but a taverna and many people take off all their clothes, to swim and sunbathe. In fact, it is a beautiful walk to here – about seven miles.

Maps show a road across this eastern wing to Vathy, a really sleepy fishing village on what looks like a lagoon but has a very narrow exit to the sea. In 1987 my friends, just back from the island, said that the tarmac disappeared shortly after the path to Analipsi, then the rough track petered out on threadbare hills. The taxi driver had phoned ahead for a tiny boat to meet them in a little cove below and take them to Vathy. That's the Greek islands!

You can sometimes get a boat to Vathy from the port. It is certainly a hideaway – a few houses, a few boats, donkeys for transport of goods and people, a taverna and one telephone. The office won't find you.

ASTIPALEA
Ferries ...... One or two weekly Piraeus, Paros, Kalymnos, Kos, Nissiros, Tilos, Symi, Rhodes.

NORTH SPORADES

Samos

Mark Antony, the playboy general of Ancient Rome, took over Samos and held a party. It lasted several months of eating, drinking and debauchery, and Cleopatra was there.

He made a wise choice. It was called the Isle of the Blessed because of its greenery and fertility, and he was unlikely to run out of food or good wine.

Later Antony's enemy Augustus Caesar made it popular for holidays by wintering there, granting it many privileges. The island produced great brains and great artists, and even the pirate tyrant Polycrates, who took over in the sixth century BC, was a patron of the arts, encouraging poets, sculptors and architects to go there from around the world.

When the Turks invaded in 1453, most of the people were able to escape to Chios, leaving their island deserted for eighty years. When the Turks were defeated in 1912, Samos smartly declared unity with Greece before Italy could invade it, thus avoiding the attempted 'Italianization' which Mussolini applied to the unfortunate Dodecanese.

After the Second World War, it was one of the first isles to have a regular air service with Athens, bringing prosperity from up-market holidaymakers, and then was one of the first to accept charter holiday flights from the rest of Europe.

Rooms are very scarce in July and August but the island is a fair size (184 square miles) and never appears to be overcrowded, except in the port of Samos when the excursion boats from Patmos are in. Natural springs make it one of the greenest of Greek islands, with pine woods, figs, olive groves and a lot of vineyards. Samian wine has been famous through history, mentioned by many writers, and holidaymakers will take little urging to follow Byron's advice to 'fill high the cup with Samian wine'. The sweet red wine is fairly easy to get but much of the better light dry white is exported to Athens.

The main town and Piraeus ferry port is called Vathi but the deep port part of it is called Samos Town. Attractively set in a U-shaped bay, it is not pretty, but is dignified, with nineteenth-century buildings, many well restored, and red-roofed houses, not concrete high-rise blocks. There are many pensions, including the Avli, made from a nunnery, where you can sleep in a converted nun's cell with your own numbered toilet in a row of them. You can eat breakfast in the courtyard where the nuns took exercise. The Xenia B-class hotel is the most attractive, opposite a fishing boat quay. Restaurant Dionysus on Sofouli Esplanade is a posh taverna with good cooking.

Even the old part of Vathi up the hill is very much a working town, too busy to pander much to tourists, but for that reason alone it is interesting to me, for you meet many more local people in the bars and tavernas than in most tourist islands. But the rest of Samos is much more attractive, and I would not stay long here. In summer the north winds pass above it and it can be stiflingly hot.

Incidentally boats go twice a day from here to Kusadasi in Turkey, weather and politics permitting, and buses in Turkey go to Izmir and Istanbul. You must give the Greek authorities twenty-four hours notice 'to complete documentary formalities' and the return journey (two hours each way) and port taxes cost 5000 drachmas in 1987 (£25 or about US $40)! I get the feeling that the Turks are happier to receive people than the Greeks are to let them go!

Parts of the north coast of Samos are rocky and inaccessible. The best beaches are in the south.

Although it has many pensions and small and large hotels, it is even more difficult to find rooms in the port of Pythagorion without booking in high summer than in Vathi. Pythagorion is very much more attractive. Package

tourists, Greeks from Athens and the Dodecanese and back-packers all make for it. So do yachtsmen. It is still a fishing port, though little ferries for the Dodecanese isles go from here and you can get boats for Turkey. There is a small sandy beach and a long pebble beach beyond the harbour. Hotel Acropole on the harbour is pleasant. The tree-lined harbourside is lined, too, with tavernas, very pleasant for a night's eating, drinking and talking after the day visitors have gone. Backstreet tavernas are cheaper. The views across the Mycale Straits to the mountains of Turkey are beautiful and inspiring for it was here that in 1824 Admiral Canaris defeated the Turks with his fire ships as they prepared to invade Samos and inspired Greece in her fight for freedom.

The port was called Tigani, but its name was changed in 1955 in honour of Pythagoras, the mathematician born here in the sixth century BC. Most of us know him for the right-angle theorem of our school days and possibly as the Father of Trigonometry. But he was also the first to show the mathematics of the stars and planets, and of music, and the beauty of proportions, on which Classical architecture and sculpture were based. He could not stomach the corsair-tyrant Polycrates who took over Samos, and he joined other Samian refugees in the Greek colony of Crotone in Italy, where he and his followers formed a religious and moral cult.

Tigani was the port and capital of Polycrates. You can still see some of the walls of the vast city and port he built here, called by the historian Herodotus 'the first among all Hellenic and barbarian cities'. In a palace occupying the lower slopes of Ambelos, he received kings and princes, architects, poets and sculptors whose statues lined the five-mile Sacred Way to the temple of Hera, which he rebuilt.

From the port he sailed with his fleet of galleys of 150 oars each and army of 1000 archers to plunder, capture and loot. Like the pirate he had been, he raided indiscriminately, attacking even his 'friends' and giving them back some of their own property afterwards.

Herodotus described his works as 'three of the greatest building and engineering feats in the Greek world'. These were the great mole protecting his harbour, on which the modern town is built, the second a tunnel through a hill to the north of the town through which a pipe carried drinking water, the third the vast temple of Hera south of the town on Cape Colonna, of which only one column survives of the original 133, though it was a wonder of the Greek world. The goddess Hera was said to have been born on Samos.

The tunnel was remarkable for its time – a mile long, eight feet tall, eight feet wide. Called after the engineer Efplinion, it was built by thousands of slaves over fifteen years, with many hundred deaths.

The tunnel was also intended as a bolthole, and was used once when the Persians attacked. Now it has collapsed in the middle, but you can get along the first 320 yards. It is now lit electrically. I remember it as dank, eerie, evil-smelling and slightly reminiscent of the tunnels built in our wartime prison camps, though bigger and more comfortable.

Polycrates got his uppance from the Persians. Tired of his marauding they lured him to the mainland and crucified him.

The rugged north coast is beautiful but I cannot say the same for the port of

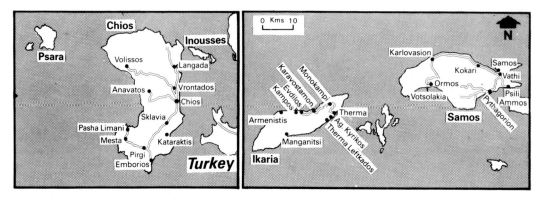

Karlovasion, where some Piraeus ferries call. It is a run-down industrial town.

If you cannot get a bed in Vathi or Pythagorian, consider Kokari which is only six miles from Vathi and has a good bus service, except on Sundays. It is building up into a package tour resort, but is still attractive, has a long pebble beach and pleasant coves nearby.

One of the nicest places to stay is Votsalakia, a modern but very Greek-style holiday development with pensions, rooms and two tavernas on a very long, sand and pebble beach with shade from trees. It is a mile or so over a headland from Ormos, a really delightful, 'old Greece' fishing and caique-building port, with an unmade road around its harbour,

rooms to rent, café-tavernas, a couple of restaurants and a large modern hotel, the Kerkis Bay.

When I last heard, the buses stopped at Votsalakia, but you can walk on to Psili Ammos, less than a mile away, passing a taverna with glorious views and good food called *Kalamaki* and the odd room to rent. You are now really in back-packers' country. At Ormos there is a just about driveable road across the island to join the northern main road. There are several of these roads into the vine-growing hills and beautifully-green southern interior of Samos, with near-lush terraces. If you leave Samos without driving inland you will not really understand why it is called a green and fortunate island.

SAMOS

Air ...... Many charter flights from Western European countries; Athens two to three flights daily (45 mins); Chios twice weekly (35 mins); Lesbos one to two weekly (55 mins); Mykonos one to four weekly (40 mins).

Ferries ...... Piraeus three to seven weekly (12 hrs); Ikaria three to seven weekly (2½ hrs); Paros three to four weekly; Chios three weekly (4¾ hrs); Samos (Karlovasion) six weekly; Lesbos (Mitilini), Limnos, Kavala (mainland), Syros, Leros, Kalymnos, Kos, Rhodes, Chalki, Karpathos, Kassos, Crete (Sitia, Aghios Nikolaos), Santorini, Folegandros, Milos all once weekly. Daily caiques to Turkey (see text).

Ikaria (Icaria)

When Daedalus, the inventor, made wings for himself and his son Icarus to fly away from Crete to escape the wrath of King Minos, he stuck them on with wax. Icarus so fancied himself as an aviator that he went soaring up towards the sun, the wax melted and he fell in the sea off this island which was named after him. The legend offers a reminder to visitors to Greece not to fly too high (especially on ouzo) nor to expose themselves too much to the fierce summer sun.

There seem to be two opinions of Ikaria. Those who like it say that it is a truly Greek, old-fashioned island where most of the visitors are Greek, and the people are friendly but rather bewildered by the funny ways of foreign tourists. Those who dislike it say that the people are uncharacteristically rude, bolshie and unfriendly, that they welcome only rich Athenians who come to take the 'cure' in the thermal spa, and that they are particularly unfriendly to the young and to back-packers without much money to spend.

They have some excuse for feeling somewhat soured. In 1912, towards the end of the Balkan Wars between Greece and Turkey, they overcame and imprisoned their Turkish rulers and declared 'UDI', shunning the rule of all outsiders, issuing their own money and stamps. But three months later the Greek fleet arrived from Piraeus and 'persuaded' them that they should join Greece after all. Since when, say the islanders, they have been completely neglected by Athens except when the Colonels' military dictatorship grabbed power in 1967 and dumped 15 000 opponents of the regime on the island's 7000 people. It became a sort of prison isle. The Colonels called these exiles 'communists' but in fact they included many leading, very democratic social democrats and liberals. It seems that they got talking to the local people in kafeneions and tavernas over ouzo and wine, and the younger ones fraternized with the young islanders, and now Athens says that Ikaria has distinctly left-wing views.

Unlike Icarus, you cannot drop from the sky onto Ikaria. It has no commercial airport. Seas are rough, landing can be difficult even in summer winds, despite the recently extended breakwater. The god of the wind is said to live on the long mountain which divides the island into north and south, and if it is calm on one side, he is sure to be blowing on the other.

People braving these elements were met, until recently, on the dock at Aghios Kyrikos, the port, with a rather discouraging notice saying: 'Welcome to the

Isle of Radiation'; it has been painted over.

The baths are at Therma, a seaside village between two hillsides two and a half miles from the port and they are certainly radioactive – the most active in Europe. One was so strong that it had to be closed. People come here to treat rheumatism, arthritis and gout. Therma also has the most hotels and restaurants. Another little spa on the other side of the port, Loutra (Therma Leftkados) has a spring so hot that people on picnics use it to boil eggs. The island's most luxurious hotel (the Toula) is here.

Ikaria has a definite season for visitors, from the beginning of June until the end of September. Outside that, most hotels, restaurants and even many tavernas are shut and there are even fewer buses than in summer. Best to share a taxi on this isle.

There is little obvious activity around the port of Aghios Kyrikos except the boats, the sea and the wind. It is in gentle decay, and listless. But it does have a lot of little hotels, pensions and rooms to rent, and some restaurants. But many close out of season.

The north of the island, with sandy beaches, shady pine woods, good roads and many pensions is the favourite for visitors, and the biggest village, Evdilos, a pretty fishing village, is also a port where the ferries from Piraeus and Samos call once a week.

The road through steep mountains from Aghios Kyrikos to Evdilos is beautiful and awesome. You pass villages clinging to the mountainside, parts of which are covered in thick shrubs like the maquis of Corsica. When the wind blows, you can smell thyme. Monokampi lies

above a deep green and fertile ravine with terraced farms, then the road snakes to the coast at the fishing village of Karavostamon, after which there are several coves of sand and shingle before Evdilos. This little port is very popular with visitors. It has quite a lot of accommodation but it can be full in July and August. The bus from Aghios Kyrikos does not return from there until the next day.

Kampos further on has the ruins of a Byzantine palace and church and a small museum. Rachis, called the Little Switzerland of Ikaria because of tall pines covering the mountainside, has a sandy beach, a taverna and some rooms, but it lures a lot of unofficial campers and beach-sleepers.

The paved road ends at Armenistis, a little port and seaside village with a big coarse-sand beach, several tavernas, rooms and even a disco, I hear, in summer (I would prefer *not* to hear it, but I am old). I used to like this place and persuade fishermen to take me out in their caiques, but I hear a sad story of a huge invasion in mid-summer of young foreigners wandering fairly aimlessly around Greece who camp out, often in makeshift tents, at the back of the beach, leaving some litter and mess around. They cannot be true island-hopping backpackers, whom I have always found to be meticulous about looking after the environment.

From Aghios Kyrikos you can get a caique to an isolated fishing village in the south-west called Manganitis. You cannot reach it by road and it has no electricity, but you can have quite a lively fish meal with wine there. That's for me!

Though rocky, Ikaria abounds in fruit trees and its apricots are the best in Greece. Honey is good and they make a fair line in raki, the fiery spirit, sometimes flavoured with apricot to make a sort of apricot brandy. And the island is known for its parties, too – old-style feasts at which you consume lots of soup, roast goat, bread and wine, with speeches, music, folk and modern dancing.

IKARIA
Weather can play havoc with ferry sailings and timetables.

Ferries ...... Piraeus daily (8 hrs) – often twice daily in summer; Samos six days weekly, often twice a day – but not Sundays in 1987 (2½ hrs); Paros four weekly; Syros twice weekly; Chios, Lesbos (Mitilini), Limnos, Kavala (mainland), Leros, Kalymnos, Kos, Rhodes, Chalki, Karpathos, Kassos, Crete (Sitia, Aghios Nikolaos), Santorini, Folegandros, Milos once weekly.

Caiques to Fourni isle subject to weather.

Chios (Hios)

Chios does not need tourism. It grew rich on shipping, chewing gum and varnish.

Twenty-two old fortified towns and villages in southern Chios are called Mastichoria. Here they grow lentisk trees. They are gashed in May and in late autumn the resin (masticha) is tapped – a clear liquid which crystallizes. For centuries it was used as chewing gum to sweeten the breath and in the making of varnish. Cellulose has replaced it, but it is still used to flavour alcoholic drinks, especially a form of ouzo, and also served as a sticky, jelly-like jam placed on a spoon in a glass of water. The Greeks call this *ypovrychion* (submarine). It is also used in pharmaceutical products.

When the Turks took Chios from the Genoese in 1566, the ladies of the Turkish harems took to the chewing gum so fervently that Chios became a chosen isle of the Sultans and mastik farmers were given special privileges – they did not have to give statute labour to the Turks or pay taxes and their churches could ring their bells. The Turks were so upset at the ungratefulness of the people in joining the fight for Greek independence in 1822 that they murdered around 30 000 islanders, took 45 000 into slavery out of 100 000 people, and destroyed towns, villages and crops. But they left the mastik villages alone. These atrocities raised the wrath of Europe and America. Victor Hugo wrote poems about it, the Frenchman Delacroix painted moving pictures. A French colonel Fabvier tried to liberate the isle in 1828 but failed. There was a small compensation for the people left when Admiral Canaris and his fire ships sank the Turkish flagship in Chios harbour as the Turks were gathering a force to invade Samos, where the people had revolted successfully. Samos at least was saved from a massacre.

I have never understood how, after the defeat of the Turks and the achievement of Greek independence, the great powers of the time, France, Russia and Britain, could have solemnly handed back the brave and suffering Greeks of Chios, Samos and the Dodecanese to Turkish rule. At least Chios and Samos were united with Greece in 1912 and did not have to go through the 'Italianization' by Mussolini's Fascists. But by then many of the beautiful Genoese buildings had been destroyed and many people killed in a terrible earthquake in 1881.

The first sight of Chios from the ferry is uninviting. Chios town does not look Greek. It is an ugly mess of prefabricated concrete, with high rise apartments and office blocks. And when you land you find too many fast-food, hamburger joints and smart plastic bars for a true Greek island port. Very many of the local people have returned from the US wealthy by island standards. Their children behave more like Athenians than islanders, although the quayside walkabout is still traditional in the evenings and there is no room for cars until the early hours, when everyone seems to jump in cars and rev up their engines at once. There are very-Greek lanes and alleys in the market area.

Do visit, suitably clad, the Monastery of Nea Moni seven miles from Chios town. It became 'new' in 1042 when three hermit monks discovered a miraculous ikon

on a church site. Considering it was looted by the Turks, who killed all the monks, in 1822 and that the dome, bell tower and vault all collapsed in the 1881 earthquake, a surprising number of the most beautiful mosaics have survived. They are masterpieces of religious art and have been sympathetically restored. Nuns have replaced the monks and they will show you round.

The poet and historian Homer was said to have taught on the hillside above the garden seaside village of Vrontados, two miles from Chios town, but Homer's Stone is now believed to have been an ancient altar. Local legend claims that Christopher Columbus stopped here on his way to America. Possible, I suppose, because he was a Genoese and Genoa ruled Chios from 1261 to 1566.

Ten miles up this coast is a delightful fishing village, Langada, at the end of a bay backed by hills thick with pines. The pretty waterfront is lined with cafés and tavernas, with a river running into the sea – when it is running. You can find rooms here. As Chios has only recently turned to tourism and is not widely visited, rooms are easier to find than on such isles as Samos.

Inland is the fortified mediaeval village of Anavatos, built up a very steep mountainside to a ruined castle standing above a near-vertical cliff face down to a deep gorge. It's an eerie place. It is almost deserted. Three people lived there when I saw it. It seems that during the Turkish atrocities 400 villagers threw themselves off to avoid capture, torture and enslavement.

Volissos, almost at the west coast, is one of many villages in several areas where Homer was born!

South of Chios town the countryside is very attractive, with orchards surrounded by mediaeval walls, some with gateways inscribed with coats of arms of Genoese families. There are many Genoese villas and gardens, particularly at Sklavia, a name derived from the Greek slaves forced to work for the Genoese. It has splendid views. Some houses have water mills and little wooden bridges.

Kataraktis down the coast is a very pleasant working fishing port, with cafés and tavernas.

The southernmost region is where the mastik is produced. The main road by-passes the delightful mediaeval village of Pirgi. It was built in the thirteenth century so that the close-packed houses formed the walls of a fortified village to protect the people from pirate raids. The houses are massive, their walls of stone, their doorways and windows framed with arches and more arches over the alley-like streets. The ground floor was used for storage and as stables for mules. On the first floor are small open courtyards with steps up to the flat roofs used as terraces, and all the upper floors have balconies with ironwork railings. But what gives the houses a beautiful, almost unworldly effect is the decorative graffiti – black and white geometric patterns engraved with

An old woman cracks almonds

black sand into the plaster. It is sheer joy to walk round the narrow streets and look up at the patterned walls and balconies. To add to the effect, thousands of house-martins and swifts make nests on the balconies and swoop and dive along the streets. And on almost every balcony plants and flowers grow. The ultimate effect is when you pass an old man or woman riding side-saddle on a donkey, possibly leading a goat.

It is a busy little town, with the co-operative of the mastik industry, and a shop where all the mastik products can be bought. The graffiti in the main square, dominated by a seventeenth-century church, are particularly ornate, and alongside is the mediaeval defence watch-tower.

The twelfth-century church of Aghii Apostoli is attractive and interesting for its octagonal tower. Inside are wall paintings by a Cretan artist from 1665.

There are several of these mediaeval

walled villages. The best preserved of them is Mesta, with the same lovely old Genoese-style houses and narrow winding lanes with arches over them. These arches were not just decorative – they were a protection against earthquake damage. Some houses are so near together that their balconies meet giving streets a tunnel effect.

Mesta is much quieter than Pirgi but houses are being restored and made into guest houses, each sleeping up to five people. Several others in a little alley off the main square have become a small hotel complex – Hotel Maion (Mediaeval Hotel). Olympoi is another attractive mediaeval village.

The surprising thing about all of them is that you see no excursion coaches and surprisingly few visitors. Some say that the shipowners of Chios are not too keen on having many tourists on their island.

Nearby Emborios is a pleasant fishing port between hills in a long narrow bay, with several tavernas and a beach of volcanic black pebbles and sand. Oddly it is rather lovely.

On the other coast westward is a port variously marked on maps as Limani Meston or Pasha Limani, growing fast as a little commercial port.

Off the north east coast is the little isle of *Inousses* or *Oinoussai*. It has a school of navigation and elegant mansions most of which are now just shells, though some are being restored. There is a mediaeval castle, an operational convent, two hotels, cafés and tavernas known for lobster. A ferry goes there from Chios town but you must stay overnight. It returns next day.

Psara, the island to the west, has three ferries a week from Chios town but the Chiots are unenthusiastic about it and its people. It is arid and not much to look at, but at least quiet and has beaches of a sort.

The Greek Tourist Organization has converted a prison into an hotel and with strange humour called it 'Alcatraz'; a pension restaurant has been made from a sanatorium and a bed and breakfast pension from a church cloister.

Psara was the birthplace of the great Admiral Canaris, hero of the War of Independence, and supplied him with several ships. The Turks, who had virtually ignored the island until then, decided to lay it waste in 1828 and landed 28 000 men who killed about 27 000 people – islanders or refugees from other isles. 3000 got away to Evia. Psara now has 500 people.

CHIOS (HIOS)

Air ...... Athens at least twice daily (40 mins); Lesbos one or two weekly (40 mins); Samos one or two weekly (35 mins); Mykonos one or two weekly (55 mins).

Ferries ...... Piraeus three to seven days weekly (10 hrs); Samos thrice weekly (4¾ hrs); Lesbos three to seven days weekly (4 hrs); daily to the little isle of Oinoussai; thrice weekly little isle of Psara (3¾ hrs – free travel off season); Tsesme (Turkey) one or two weekly (returns same day); Limnos, Kavala (mainland), Ikaria, Leros, Kalymnos, Kos, Rhodes, Chalki, Karpathos, Kassos, Crete (Sitia, Aghios Nikolaos), Santorini, Folegandros, Milos once weekly.

SPORADES

Skiathos

Skiathos is a gorgeous island, smiling and happy. It is an isle of gentle hills, pine and olive groves slipping down to the sea, woods so dense that it seems to be smothered in green, of long, indolent sand beaches and wild and magnificent shores, all capped to the west by mountains so rugged that you can enter only on foot or mule. All this is packed into an island just eight miles long.

Perhaps it is a pity that so many visitors now arrive by air on charter flights or from Athens. From the sea Skiathos looks so lovely. Through calm sheltered waters you pass the deep green hills, waterside hamlets of white houses, the occasional big white hotel on a hillside, sand beaches with a few small boats at anchor. Then you round the southern point Kalamaki, cutting inside little islands, and sail into the even more protected waters approaching Skiathos port, with one of the safest anchorages in the isles.

Once the airport had been built back in the 1960s, Skiathos was sure to become a holiday island. Happily, the holiday business grew fairly gradually and although the visitors have turned Skiathos town into a very lively cosmopolitan happy place, they have not swamped the isle or the beaches. There are sixty-six beaches to choose from, and as some of them can be reached only by caique, there are still places to hide. It is an island for those who want some sophistication and comfort but not the highly organized tourism of Rhodes.

Although Skiathos has its share of first and second class hotels, mostly new, plenty of small hotels, and has built very many villas to let to tourists who like more freedom, you may find difficulty in getting a room mid-summer because so much accommodation is booked by package companies. Unofficial camping is strongly discouraged. So if you intend to stay at least a week or to use it also as a base to see one or two neighbouring isles, such as Skopelos, do as we have done several times and take a cheap air package with bed and breakfast or rooms.

Roads on Skiathos are good but few. So be prepared to take caiques or small boat excursions from Skiathos harbour to reach the beaches of the north – Kastro and Lalaria, an enchanting beach of silver pebbles with a holed rock like a gateway to nowhere in the water and sheer grey white rock behind. Boats can take you to three sea caves here.

You can walk in two and a half to three hours to Kastro over the mountains, reckoned to be the best walk on the island. From the ring road round Skiathos you go to the summit near Aghios Konstantinos by a path marked by red blobs of paint and then continue down to the coast at Kastro.

Up steps you reach the crumbling walls of the old Byzantine fortress-village at the end of a point. Once it had 300 houses and twenty-two churches; now there is an entrance gate, two ruined churches and a hammam (Turkish baths). Views from the end are beautiful. When piracy was rife in the Aegean in the sixteenth century, the people of Skiathos would trek across the mountains at the first sign of trouble and hide safely in this fortress, which they entered over a wooden drawbridge.

The paved road goes from Skiathos town to the airport and the other way all along the south coast to Koukounaries Bay, but cutting across the Kalamaki peninsula. It passes many beaches with tavernas and restaurants, hotels of different types and sizes and self-catering villas, but they are never obtrusive. Tzanerias (Kanapitsa) has a big hotel like white honeycombs on the hillside (Nostos) and Akhades Bay has sands with a hotel-restaurant with gardens (Achladia) and a good taverna.

Koukounaries has one of the best stretches of sand in Greece, backed by shady trees, with a little harbour at one end, used when I was last there as a base for a British flotilla sailing club. There is a water-ski school, too, which is a pity, for it does spoil the calm of this almost-idyllic beach, and a new concrete taverna which is more useful than ornamental. The same is true of the luxury Skiathos Palace Hotel of boxes with balconies on a hillock overlooking the beach at one end. But it must be a wonderful place to stay for beach loungers and sun-addicts. Behind the beach and the trees is a big lagoon, Lake Strofilias, which is delightful and gives the beach an extra dimension of beauty. I have seen kingfishers diving here.

Just across the point from this bay lies Krassa, now called Banana Beach (where you can peel off everything!). It has a taverna. You can strip (unofficially) on the next beach, Aghios Elenis, the last one accessible by road. By footpath from the road behind the lagoon at Koukounaries you can reach Mandraki, a lovely sand beach with a snack bar in the Bay of Xerxes. Here on his way to fight Athens in 480 BC King Xerxes of Persia lost many ships in a terrible storm. He took the island and repaired all the ships he could salvage. On a rocky reef called Lefteris between Skiathos and the mainland he built the world's first lighthouse. To avoid attack by the larger and more modern Athenian ships and to save his rowers from thirst in the heat of the day, he took the unusual course of moving his fleet at night. It all did him no good. He was on his way to defeat at Salamis.

There is a good bus service on the coast road but buses are crowded in summer.

Taxis cruise and when shared the cost is reasonable. I like Skiathos town. It is a jolly, happy place where everyone – visitors of many nations and islanders – seems to be enjoying life. The port is divided into two by Bourtzi, once an island, now joined to the mainland by a bridge. Its much-restored Venetian castle is used as a primary school. The original south-facing port is now used by fishing boats. The main port where ferries and small cargo boats arrive always seems to be in a state of alteration and extension, like an airport. White buildings with red roofs are packed in streets which are crammed with cars and people in summer, but blessedly there are no high-rise buildings. The tavernas on the harbour road have a pleasant atmosphere at night – a bit noisy but happy. I love the tiny fish tavernas up the steps towards the pink church at the south end of the harbour – just a few tables under trees against a wall, with waiters bringing the food across the narrow street from the kitchen. Cramped, but a pleasant position over the fishing harbour.

There are music bars and simple discos for those who want them, but I am a taverna man.

The best time for me in Skiathos is in May when the island is awakening from its winter sleep and everything is opening up. Late October is rather sad as the tired people close things down one by one. But they do have more time to talk to you.

SKIATHOS

Air ...... Many charters from Western Europe, especially Britain and Germany. Athens: three to seven flights daily (50 mins); Thessaloniki thrice weekly was suspended, so check.

Ferries ...... Volos on mainland two to five daily (3 hrs), with bus connections down to Athens; most days from Aghios Konstandinos (3 hrs); one to three weekly Kimi on Evia (4½ hrs); Skopelos one or two daily (½ hr); Alonnisos one or two daily (2½ hrs); one to four weekly Skyros. Lemnos boats one or two weekly (8 hrs). Also summer excursions to Skopelos.

Skopelos

Skopelos is for dreamers and for walkers. It is nearly twice the size of Skiathos and has more people living there permanently but in summer that is very difficult to believe. It is much less developed and to get around it you must do some delightful but pretty hard walking. Bus services are not frequent. Boats are used for local transport.

The island is hilly and covered with trees – pine and plane trees, silver-leafed olives, almonds and other nuts, quinces and plums. To visiting Greeks used to arid isles or rocks, it is dramatically beautiful.

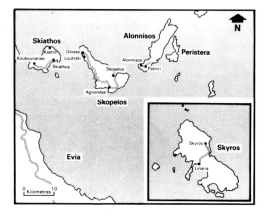

Though the welcome is very friendly, the people do not go out of their way to attract and entertain visitors as on Skiathos. Most of the young men go to sea or work abroad to make some money before returning to marry and settle, and not many are interested in tourism. So many bars, restaurants and even pensions are run by people of other isles or the mainland, who leave at the end of the season. There are no big holiday hotels. But lots of yachts call in summer.

The main port and town, Skopelos, is delightfully attractive. It is built on a steep amphitheatre round the port, its houses with roofs of blue slate and red tiles seeming to look over each other's shoulders at the boats, the quay and the café tables below. White paved streets, shutters and balconies painted blue and green with many flowers add just enough colour to the whiteness. Houses tend to be taller than on most islands. Mixed with stone buildings are Venetian houses with projecting upper storeys held by wooden beams and secretive courtyards packed with plants. Some are joined by bridges over the street.

Above it all is a Venetian castle used by Philip Gizi when he turned pirate and made his base here until he was captured. The dreaded pirate-Admiral of the Turkish Empire Barbarossa arrived in 1538 and butchered the people for daring to defy him for a few days. The isle was deserted for eighty years. In the War of Independence Skopelos and its Venetian fort were headquarters for leaders of the Greek insurrection and the Turks did not attack it. It joined Greece in 1830. Now the fort is in ruins, the dusty road to it the home of goats and donkeys and the view from it superb.

There are 123 churches in the town. The few discos and most hotels are tucked away on the far side of the bay but on the harbourside is 'O Platanos', one of the few jazz clubs in the Greek isles. The evening entertainment begins with the volta – families walking up and down the harbourside under the plane trees, men drinking ouzo outside cafés and tavernas. Then the tavernas serve dinner and someone may play an instrument – the taverna owner perhaps, or a waiter.

A bus goes along the only paved road round the coast to the little port of Loutraki and the lovely town of Glossa, and I prefer a bus to a taxi because you can see more of the beautiful scenery. Anyway, taxis are few. The road passes first Staphylos beach, most popular because you can walk to it in about half an hour and it has a good taverna. At Velanio, over a headland, is the unofficial stripping beach, secluded by high cliffs.

Agnondas, next stop, is used as an emergency port when rough seas prevent the ferries landing at Skopelos town and it has another good taverna. A road has been built to Limonari beach, accessible only from the sea until 1986.

From Agnondas the road is beautiful – one of my favourites on the Greek isles. It is shaded by pine groves, olive trees intermingled with almonds, quinces and plums which are used for making prunes. You can visit the huge prune-baking oven in Skopelos, but the trade is unreliable because old trees produce very varying crops. Quince is traditionally made into a jam which is eaten with a spoon. To be given a spoon of it is a symbol of genuine welcome.

The road nears the coast again at Panormos, a large sheltered bay where many camp in summer. An inlet at the end of the beach is used as shelter by caiques and holiday yachtsmen. There is a taverna at Panormos and boats for hire. To get away from this 'crowding', walk along a path to Milia, a mile-long beach of tiny pebbles beneath the shade of a terrace of pines. It has no taverna so far. Opposite is the little isle of Dasia. A track continues to an even-more secluded spot, Chovola.

Elios beach further on has some concrete bungalows looking like a holiday club. They were built as emergency shelters after the 1965 earthquake.

Except in mid-summer, you are now likely to meet as many donkeys as cars, most joining from tracks going into the woods and hills. Glossa is beautiful. Built mostly during the Turkish occupation in woods high above the sea, it blessedly survived the 1965 earthquake which ruined much of old Skopelos, and it remains an agricultural market village, immune to visitors and tourists. Yet there is a bank and even a disco on the outskirts! Animals are everywhere, chickens scratch in the dust of the cobbled alleys. I have found no rooms to let and only a very simple taverna. Its white and orangey-ochre houses dot the hillside down to the

little port of Loutraki, called Glossa by the ferry companies.

Loutraki has an enormous quay which seems quite out of place in a fishing village tucked in a deep bay, with boats pulled up on its shingle beach, two beachside tavernas, a small hotel down the road, a few houses and little else. The reason is that the ferry calls here as well as at Skopelos town, which shows the importance of Glossa.

At other times, Loutraki is a charmingly quiet, listless place where you can find true peace. I can remember spending a whole day sitting under plane trees outside a taverna, occasionally ordering another bottle of wine or walking around a little, calling at lunchtime for a Greek salad and *tsatsiki*, otherwise doing absolutely nothing except read while Barbara sunbathed on the beach and went for a little sail in a fishing caique. I was reading *Gates of the Wind*, a delightful book about Skopelos by an Englishman, Michael Carroll, who built a house here on a cove near Panormos. You can learn more about the isle and its people from this lovely story than from any erudite work concentrating on its history and monasteries.

When Barbara came back from her

caique trip we dined outside the taverna – more salad, freshly caught fish, and pork chops served with local prunes.

You can possibly find rooms in Loutraki or three villages south of Glossa – Makhalas, Kato Klima and Ana Klima, on the road. A mule track from Makhalas, becoming a footpath, takes you in an hour across the island to the church of Aghios Ioannis, reached by a hundred steps and perched like an eyrie over the sea. Inside is a mural of St George killing the dragon.

There are 360 churches on Skopelos and several monasteries. Four are within reasonable walking distance of Skopelos town. Aghi Barbara is fortified, with fifteenth-century frescoes. Evanelistrias was founded by the monks of Mount Athos on the mainland, who won't allow a woman into their own monastery to this day. Ironically it is now a convent. It has fine views of the town and you can buy woven goods. Metamorphosis monastery was recently abandoned, but is used for a big August festival. Prodomos, looking out from a craggy height to the isle of Alonissos, is still used by nuns.

In good weather, caiques from Skopelos town take you off the east coast to the little isle of Aghios Georgios, with some ruined fishermen's cottages, a seventeenth-century monastery, and a herd of wild goats.

Go to Skopelos at the end of May and in early June, when it is quiet, serene, not too hot and even greener than later. Most visitors fly into Skiathos and take the ferry (an hour). But there is still no love lost between Skiathos and Skopelos, so don't be put off by what the people say about each other's island.

SKOPELOS

Most people fly to Skiathos, then take the boat. Ferries from mainland call at Skopelos town and Loutraki (Glossa).

Ferries ...... Volos two to five daily (3¼ hrs), with bus connections to Athens; most days Aghios Konstandinos (4 hrs); one to three weekly Kimi (Evia – 3½ hrs); Alonisos one to two daily (½ hr); Skiathos daily (½ hr); one to four weekly Skyros; Lemnos one to two weekly (7 hrs).

Alonnisos (Halonnisos, Alonysos)

Alonnisos has a bus. Anyone who knew this strange little isle of pines, clean blue sea and strange rocks where lobsters lurk before about 1975 will simply not believe that it has a bus. Furthermore it has taxis and one of the drivers also plays the bouzouki in a taverna in the old Chora up the hill.

Before 1975 the island did not even have a proper road – just an old mule track – and in 1980 the Chora was still abandoned after the 1965 earthquake. Mind

you, all six miles of paved roads are in the south-west – others are still tracks. And the Chora is deserted in winter. But in summer it sings.

When the 1965 earthquake devastated Chora, the authorities built up a new town from a seaside village, Patitiri, which has gradually merged with the fishing hamlet of Votsi. There was virtually no tourism. Then in the 1970s a French architect built on a peninsula at Marpounta in the far south a club hotel. It was not unlike a Club Méditerranée except that it had more of a Greek atmosphere than French. Simple but comfortable accommodation was laid out like a Greek village, with white bungalows with green shutters hidden among trees. There was a restaurant with an outdoor area, bar, lounge, tennis courts, open-air dance floor, sailing, canoeing, water-skiing, two pebble beaches, a beach of yellow sand, all imported, matched sunshades and a beach barbecue serving chicken, chops, souvlaki and pizza for lunch. Also a rocky inlet for topless bathing when such exposure was banned on more sophisticated Greek islands.

When I saw it a British tour operator who was sending customers called it 'a place for a civilized gin and tonic in the wilderness'. But it was certainly a tonic to the local people, who had not only suffered a devastating earthquake, but had also lost their main crop, grapefruit, to disease, and their other great crop, wine-producing vines, to phylloxera.

It is still there, is still the biggest hotel on the island and, considering it rates only Class C, with appropriate prices, is excellent value if you like that sort of holiday.

Patitiri no longer looks like a concrete building site. Its houses rise in a pleasantly disorderly fashion among trees up

its hillside above the port, flowers adorn its balconies, and the tavernas on the quayside look already as if they are part of Old Greece. They are known for *astakos* – a type of lobster (pricey). The Greeks have a genius for making new places built of necessity look old and venerable. There are several smallish hotels, and a lot of rooms to let considering the population is only 1530. Furthermore, yachts of many colours and sizes come and go and there are anything up to 100 fishing boats using the harbour.

You can hire boats to take you to many of the little coves hidden away around the coast and there are excursions in summer to two east coast beaches – Steni Vala and Kalamakia, which both have a small hotel, tavernas and some watersports. An unpaved road leads to Kalamakia, and taxis will take you. The only paved road goes to Chora. It is no longer deserted – except in winter.

Germans have been buying up the old earthquake-damaged houses in the narrow streets and lanes of this once-beautiful hilltop town and using them for summer houses. Now a few local families are moving back, there are two tavernas, two shops and rooms to let in summer. Paraport taverna is very good. But Chora still has a hauntingly deserted atmosphere, with lovely old buildings roofless and exposed to rain and sun, iron balconies twisted, courtyards and alleys overgrown with vegetation, to the joy of donkeys and chickens who live happily here. Here and there you see a house renewed, with tended flowers in its courtyard and on its balconies. Local owners of ruined houses are selling and building themselves nice houses down by the sea.

I wrote some years ago that a compass was more use on Alonnisos than a map, and that is still true. There is a driveable track from Votsi to Vrsitsa on the west coast, where there is the only sand beach, otherwise you must walk the mule tracks. And it is a lovely island for walking. You will come across a very few houses or farms near former vineyards, and you will meet people on donkeys, but mostly you are on your own. And with luck you will find a deserted cove. Take some water and

something to eat, but do not worry if you become temporarily lost – the whole island is only twenty miles long by two miles wide.

Much of the east coast is sheltered by the isle of Peristera (Xiro) which can be reached by hired or excursion boat from Patitiri. A few shepherds live there and there are good sand beaches; that is all. It was once joined to the mainland, and the sheltered stretch of water between would seem to be made for watersports. It is one of a group of uninhabited isles, if you call islands with wild goats on them uninhabited. The most beautiful is Panayia Kyra (Pelagos), which has pleasant beaches and one of many caves said to have been the home of the legendary Cyclops. It belongs to the monastery of Mount Athos and once had two monasteries, but now wild goats are the only locals, though divers have used it as a base for finding sunken Byzantine ships. It is a charming place but it takes two hours to reach it from Alonnisos, so take some supplies – just in case the weather turns nasty!

ALONNISOS (ALONYSOS)
Most visitors fly to Skiathos from Athens or on charters and take the ferry.

Ferries ...... Volos five to eleven weekly connects with Skiathos, Skopelos (5½ hrs); Aghios Konstandinos one to three weekly (6 hrs); Kimi (Evia) one to three weekly (2½ hrs).

Skyros (Skiros)

'If I should die, think only this of me:
That there's some corner of a foreign field
That is for ever England.'

'The Soldier'

And Rupert Brooke, poet and soldier, was buried on St George's Day, 23 April 1915, among blue flowering sage in an olive grove on the isle of Skyros, after dying of blood poisoning in a French hospital during the Gallipoli campaign against the Turks.

The people of Skyros have made him their hero. His statue, cast in the heroic role of a Greek athlete, stands looking out to sea on a headland near Skyros town. It is called 'The Statue of Immortal Poetry'. Until recently it was fashionable among intellectuals not to like it, just as it was fashionable not to like Brooke's poetry. Times change, Brooke is getting his deserved appraisal, and the statue is forgiven for not being abstract. But older local ladies still avert their eyes from this heroic nude.

Skyros was almost isolated until 1980. Inter-island ferries were infrequent and unreliable in winter and bad weather. Sporadic, so to speak. There was not even a senior school on the island and more affluent parents sent their children to Kimi, on Evia, which is joined to the mainland by a bridge. Young men found jobs abroad and few returned. The islanders raised the money and started their own ferry company, and now there is at least one boat a day to and from Kimi, which has bus connections direct with Athens and via Chalkis. And now there is a senior school and embryonic tourism. The truth is, though, that Skyros is not so attractive as Skiathos or Skopelos. Much of its charm comes from its isolation and backwardness.

For centuries the island was virtually cut in half, with nearly all the people living in the wooded, cultivated fertile north. The south is mostly stony slopes with scattered olive trees and goes brown in summer. But the south has been the home since earliest days of wild ponies, Pickermes, a breed about the size of Shetlands and found nowhere else in the world. The north islanders used to round them up to use during the harvest, then let them loose again to fend for themselves when they were no longer needed. Now the Greek government protects them, and you are most likely to see them at summer shows organized by the islanders.

Two bays give the island a slim waistline at the centre, making an hour-glass figure. The large natural-harbour bay of Kalamitsa in the west is less than five miles away from the smaller, more ex-

posed Achilles Bay in the east, south of Skyros town. The only paved road on the island joins these three and carries on to Molos, two miles north. Even this road is so narrow that there can be passing problems with the island bus. Unpaved roads, mostly in the north but one south to Rupert Brooke's grave, are fairly good and driveable. There are seven or eight taxis.

At the head of Kalamitsa Bay, in lovely surroundings, is the little port of Linaria, where the ferries arrive from Kimi. It has cafés, tavernas, a few tourist shops and rooms to rent but no hotel. I have seen the little horses of Skyros grazing in the churchyard – domesticated, I am sure.

In 1986 we found only one real hotel on Skyros – the Xenia at Magazia, the beach of Skyros town. There were two small pensions and about 100 rooms, mostly in Skyros town. In mid-summer Athenians fill a lot of these. They have just discovered the island.

Several beaches along the west coast have tavernas and can be reached by dirt roads from Linaria. Southward is Kalamitsa, northward are Pofkos and Atsitsa, where they drain resin from the pines for retsina and turpentine. I hope that you can tell the difference. They can be dangerously similar.

Skyros town, known locally as Chora, is a delightful place. It is built down the landward side of a massive craggy rock overlooking the sea, from which King Lycomedes pushed the Athenian hero Theseus to his death when he sought sanctuary here, giving Athens an excuse to invade, enslave the people and put in Athenian colonists. The rock is crowned by the ruins of a Byzantine and Venetian fortress, and below is the monastery of Aghios Georgios (St George), now being

repaired after being shaken by a tremor in 1983.

The town stretches from the top of the hill to a sandy beach in a higgledy-piggledy maze of narrow twisting streets, flagstone paths and steps and white cube houses which look as if they have strayed from the Cyclades. No cars can penetrate most of it, and it is more suitable for mules than for people. It is a photogenic town where many old men still wear baggy blue trousers and square-soled Skyrian sandals every day and women wear yellow headscarves with a black pattern and their hair in two plaits.

In the evening doors are often left partly open to show off the family display of copperwear and painted plates and lovely carved furniture of Byzantine origin. Two model houses are open to visitors and furniture, copper dishes, ornaments and plates are excellently displayed in the Faltaits Museum, where there is also a fine collection of seventeenth-century embroidery. Wood carving and hand-made furniture are living crafts. The museum also has masks and costumes used in the annual carnival where they perform still a Goat Dance left from primitive days of goat worship. The word 'tragedy' (goat song) was derived from it.

Plate collecting started in Byzantine days. Dissident Byzantine families were exiled to Skyros. They were wealthy and lived well. But as their power declined under the Venetians they sold their belongings, including dining plates. Collecting dinner plates became an island hobby, and every local boy sailing the world would bring back new ones for the family, even from China.

There are wide beaches below the town and northwards at Basales and Molos and here are the few tourist facilities such as windsurfing, sailing, tavernas, cafés and boats to take you on round the island excursions. The stripping beach is a remote one down in Achilles Bay among sand dunes. From here Achilles sailed with Odysseus to fight at Troy, where he was killed by an arrow in his heel. His doting mother, the goddess Thetis, had hidden him in the court of King Lycomedes at Skyros dressed as a girl to stop him being called up for the Troy War.

That probably helped him to seduce a local girl and father a son, Neoptolemos.

A prophecy said that the Greeks could not win the Trojan War without Achilles, so Odysseus went hunting for him on Skyros. He brought a chest full of treasures for the court ladies – perfumes, jewellery, finery – and one sword. The 'girl' who grabbed the sword was Achilles.

The grave of Rupert Brooke is way down south at Tris Boukes, once a hideout for navies and pirates, now deserted because the water is deep, the wind too gusty for yachtsmen. His grave is well tended. You can get a taxi to take you there, but it is more romantic to arrive in a caique through one of the three channels which give Tris Boukes its name.

This is one of the quietest spots in Skyros. The tavernas of Skyros town's main street are far from quiet on summer evenings. The locals are known for their enthusiasm for wine and ouzo, the younger islanders who work in Athens most of the year are home for the summer season, and the Athenian holidaymakers join in enthusiastically. It is pure Greek and great fun.

SKYROS (SKIROS)

Air ...... Athens daily in season, less frequently in winter.

Ferries ...... Kimi (Evia) daily (4 hrs); Volos occasional boats; Skiathos, Skopelos, Alonnisos one to four weekly.

NORTH AEGEAN

Lesbos (Lesvos) – Mytilini

The third largest of the Greek isles, Lesbos, has two different names, two distinctly different major towns and surprisingly few visitors.

The Greek government call it Lesbos but the locals and the ferry companies call it Mytilini, the name of the ferry port and capital. Mytilini town is mainly industrial and certainly no charmer while Molyvos (Mithimna), two hours by coach away in the north, is pretty and delightful. Some visitors simply adore the island and keep returning. A few complain that it is not easy to see much of the island without long, tiring bus journeys or hiring a car, which can be expensive.

Frankly, Lesbos is very different from the traditional dream of an idyllic little Greek island. In many places the people have more important things to do than devote all their time to tourists, such as tending 11 000 olive trees which turn whole hillsides silver and provide some of the best olive oil in the world with only 0.2 per cent acidity.

Barbara adores Lesbos, and, as one of the leading Greeks in the tourist trade said of her, she is a most unlikely Lesbian. But, like me, she is prepared to drive over rough mule tracks marked on local maps as 'unpaved roads' to find villages where

life goes on unchanged by machine-living.

The lyric poetess Sappho, born on the island, was responsible for the connotation of the word Lesbian. She ran a school and wrote passionate verse to and about her female friends and charges. But very little of her work survives because the Orthodox church in Constantinople banned and burned her poems. Her main theme seems to have been love, or some say sex, but she may well have been misunderstood, for such poems were fashionable as poems by men to young men were in Elizabethan England.

The women of Lesbos were famed for their beauty, and they held an annual 'Miss Lesbos' beauty contest, though the girls paraded in robes in those days. Agamemnon, trying to bribe the angry, sulking Achilles into continuing the fight at Troy, offered him a bribe of seven women from Lesbos, chosen for their exceptional beauty.

Even in Sappho's day there was a political feud between Mytilini town and Molyvos, and they are still rivals. Mytilini, where the ferries come in and near to the airport, is a busy place but the people are friendly. It has two harbours, divided by a pcninsula topped by an attractive castle bordered by trees and with grass paths between its ruined walls. In ancient times this peninsula was a little island and the whole city fitted into it. It was joined to the mainland by a marble bridge. The original castle was sixth-century but it was rebuilt by the Genoese in the fourteenth century using a lot of old materials. In the sand which accumulated to join the islet to the coast was quite recently found an ancient trireme, the type of boat with over 100 oarsmen the Athenians used so effectively to defeat the Persians at Salamis.

The northern harbour is commercial and unattractive. In the south harbour you see fishing caiques and yachts. The waterfront is still the heart of the city, with everything from quick-food counters to banks, hotels and restaurants. The Sappho Hotel (C-Class) is attractive. Blue Sea on the harbour end is more comfortable. There's a simple very cheap E-Class hotel called Great Britain. Lesbos is well off for restaurants and tavernas, with locally caught fish, local beef and vegetables from island farms – unusual for Greece. Try Asteria restaurant in Mytilini.

There are some 'folk-art' (that is, souvenir) shops but mostly the shops are for the locals with that remarkable Greek contempt for window and shelf display which leads to an attractive confusion. At Kioski, under the castle, and the south end of the town near the yacht club at Makriyialos are some delightful old mansions with pillars, turrets, balustrades, and carved cornices.

The Archaeological Museum in a fine old mansion has good Roman mosaics and the Byzantine museum has beautiful icons. But the one I love is Theophilos Museum two miles south of Mytilini at Varia, housing eighty-six works of the primitive folk artist Theophilos. Born in 1873, he was a painting tramp, roaming round painting walls in churches, tavernas or houses where people would give him food and ouzo. Teriad, the Paris critic who lived on Lesbos, persuaded him to paint on canvas, and there are some wonderful primitive paintings of Greek island scenes and people. I love especially one called 'The Megarian Dance', a superb country barbecue scene with a row of dancers in folk costume, musicians, a man cooking over an open fire and a mouth-watering table of fish, fruit and wine awaiting. It makes you want to join the party. Teriad used his influence for a show of these paintings in the Louvre, but Theophilos died in poverty in 1934.

Nearby in the same olive grove is another superb museum which Teriad built and set up, with the forty of Theophilos's paintings which were shown in the Louvre and works of Matisse, Chagall, Miro, Picasso, Le Corbusier and many others. Chagall's works are illustrations for five books, including Gogol's *Dead Souls*.

Another rewarding visit in Mytilini is to the typical nineteenth-century Lesbian house (in Mitropoleos Street).

On pine-forested heights to the north is the ancient theatre which so impressed Pompey on his visit in 62 BC that he had a similar one built in Rome. One of the biggest in ancient Greece, it could take an audience of 15 000.

The Mytilini beach is organized, with shaded areas, comfortable chairs, snack bar selling the inevitable Greek cheese pies and drinks, and, shades of my youth, changing cubicles!

It is only forty miles on a paved road to Molyvos in the north but it takes coaches two hours and buses longer because it is a

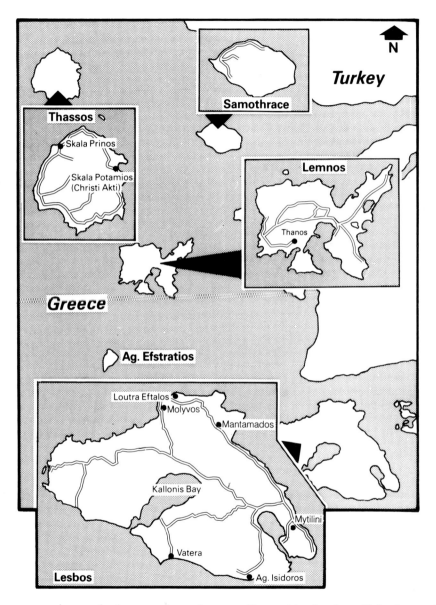

tortuous mountain road. A second road hugs the coast to just before Mantamados, which has a famous church, but in 1987 the rest of the road was closed, having collapsed in the dreadful winter of '86–7.

The road that is open passes the big almost-landlocked bay of Geras, then crosses the mountains to Kalloni, a busy market town where the ancient city of Arisbe stood. The boys of this city made the mistake of abducting some girls from Molyvos, so the boys of the bigger city destroyed Arisbe and enslaved its people. Now Kalloni is known to visitors for Skala Kalloni, its fishing village on the huge gulf of Kalloni. It is renowned for its sardines, which used to be salted and taken to Melyti. Some still are, but sardines are not so easy to catch these days, and a lot are consumed by visitors staying in the bungalows and villas. One British package-tour company discovered Kalloni and has rather cornered it, but you can find rooms. The attractions are a good sandy beach, a pretty fishing harbour and tavernas and cafés. A local way of cooking sardines is to bone and mash them, then cook them in oil like an omelette.

Just before Kalloni is a road to the right into the hills to Aghia Paraskevi where they breed horses. You can see white mares with black foals in the fields. They do not turn white until later. North of Kalloni is the impressive Leimonos monastery of 1523. It comes under the monks of Mount Athos and no women may enter. It has a library of books and manuscripts, interesting to scholars but all Greek to me, and some magnificent carvings and icons.

Molyvos (officially Mithimna, but not to locals) is a truly delightful place and the annual target for lovers of Lesbos. It is a tourist town, but still a thoroughly Greek fishing village. The harbour is lovely and filled with real old-style wooden caiques, often with nets hung from the mast to dry. Elegant stone houses with red roofs rise in steep stone-paved lanes and cobbled steps to impressive ruins of a Genoese castle atop the hill from which there are wonderful views to Turkey.

Among fish tavernas alongside the water on the harbour road is our favourite, Nassos, where the choice is unusually good for a Greek isle – lobster and sardines, red mullet, sea bream, swordfish, octopus, good steak from island cattle, lamb. Tzatziki is good too, and a nutty mixed salad. Sea Horse pension on the harbour is a convenient place to stay. Molyvos 1 pension is pleasant, so is Poseidon, but with only six bedrooms. For something more comfortable and quieter Hotel Alkaios, on a hill with good views, a swimming pool and a pebbly beach 100 yards away. But you have a mile uphill walk back from the tavernas in the evening. The A-class hotel Delphinia is a good twenty minutes' walk away in the hills.

In summer there are theatrical performances in the old castle. Barbara was told by the locals that one was in English. It was in Greek!

Molyvos's long pebbly beach is a bit disappointing to sun loungers but there are buses to the quieter little village of Petra with a sand beach, cobbled streets, red-roofed houses and, 114 steps up a rock, wonderful views from outside a church. Sunsets can be spectacular. You will find tavernas and shops in the main square and beside the beach, including Taverna Georgios, under vines with several rooms behind, and Blue Sea taverna with rooms and a lot of music. The new hotel Theofilos is comfortable but a good five minutes walk outside town.

Petra was the first place in Greece where the authorities set up a Women's Agricultural Co-operative to let out rooms to tourists. Some are among orchards and olive groves. A partly paved road leads south-west to the very quiet hamlet and beach at Anaxos.

Preparing whitewash

An unpaved road east from Molyvos leads to Loutra Eftalos, a spa with hot springs right by the sea – so hot that most people nip in and out, then jump into the sea to cool down. There is a small beach, tavernas and two fairly good hotels, Alkeos and Molivos 2.

A winding, mountainous but paved road west from Kalloni leads to Antissa. Straight on is the quiet fishing village of Sigri, known for lobsters. There are several good beaches along the coast and a castle built by the Turks in 1757 is in good order. The petrified forest nearby is not worth the long walk. One expert says that the trees are 500 000 years old, another, twenty million years old!

The south fork from Antissa takes you to Erossos and its beach resort Skala Erossos. Both are delightful. The town, birthplace of Sappho, has a superb main square under an enormous plane tree and a lively market around it. The resort has a one-and-a-half-mile sand beach, 230 feet wide, which not surprisingly lures many tourists. They stay in rooms in the pleasant red-roofed houses among trees alongside the beach which they share with the blue boats and orange nets of local fishermen. There are tavernas with tables on the beach and small hotels, too.

Some of the most beautiful routes are in the south, with lovely mountain views, but they can be rough, and the tracks posing as roads need some courage – wiggling and winding, with sudden boulders in the tracks and sheer drops alongside. A paved road crosses from Mytilini to Polychnitos and its beach on the shores of Kallonis bay. A very tortuous and lovely road off to the left takes you to Agiassos, a charming, interesting old village in a gorgeous setting among apple orchards and woods of olives, plane, chestnut and pine on the slopes of Mount Olymbos. Old wooden houses with balconies decked in flowers stand in steep cobbled streets. There is a mediaeval castle, too, and a twelfth-century church.

Polychnitos, an elegant spa in lovely country, has five hot springs claimed to be the hottest in Europe – 76–87.6 degrees centigrade. Its fishing village Skala has a pleasant harbour, beach and tavernas and rooms to rent, and Nyfida westward has a marvellous beach.

Down south is another village, Vatera, among orchards and vineyards, with a wide sand beach five miles long, a few pensions and few people. The unpaved road turns east and inland. Views are magnificent, surfaces sometimes dodgy. But a paved road leads to Plomari down a long winding hill with superb views over the rooftops to the sea. The second biggest town on the island, Plomari has an old city on one side, a new on the other, both packed tight on a hillside with dignified tall houses, though the new has a few modern apartments by the waterfront. The port is busy, the fishing fleet active, and they make the best ouzo in Greece, they claim. Certainly Aphrodite at ninety per cent proof is formidable. The town even smells of ouzo. The best beach Aghios Isidoros is outside the town.

Lesbos is big enough, varied enough and has so many good beaches that it could take a lot more tourists and hotels without anybody noticing significantly. A holiday at Molyvos with a car for some days to explore wilder places is a superb combination.

LESBOS

Air ...... A few charters from Britain including Skyworld and Intasun. Athens – up to six flights daily (45 mins); Thessalonika on mainland six to seven weekly (1 hr 20 mins); Chios (40 mins), Samos (55 mins) one or two weekly; Rhodes three weekly (1 hr 20 mins); Lemnos four weekly (45 mins).

Ferries ...... Piraeus two to four weekly; Chios five weekly; Kavala (mainland), Lemnos, Samos twice weekly; once weekly to Thessalonika (mainland), Leros, Karpathos, Crete, Santorini, Folegandros, Milos.

Lemnos (Limnos) and Samothrace

Lemnos is not to me a holiday isle and not exciting to travellers. Hilly, but almost bare of trees because of the fierce winter winds that sweep across from the Dardanelles, it has a few sheltered spots growing corn, sesame and cotton, with scrubby hillsides where tens of thousands of goats and sheep graze. But what spoils it for visitors is that it is a big military base, vital to Greece because it is so near Turkey, opposite the Dardanelles, not far from Eastern Europe and has a splendid natural harbour at Moudros Bay.

There are many military installations round the coast, and most planes coming in to the airfield are Greek Air Force or military supply carriers. The young soldiers are friendly enough, especially to visiting young ladies, and the presence of officers and their families and visiting friends means that there are quite good shops, some good hotels and all services, but few paved roads – just one joining the military area of Moudros Bay, the airfield and the capital Myrina on the west coast. I suppose that tanks and military vehicles spurn roads. But the unpaved roads are well kept.

It was the Allied base for the disastrous Dardanelles attack in 1915 conceived by Winston Churchill to land on the Gallipoli peninsula and seize the Turkish ports guarding Constantinople. Nine months of fighting brought the British, Australian and French troops nothing but disease and death, and many were brought back to Lemnos for burial. As time passes, few visit the British cemetery north-east of Moudros town.

Moudros is disappointing. The capital Myrina is the ferry port. Dominated by a Venetian castle from which there are wonderful views of Mount Athos, thirty-six miles away, especially at sunset. Myrina has some nice gardens and houses. The long beach is protected from winds and lined with restaurants and cafés, it is the centre of what little tourism there is and of night life. There is a huge luxury bungalow hotel Akti Myrina with bedrooms in wooden bungalows, four restaurants, a night club, private beach, swimming pool and its own caique. The C-class Lemnos is nearer my style.

The most pleasant part of the isle for scenery is south-west in the wine-growing area around Thanos. There are some archaeological sites with ancient remains but they are of interest only to serious students.

It takes one and a half hours by caique to reach the islet of *Aghios Efstratios* and when you get there the fishermen's village is of box-like prefabs put up after an earth-

quake, and beaches a one-and-a-half hour walk away.

Samothrace does not seem like a Greek island. Sombre, stern and windy, it is a big rocky mountain which is snow-capped nine months of the year. A small strip of wheat and olives rims part of its coast. Yet it was a place of great religious importance to the people of ancient Greece and its archaeological sites are still providing scholars with much material to unravel the mysteries of old Greek myths and religions.

Even Greeks regard it as inaccessible. There are daily ferries from Alexandroupolis, but that is in the far right hand corner of Greece on the Turkish borders. The Kavala ferry, more convenient for Athens, sails only weekly.

Mount Fingari, 5500 feet high and called Mount Saos locally, is where Homer put the sea god Poseidon to watch the long siege of Troy, which was over on the mainland, and you can get up there to see Poseidon's dramatic view of the North Aegean, even to Mount Athos in the west. You start from Chora, the quiet, attractive capital well up the mountain and you should really get a guide. The 'walk' takes four to six hours and paths are not clearly marked.

You take a bus from the port of Kamariotissa to Palaeopolis, where the Sanctuary of the Great Gods has been excavated. Happily the excavations were taken over in 1948 by the Americans Dr Karl and Phyllis Williams Lehmann, so there are excellent guides in English and

Greek. It includes a plaster copy of the Nike, called Winged Victory, the headless statue given to the sanctuary by one of Alexander the Great's generals Dimitrios Poliorketes in thanks for a naval victory in 305 BC. It once stood as figurehead of a marble ship but the original is in the Louvre in Paris, at the top of a main staircase. Philip II of Macedonia met his future queen Olympias in the sanctuary; their son was Alexander the Great.

The Great Gods (Kaberoi or Cabeiri) worshipped here were older and more powerful than the Olympian gods, and mysterious rites of initiation were taught and performed in the sanctuary, with two levels of membership. But anyone could go through them, man or woman, rich or poor, freeman or slave, and many famous people did. As time went on, the Thracian Great Gods and the Greek Olympian gods tended to become merged, and even the Romans adopted the sanctuary, for the island was associated with the ancestors of Aeneas, regarded as founder of Rome.

Unfortunately the buildings were much dismantled by the Genoese to build their mediaeval castle by the Nike fountain. But what is left is impressive, evocative and well labelled.

There is a B-class Xenia hotel in a grove by the site, or you can get rooms in the embryo beach resort of Therma, reached by an unpaved road east from the site. There are tavernas there, too. There is a good new class C hotel by the sea at the port of Kamariotissa, Niki Beach Hotel, but the nicest place to stay is in Chora, with Thracian style houses with balconies and red roofs weighed down with stones against the wind, spread in an amphitheatre on the mountain slopes. Here are pensions, rooms and tavernas, though even here the tavernas seem to shut in winter.

Winters must be very sombre indeed, with the wind, the snow-topped mountain and the spirit of the Great Gods hanging over the island.

Two ferries a day run to and from Alexandroupolis in summer, so you could just stay nine hours to see the Sanctuary and Chora, but you would be stuck in Alexandroupolis.

LEMNOS (LIMNOS)

Aircraft seats to Athens often booked two or three weeks in advance by military or their families. Piraeus boat goes a long way round.

Air ...... Athens two to three daily (45 mins); Thessalonika on mainland daily (1 hr 10 mins); Lesbos four weekly (45 mins).

Ferries ...... Kavala (mainland) four boats weekly (5 hrs); Piraeus weekly; once weekly to Lesbos, Chios, Samos, Ikaria, Leros, Kalymnos, Kos, Rhodes, Karpathos, Kassos, Crete, Santorini, Folegandros, Milos, Skopelos, Kimi (Evia).

SAMOTHRACE (SAMOTHRAKI)

Ferries daily to Alexandroupolis (mainland) – (1 hr 50 mins) which has an airport connecting to Athens; Kavala (mainland) – (4 hrs) one or two weekly.

Thassos

Thassos is undramatically beautiful – a round mountain decked with luxuriously green pine woods, plane trees, chestnuts and walnuts, watered by the torrents which have carved valleys in the mountainside, all sloping down to a ring of sand beaches. Where the rivers run into the sea, the beaches are backed by vineyards and olive groves, wheat fields and vegetables. The idyll is broken only by a few ugly iron ore and cadmium mines on the west coast.

Because it is only seven miles from the mainland of Macedonia, it is not afflicted by the meltemi winds, and in summer it has that languid atmosphere of hot sun, sand, sea and the smell of pines.

It has long lured mainland Greeks for holidays and weekends, so it has good accommodation and tourist facilities, and bus services all round the island, but it has not been vulgarized by tourist hordes. Comparatively few foreigners go to Thassos, so notices and menus tend to be in Greek only and few people speak English. One British company, Intasun, discovered it in 1987 and run one charter plane a week to villas and hotels. They fly to Kavala on the mainland and take a ferry. Winters are cooler and damper than on most Greek isles.

Thassos town is called locally Limenas (or Limen) which can be confused with the second biggest town Limonaria, a seaside resort. Like Kos town, Limenas has ancient remains mixed up with its modern buildings. They are not only interesting but often beautiful, for the central peak Ipsarion is virtually a massive block of marble, and it was used for buildings, statues and streets.

The main excavations are the Agora, entered from beside the museum. You will need a guide book, for there is little labelling. There are first century AD Roman stoas and remains of passageways, shops and monuments of the classical city. The earliest finds are a passageway and an elaborate temple of Artemis from the seventh century BC.

Exploring the ramparts means a strenuous but rewarding three mile walk. You take the steps above the town to the ancient theatre, set dramatically among pines overlooking a wide expanse of sea. Here performances of ancient drama are given on Saturdays from late July to mid-August – in Greek, of course. A path leads on to the remains of a Genoese acropolis and here you can follow the old walls past the foundations of a fifth-century temple of Apollo to a small sanctuary with a relief of the god Pan and his goats. Descend with care the 'Secret Stair' carved into the rock in the sixth century BC to the Gateway of Silenus, the phallic god. Alas, his massive phallus (a fertility totem) was chiselled away in the 1930s during one of those periodic campaigns of 'moral cleansing' which the Greeks have thrust upon them.

The town has a nice little fishing harbour, very-Greek shops, cafés and tavernas and rather scruffy beaches. Try to walk the waterfront and streets in early evening when some streets are closed to traffic and families stroll in volta before going home to supper.

A few of the main ferries from Kavala on the mainland come to Limenas but many stop only at the little port of Skala Prinos ten miles west, from where you can get a bus. Bus services are good and frequent on Thassos. But ferries also go from Keramoti, twenty-seven miles south-east of Kavala, to Limenas many times a day.

South of Limenas is a very good beach with tourist facilities for watersports, but it is mostly the private domain of the Makriammos Bungalow Hotel, A-class. Limenas has hotels of all grades from A–E, pensions and rooms to rent (although it is forbidden to let rooms in Thassos between mid-September and mid-May). The B-class Timoleon hotel is good value, the Lido is cheaper, and the Akti on the waterfront cheap, cheerful and clean. There are three camp sites.

A paved road runs round the island through delightful scenery and there are several buses a day doing this fifty-mile trip. It is better by car because there are many roads leading to beaches and to picturesque mountain villages.

Loveliest of the inland villages is Panagia, on the side of Mount Hyparion among forests and springs. Its slate-roofed Macedonian houses with carved wood decorations are along winding stone alleys leading to a tree-shaded square. Sea views are a delight, and this is a good place to stay at least one night, for it has a pension, Chrystis, rooms and tavernas up here and down on the beaches of Potamia Bay. At Christi Aktri on this bay fishing boats still go out at night, and fishermen's cottages have shaded outside tavernas where you can taste the catch.

Round the coast at Archangelos is a convent where nuns will show you the spot where St Luke is said to have knelt in prayer, his knees making hollows in the stone. Clothing rules are strict but the nuns rent long skirts and men's jeans. Ironically, the inlet below is used for nude bathing!

The road passes good beaches to Potos, with a very good beach lined with tavernas. The modern Olympion hotel is comfortable. A road through a lovely valley leads to the old capital, Theologos, beautifully situated, with water from springs channelled to run through the streets to irrigate gardens. Here you can buy the famous Thasian honey and a sticky preserve of figs or green walnuts in honey.

Beyond Potos is Limonaria, really an overgrown fishing village with narrow streets sloping steeply down to a sand and pebble beach. Quiet by day, it wakes up at night to the sounds of taverna talk, bar music and four discos. Plenty of tavernas serving Greek food, including a modern one opposite the beach called Ralitsas above which are rooms with shower, wc and balcony. Other little modern hotels with these facilities include the vine-clad Haztichristos on the beach and the Samaras. E-class hotel Papageorgiou is good value.

An island as attractive as Thassos has to have *some* fault. It is mosquitoes. But modern electrical devices will deal with them at night. Forest fires, too – so be careful especially if camping. The journey to Lesbos and Thassos may be more difficult than to some isles, but they remain staunchly Greek in atmosphere and that is what most visitors want.

THASSOS

Ferries ...... Kavala (mainland – 1 hr 45 mins) daily; Keramoti (mainland – 45 mins) – twelve daily, every hour in summer; six in winter.

INDEX

Index compiled by Peva Keane